History of Academic Psychology in Canada

History of Academic Psychology in Canada

2nd Printing

Compiled and Edited by

Mary J. Wright
University of Western Ontario

and

C. Roger Myers†
University of Toronto

Hogrefe & Huber Publishers
Seattle · Toronto · Göttingen · Bern

Canadian Cataloguing in Publication Data

Main entry under title:
History of academic psychology in Canada

Includes index.
ISBN 0-88937-004-4

1. Psychology – Study and teaching (Higher) – Canada – History – Addresses, essays,
lectures. 2. Psychology – Canada – History – Addresses, essays, lectures. I. Wright,
Mary J., 1915–   II. Myers, C. Roger (Charles Roger), 1906–1986

BF80.7.C3H57   150'.971   C82-094469-6

ISBN 0-88937-004-4
Hogrefe & Huber Publishers, Seattle · Toronto · Göttingen · Bern
ISBN 3-8017-0803-9
Hogrefe & Huber Publishers, Göttingen · Bern · Seattle · Toronto

© Copyright 1995 2nd printing by Hogrefe & Huber Publishers
© Copyright 1982 1st printing by C.J. Hogrefe, Inc.
USA: P.O. Box 2487, Kirkland, WA 98083-2487,
Phone (206) 820-1500, Fax (206) 823-8324
CANADA: 12 Bruce Park Avenue, Toronto, Ontario M4P 2S3,
Phone (416) 482-6339
SWITZERLAND: Länggass-Straße 76, CH-3000 Bern 9,
Phone (031) 300-4500, Fax (031) 300-4590
GERMANY: Rohnsweg 25, D-37085 Göttingen,
Phone (0551) 49609-0, Fax (0551) 49609-88

Printed in Canada

Acknowledgments

This book has been published with the help of a grant from the Social Science Federation of Canada using funds provided by the Social Sciences and Humanities Research Council of Canada. Its preparation was funded by the Faculty of Social Science of the University of Western Ontario through a series of grants awarded in each of three academic years and by the Department of Psychology at the University of Toronto which provided funds to support a research assistant during one summer session. The editors are also indebted to the Heads of all of the Departments of Psychology in Canada who provided information about their universities and departments, especially to those in the twelve departments which are dealt with in depth for either writing the chapter on their Department or supporting the efforts of their designates to do so.

Contents

Preface

It was in 1879 that Wilhelm Wundt established a psychological laboratory at Leipzig University and thus publicly launched psychology as a laboratory science. This book was being prepared in 1979, at the time when psychologists around the world were celebrating their centennial. Its purpose was to describe the development of psychology in Canada as an academic and scientific discipline. No such book was available. The only published records of psychology's past in Canada were scattered in the pages of the Canadian Psychologist or the Bulletins and Newsletters of provincial psychological associations. Psychology's centennial year appeared to be a most appropriate time to review Canadian psychology's past accomplishments.

The project was launched in May 1975. The first task was to delineate the scope of the book, or how many and which universities should be given the most extensive coverage. Finally it was decided that the focus should be on those universities in which doctoral programs in psychology had been developed before 1960, and which had, therefore, been able to contribute qualified teaching staff to the universities during the great expansion that then occurred. In order to determine which universities these were, a questionnaire was sent to the Chair of every known department of psychology in Canada requesting information about when graduate training had begun and when the first M.A. or Ph.D. degrees in psychology had been granted. Twelve departments met the criterion. They were Dalhousie, McGill, Montreal, Ottawa, Queens, Toronto, Western, McMaster, Manitoba, Saskatchewan, Alberta, and British Columbia. The Chairs of these twelve departments were then asked to nominate a member of their staff who would be the most appropriate person to prepare a history of their department. The nominees, thus obtained, were then invited to write such a history.

The book begins with an Introduction which is followed by four Parts. The Introduction deals with the ethnic backgrounds of the people who played the most significant roles in the development of Canada's first universities. It describes the course of development of higher education across the country from east to west, and it provides a chronology of the founding of the twelve universities which, in this volume, are dealt with in depth. Parts I, II, and III describe the development of psychology in the English universities of eastern and central Canada, the French universities of central Canada and the English universities of western Canada respectively. Part IV describes the rapid expansion of psychology during the decade of the 1960's and the development of new departments of psychology in newly established universities across the land.

Each of Parts I, II, and III begins with an Introductory section which not only summarizes the developments described in detail in the chapters that follow, but draws attention to how events, such as the two World Wars, influenced the course of those developments and affected the universities, often in similar, but sometimes in different ways.

Mary J. Wright
London

and

C. Roger Myers
Toronto

April 1982

Introduction

Canada Before Confederation: The Beginnings

Psychology first came to Canada through its universities. That is why any history of psychology must start with "academic" psychology. It came as mental and moral philosophy and as such had a long history which pre-dated confederation by more than half a century. In British North America its arrival coincided with the founding of the first colleges, the forerunners of the universities, for mental and moral philosophy was invariably one of the first college courses taught.

In the eighteenth century, when this chronicle begins, views about the nature of man and about moral and mental philosophy varied widely. Yet only one particular kind of mental philosophy was widely espoused in Canada's early English colleges. To understand why, it is necessary to examine the roots and biases of the men who founded them.

In the British colonies of North America the demand for higher education came in the late 18th century with the flood of United Empire Loyalists who fled to them from the "republicanism" of the south, following the War of Independence against Britain. These Loyalists, had lost their wealth. They could not afford to send their sons to Oxford or Cambridge and would not permit them to return to the United States to attend Harvard or Yale. They sought to bring educators to their new land and it was these British who played a major role in bringing about the establishment of the first universities in the Maritimes. There was, however, a second stream of English-speaking immigrants, which paralleled the first, which played perhaps an even greater role than did the Loyalists in determining the character of the new colleges and the kind of psychology that was taught in them. These were the Scots.

In the century between 1750 and 1850 the economic and social conditions in the Highlands of Scotland were greatly disturbed and highly unstable. Modern technology and changes in the economic base of the country from mixed farming to sheep raising displaced the population and destroyed the feudo-clan system. Farms were cleared for sheep-walks and many clansfolk lost their homes (Prebble, 1963). Other economic disasters, including the failure of the kelp industry and a series of potato famines impoverished even the Lairds, many of whom lost their ancestral estates to "foreign" (English) speculators. At the same time the population increased remarkably (Adam, 1952, pp 85–92). Hence it became expedient for many to emigrate and these found new homes in the maritimes and Upper Canada (Ontario). These Scots valued higher education and exercised much influence in the selection of teachers for the new colleges, many of whom were imported from Edinburgh. As a result, the philosophic system propounded in the Canadian English-speaking colleges of a century ago was that which had been developed by the Scottish Common Sense School (Harris, 1976, p 52).

In colonial New France relatively little higher education was offered, because it was customary to send the young for advanced training to the great universities of Europe. But, after the Treaty of Paris in 1763, when New France became a British Colony, the desire for such education increased. Education in Quebec was, however, under the firm control of the Roman Catholic Church, and the Protestant British were suspicious of "Romish" education. At least in part because of this, for nearly a century the efforts of the French to obtain a French language University were unsuccessful. In 1852, Archbishop Turgeon wrote in a pastoral letter "It is with feelings of deep pain that we have seen our Catholic youth obliged to pass into foreign countries either to procure academical honours or to follow the study of medicine or jurisprudence" (Harris, 1976, p 23). Thus the major French-Canadian universities of Quebec had their origins in the mid-nineteenth century. Their history bears the marks of French educational traditions and the way in which psychology developed in them was very different from the way in which it developed in the rest of the country. In these universities the first type of mental philosophy taught was that of Thomas Aquinus.

The extent and development of the country in which Canada's first colleges and universities were established has been described as follows:

"Before the end of the eighteenth century there were seven provinces in the new British North America. Out in the Atlantic there was Newfoundland, a great island with an interest in Labrador. Two other island provinces, Cape Breton and Prince Edward Island, lay in the Gulf of St. Lawrence. On the Atlantic shore of the mainland were Nova Scotia and New Brunswick. These five were the "Maritime" provinces, all alike dependent upon the sea and ships. To the north and west Lower Canada stretched along the banks of the St. Lawrence, French in speech and manner of living. In the most westerly province Upper Canadians were cutting down the forests about the lower lakes, making themselves as comfortable as they could in a wilderness of wood and water" (Creighton, 1960, pp 390–391). "Thousands of Loyalists flocked to the Maritimes and to Upper Canada, and the new provinces of New Brunswick and Upper Canada were created to help solve the problem of governing this new population" (Creighton, 1960, p 376).

In general Canada as a nation developed from east to west, although this is not fully apparent from the formal record of when Canadian provinces were created or when they became part of Canada. In 1867 when the Dominion of Canada came into existence it united only the four provinces of Nova Scotia, New Brunswick, Quebec, and Ontario. The other provinces, some yet to be created (Manitoba, Saskatchewan and Alberta) joined later, Manitoba in 1870, British Columbia in 1871, Prince Edward Island in 1873, Saskatchewan and Alberta in 1905 and Newfoundland not until 1949. Yet it is a fact that, except for British Columbia, which at the time of Confederation was relatively well-populated, the concentration of population began in the east and spread gradually westward. The development of the first universities reflected to some extent, though not entirely, the increases in population density, and also proceeded from east to west.

Establishing the exact dates of origin of the earliest Canadian universities is extremely difficult because some began as secondary schools, others began as colleges and most were "chartered" long before they were able to offer any instruction. Frequently, when a university was established, two or more existing colleges were amalgamated and these provided its initial faculties and facilities. For example, King's College, founded at Windsor, Nova Scotia, in 1790 by United Empire Loyalists, came into association with Dalhousie College, which had been chartered in 1818, to form in 1923 a University College which was the beginning of Dalhousie University as it is known today.

A chronology describing the history of the founding of the twelve older universities, whose work in psychology is dealt with in depth in this volume has, however, been attempted and is appended to this chapter.

References

Adam, Frank. *The Clans, Septs and Regiments of the Scottish Highlands.* Fourth edition, revised by Sir Thomas Innis of Learney. W. & A.K. Johnston Ltd., Edinburgh, 1952.

Creighton, Luella B. *Canada: The Struggle for Empire*. Book I in the Aldine history series, revised edition. J.M. Dent & Sons, 1962.

Harris, Robin S. *A History of Higher Education in Canada, 1663–1960*. University of Toronto Press, 1976.

Prebble, John. *The Highland Clearances*. Martin Secker and Warburg, 1963, published in Penguin Books, 1969.

Chronology

Developing an accurate chronology for Canada's universities is not difficult – it is impossible. This is because of disagreement among sources, and also because there was usually a lag between decision and achievement. Charters were granted but allowed to lapse. Some colleges were founded, but failed to offer instruction until a decade or so later. Others made brave starts, but were shortly closed down again for several years. Sometimes what appears to have been a College is referred to as a University and sometimes what appears to have been chartered as a University is referred to as a College. It is not surprising, therefore, that there is disagreement about what particular events or dates marked the real beginnings of our modern universities. Most of them did begin as colleges and claim their founding dates to be those on which their first colleges were established, but others prefer to define their beginnings at the point at which a University as opposed to a College was chartered and given its modern name. Here, an attempt has been made to deal uniformly and fairly with all, by giving, where applicable, the founding dates of the first Colleges. Also, the chronological order in which the Universities are dealt with below is based on the dates when the first colleges were established.

Dalhousie University

The University of King's College at Windsor, Nova Scotia, was, according to Harris (1976, p 4), "the first institution outside the British Isles in what was to become the British Commonwealth to be granted a University charter". It was founded by United Empire Loyalists in 1790. It was under the firm control of the Church of England and, in 1802, when it obtained degree-granting powers, one of its new statutes stated "No professor directly or indirectly shall teach or maintain any atheistical, dieistical or democratical principles, or any doctrine contrary to the Christian faith, or to good morals, or subversive of the British Constitution ... No member of the University shall frequent the Romish Mass, or the meeting houses of Presbyterians, Baptists, or Methodists, or the

Conventicles, or places of Worship of any other dissenters from the Church of England ..." (Harris, 1976, p 29). This so insulted and riled the non-Anglican community that King's gradually lost almost all of its one hundred or so students and the cry went up for a new college with more liberal views.

The College of Halifax was founded by Methodists and chartered in 1818. In 1820 Lord Dalhousie, at the laying of the Cornerstone of this college, which was later to bear his name, said "... it is formed in imitation of the University of Edinburgh ..." (Harris, 1976, p 32), but in 1838 President McCulloch, on the point of assuming the Presidency of Dalhousie University rejected this claim and said "If Dalhousie College acquires usefulness and eminence it will be not by an imitation of Oxford, but as an institution of science and practical intelligence" (Harris, 1976, p 38).

In 1920 the main building of King's College was destroyed by fire and this led to a decision to move the campus from Windsor to Halifax. Finally, in 1923 King's College and Dalhousie College came into association to found a non-sectarian University College which was the beginning of the modern Dalhousie University.

McGill University

McGill College at Montreal was granted a Royal Charter by King George IV in 1821. In its early years it provided training for only medical students. Arts courses were first offered in 1843. It is noteworthy that McGill was non-denominational from its inception.

University of Toronto

King's College at York (later Toronto) was granted a charter by King George IV in 1827. It did not, however, offer instruction until 1843. It was an Anglican College, but was secularized in 1850 when it became the University of Toronto, a non-denominational institution which was declared by the Ontario legislature to be "the" provincial university for Ontario.

Queen's University

Queen's College at Kingston (Upper Canada) was chartered by Queen Victoria in 1841. Its founders were Presbyterians.

Ottawa University

The College of Bytown, a classical bilingual College for men, was founded by the oblate fathers of the Roman Catholic Church in 1849. When Bytown was re-named (Ottawa) in 1861 it became the College of Ottawa. In 1866 it was chartered as the University of Ottawa (Harris, 1976, p 24).

University of Manitoba

St. Boniface, a Roman Catholic, French-speaking, classical college was founded in St. Boniface in 1855.

St. John's, an Anglican, English-speaking college in Winnipeg, began teaching Arts & Theology in 1866.

Manitoba, a Presbyterian, English-speaking college in Kildonan began teaching work beyond the secondary level early in the 1870's and moved to Winnipeg in 1874.

In 1877 the University of Manitoba was chartered by the legislature of the province to be an examining body which would set academic standards for the colleges of the province and coordinate their efforts. The University itself did not offer any instruction until the early 1900s.

University of Montreal

The University of Montreal was established in 1919. Its founding followed that of Laval University, which was chartered in 1852. Laval was located in Quebec City, but in 1878 established a branch in Montreal. The location of Laval University in Quebec City, created an "academic civil war" between the Roman Catholic dioceses of Montreal and Quebec, because it put the control over higher education, in the whole province, under the Archbishop of Quebec. This could not be tolerated by the Bishop of Montreal, who, by enlisting the support of Rome, achieved his goal of establishing the University of Montreal, and in so doing, created conditions "which contributed in no small measure to the failure of the Université Laval to achieve the desires of its founders for the best part of the century" (Harris, 1976, p 23).

University of Western Ontario

Huron College, in London (Upper Canada) was established by the Church of England in 1863. It was this college that promoted the founding of Western University in 1878. Training in the arts, medicine, and theology began in 1881 when Huron College became the Faculty of Theology. Between 1885 and 1895 instruction in arts was offered only intermittently, but training in medicine was provided continuously (beginning in 1882) throughout this period. In 1923 Western was re-named The University of Western Ontario. It claims its founding date as 1878.

McMaster University

McMaster University's first charter was granted by the Ontario Legislature in 1887 and instruction was offered shortly thereafter. It was located originally in Toronto, but moved to Hamilton in 1930. This university was founded by Baptists.

University of Alberta

An Act to establish the University of Alberta was passed by the Alberta legislature in 1906. In 1908 the University, which was located in Edmonton, opened and began offering instruction. It was "the" provincial university and was non-denominational from the start.

University of Saskatchewan

An Act establishing the University of Saskatchewan was passed by the Saskatchewan legislature in 1907. In 1909 the University, which was located in Saskatoon was opened and began offering instruction. It was "the" provincial university and was non-denominational from the start.

University of British Columbia

An Act to establish a university in British Columbia was passed by the legislature in 1890, but was allowed to lapse. In 1908 an Act to establish the University of British Columbia was passed. However, "much time was spent in choosing a site (1908–10), in selecting a President (1910–13), in holding a competition for an architect (1912), and in selecting a Chancellor and members of Senate and in appointing members of the Board of Governors (1912–13) and in drawing up and then pruning an operating budget (1913–15), but in September 1915 the University of British Columbia did open ..." (Harris, 1976, p. 227).

PART I

The English Universities of Eastern and Central Canada

Introduction: An Overview

This overview provides a summary description of the origins and development of psychology in the major English universities of eastern and central Canada: Dalhousie, McGill, Toronto, Queen's, Western Ontario, and McMaster. The development of psychology in the English universities in western Canada is reviewed in Part III.

Eastern Canada is dealt with separately from western Canada because the ways in which psychology developed in these two major regions of the country were different. This was in part, because the eastern universities were established earlier than the western ones, before Confederation rather than after it, and, with the exception of Manitoba, were more affected in their early years by sectarian interests and influences from abroad. It was also because, unlike the western ones, they were established before psychology was recognized as an independent scientific discipline rather than a part of philosophy.

The early years

Pre-scientific psychology in the eastern universities of Canada had an eventful history. Since one of the primary aims of these early institutions was to produce an educated clergy, psychology, usually taught as mental and moral philosophy, was invariably an important part of the curriculum.

The first course in psychology offered in Canada was taught as early as 1838 at Dalhousie, by no less than the president of that institution, Thomas McCulloch, an Edinburgh-trained Scot. However, for many years following its brave start, Dalhousie functioned only sporadically. Having neither permanent faculty or students it did not resume continuous teaching for a quarter of a century.

It was in the early 1850's that the teaching of pre-scientific psychology in Canada seems to have begun in earnest and on a continuing basis. This occurred at about the same time at both McGill and Toronto. The first instructors were W.T. Leach (an Edinburgh-trained Scot) at McGill and James Beaven (an Oxford-trained Englishman) at Toronto. It has been said that the values of English Canada were moulded by the Scots. Certainly, during the 19th Century, most of the educated elite received their formal training in ethics from them. Queen's was dominated by the Scots, as were Dalhousie and McGill and Beaven's successor to the chair in Toronto in 1871, George Paxton Young, was also an Edinburgh-trained Scot.

The first textbook is psychology to be written in Canada was published in 1885. Its author was William Lyall who came to Halifax from Glasgow and Edinburgh to teach in the Free Church College of Halifax. His book, *The Intellect, the Emotions, and the Moral Nature* was, apparently, a success because, eight years later, in 1863, when Dalhousie re-opened its doors Lyall was invited to join its faculty. The second Canadian book on psychology was written by John Clark Murray of McGill. His *Handbook of Psychology* was published in 1885. The first psychology text to be written by a modern psychologist in Canada was the second volume of James Mark Baldwin's *Handbook of Psychology* which was published in 1891 while Baldwin was at Toronto.

Thus it can be said that psychology in Canada is as old as its universities. However, until well into the 20th Century it was taught as philosophy in all institutions. The first modern psychologist appointed to a faculty in Canada was James Mark Baldwin. He came to Toronto in 1889. Baldwin had received part of his advanced training at Leipzig and he taught in the Wundtion tradition. He established at Toronto a psychological laboratory, the first such laboratory on British soil and he initiated a program of experimental research. He also persuaded the University to approve a new curriculum for students who wished to specialize in experimental psychology.

Baldwin's stay in Toronto was short-lived, only four years. In 1893 he accepted an invitation to return to Princeton, which had been his original Alma Mater. However, the psychological laboratories survived. This was in part because of the enthusiasm he had engendered in a group of graduate students who continued to use them, but also because, at his urging, the University had decided to import another student of Wundt's to assist in their management. This student was a German named August Kirschmann. He arrived in 1893 and, after Baldwin's departure, was put in charge of the laboratory.

Kirschmann was an active researcher. His main interests were in the psychology of vision and during his tenure the laboratories were substantially expanded. He was a friend of E.B. Titchener's and a member of the group which promoted the establishment of the Society of Experimental Psychology.

Kirschmann was at Toronto for 16 years. He appears to have become well established and valued there because, for six years following his return to Germany (in 1909) on sick leave, he continued to receive a salary. Presumably Toronto hoped he would come back. This hope seems to have protected the laboratories and these were maintained. They were also actively used during the decade following Kirschmann's departure by at least two graduate students who were destined to play, in the future, important roles in Canadian Psychology. These students were E.A. Bott, who would determine the fate of psychology at Toronto for more than 40 years and R.B. Liddy who would guide the development of psychology at The University of Western Ontario for a quarter of a century.

It was not until the 1920's, some 40 years after the establishment of Wundt's laboratory, which announced to the world that psychology was a science rather than just a part of philosophy, that the first separate departments of psychology in Canada were finally established. In that decade new departments of psychology were created at McGill and Toronto. The head at McGill was W.D. Tait, a Canadian who had been trained at Harvard with Munsterberg. The Head at Toronto was also a Canadian. He was E.A. Bott who, first as a student, then as laboratory assistant and finally as an instructor had managed to keep the psychological laboratories, founded by Baldwin at Toronto, functional.

Thus Toronto and McGill were the forerunners of modern psychology in Canada. They provided models for their smaller, slowly developing sister universities, but it would not be until the 1940's that any other universities in Canada took the momentous administrative step of finally and permanently severing the ties between philosophy and psychology which had existed for so many years.

Dalhousie established a chair of psychology and began teaching courses in modern psychology in 1923. However, in 1929, a philosopher, Hilton Page, was appointed to that chair and Page directed the development of psychology at Dalhousie for 34 years. He was even made Head of the new separate Department of Psychology which was established in 1948 and he remained in that post until his retirement in 1962.

Queen's, which began teaching psychology as moral and mental philosophy in 1847, kept on teaching, even modern psychology, under the label philosophy until 1949. It is startling to discover that even the courses in experimental psychology taught by D.O. Hebb, who instructed at Queen's between 1939 and 1942, were listed in the calendar as philosophy courses. This was probably due, at least in part, to the influence of John Watson, which was exercised over a period of more than 50 years. This prestigeful scholar, who held the Chair in Mental and Moral Philosophy from 1872 to 1924 was, throughout his entire career, an exponent of British idealism and was highly critical of all of 20th Century modern psychology, especially of experimental psychology. Watson was succeeded, however, by a philosopher with considerable training in psychology, who was asked by the University to build up the psychology side of the Philosophy Department. This was George Humphrey a man who had been trained first at Oxford, then at Leipzig in Wundt's laboratory and finally at Harvard where he obtained his Ph.D. Humphrey promoted the interests of psychology both at Queen's and in Canada as a whole. He was clearly identified with the psychological community as evidenced by his active participation in the affairs of the Canadian Psychological Association (Wright, 1974). In 1949, the year that he left Queen's to return to Great Britain, a separate Department of Psychology was established. The modern era in psychology at Queen's then began under the leadership of Julian Blackburn, a psychologist imported from England who had been trained at Cambridge.

The University of Western Ontario began teaching psychology in 1898. The textbooks used were those of Angell and Stout but, until 1929 the instructor was the Reverend George B. Sage, an Anglican Priest. The first "full-time Director in Psychology," Desmond Humphreys Smyth, was appointed in 1929. The significance of the title "Director" was that the appointee was to establish and "direct" a laboratory. Smyth, fresh from McGill with a 1928 Master's degree, lasted at Western for only two years. He established a modest laboratory, but did little in it. In 1931 he was replaced by Toronto-trained Roy B. Liddy. A new department of Philosophy and Psychology was established that year and Liddy was made its Head. Although by formal training a philosopher, Liddy had a keen interest in psychology. This had been developed during his graduate student days in Toronto where he had spent many hours with E.A. Bott in the psychology laboratories. By 1932 Liddy had established a complete honors program in psychology at Western, had added a psychologist (Douglas J. Wilson, also trained at Toronto) to his staff and had begun training graduate students. The first Western M.A. degree in psychology was conferred in 1933. Liddy continued in charge of psychology at Western until his retirement in 1954. He was the first Head of the new separate department, which was established in 1948.

At McMaster the teaching of psychology began in 1888. The courses were offered by the Department of Philosophy, although by 1940 they were listed as courses in psychology. A Department of Philosophy and Psychology was established in 1947, but no psychologist was appointed until 1953 when R.H. Nicholson joined the staff. Nicholson remained at McMaster for only two years and in 1955 was replaced by P.L. Newbigging. It was Newbigging who first promoted the interests of modern psychology at McMaster in a forceful way. By 1957 he had obtained approval for an honours program and by 1958 a separate

Department of Psychology had been established with the authority to commence training at the graduate level. It was Newbigging who shaped the beginnings of the strong department that exists at McMaster today.

Thus modern psychology came to Canada first at Toronto and during the Baldwin and Kirschmann years experimental psychology of the Wundtion type prospered there. Research was done, graduate students were trained, monographs and papers were published. The psychology of vision flourished and important work on, for example, colour vision was done.

At McGill, in 1903, the Chair in Mental Philosophy became vacant and consideration was given to hiring a modern psychologist to fill this post. Titchener who, during the Kirschmann years, had tried to obtain a position at Toronto, now applied for the vacancy at McGill. Although well recommended he was not appointed, perhaps because, as George Ferguson suggests, the "tight-fisted Scots" at McGill were unwilling to under-write the costs of the laboratories Titchener would require. Although another Edinburgh philosopher, William Caldwell was appointed to the Chair, he gave strong support to the development of psychology. He obtained private funds for the support of experimental psychology and shortly appointed a psychologist to his staff. J.W.A. Hickson, a Canadian who had done his graduate work in psychology at the University of Halle in Germany, became a member of the Department in 1905. An honours program in psychology was instituted in 1904 and by 1909 the burgeoning number of students in it justified the appointment of a second psychologist. The second psychologist was W.D. Tait, the man who would shape the image of psychology at McGill for many years.

Tait's first job at McGill was to establish a laboratory and this he did during his first year there in 1909–1910. During World War I Tait joined the armed forces and went overseas. His experiences there seemed to diminish his interest in psychology. However, he returned to McGill after the war and when the separate department of psychology was established in 1924, he was made its Head. In this same year, Hickson resigned and was replaced by Chester E. Kellog. Kellog was an American with a Ph.D. from Harvard, a man who was to remain at McGill until 1947. Thus, until the end of the second world war, Tait and Kellog represented psychology at McGill. A few others came and went but these two men determined its character. It was not until 1946, after Tait's retirement, that a new era began at McGill and this was initiated by Robert B. MacLeod.

The Period between the Two World Wars

Between the two great wars psychology in Canada (and also in the United States, O'Donnell, 1979) was largely applied. Little experimental work was done and the laboratories lay idle. Three factors were probably the most important determiners of this situation. First, having so recently gained recognition as an independent discipline, there was a felt urgency to demonstrate that psychology could be used to solve practical problems. Second, following the first great war, there were urgent demands for help from the social sciences. Many were appalled at man's inhumanity to man and his potential capacity for self-destruction. Faith in science was strong and there was hope that the social sciences might be able to find ways and means of changing human beings which would make them capable of coping with the demands of a modern technologically sophisticated world. Thirdly, there was little or no money for basic research. There were, however, funds for applied research.

During the twenties and thirties the psychologists at both Toronto and McGill were busily engaged doing a variety of things in mental hospitals, schools and industry. The mental hygiene movement sparked by Clifford Beers (1931) was gaining wide attention and support. The Canadian National Committee for Mental Hygiene, established in Toronto under the direction of Clarence Hincks, raised funds for research and promotion in the mental health field. Much of this was invested in enterprises undertaken by the staff in psychology at Toronto which by this time had expanded to include besides Alexander Bott, Earle Mac-Phee, William Blatz, Sperrin Chant, Davidson Ketchum, Winfred Bridges, and later William Line (who replaced MacPhee), Karl Bernhardt, Gerald Cosgrave, and Roger Myers.

While Toronto was focusing on community psychology and the improvement of mental health, McGill was studying the psychological effects of unemployment. The stock-market crash in 1929 and the great depression which followed, prompted the Canadian government to invest as much as $15,000 a year for five years, a substantial sum in those days, in research in this area. These funds were entrusted to McGill and they sustained the work of the psychologists there during this difficult period.

It was also in the early 1920's that money began, for the first time, to become available for the study of children and family relations. Early intervention and parent education were viewed as essential elements in any mental health promotion program. Encouraged by Hincks the Laura Spelman Rockefeller Memorial Foundation provided sufficient funds to establish at both McGill and Toronto a nursery school and child study centre. Although the centre at McGill, directed by J.W. Bridges and his wife Banham Bridges did not thrive, perhaps because the research interests of the directors were not appropriate, and support for it was withdrawn at the end of five years, the centre at Toronto was a striking success. Under the direction of W.E. Blatz it became the Institute of Child Study, one of the first of such Institutes on the North American continent and, for a number of years, enjoyed both national and international respect.

World War II

Certain events occurred during the second world war and immediately following it which laid the foundation for the resumption, during the post-war period, of experimental research. The most important of these was the securing of a source of funds for the support of basic research. This was achieved through the efforts of the Canadian Psychological Association (CPA) which was established in 1939. The CPA was formed primarily in response to the desire of its members to insure that their expertise was used appropriately and effectively in the war effort. The psychological resources available in Canada were mustered and initially put to work on the development of armed forces' manpower selection procedures. The Initial work was funded from private sources, but as its importance was recognized public funds from the National Research Council were made available. The valuable contributions made to the war effort by psychologists ultimately assured the recognition of psychology as a useful discipline worthy of financial support. After the war both the National Reasearch Council and the Defence Research Board allocated funds for training and research in psychology. A third national source of funds was also obtained. This was the Ministry of Health and Welfare (Wright, 1974).

Post World War II

After the war the move back to basic research was made first at McGill and not until much later at Toronto. It was Robert MacLeod who changed the course of events at McGill. He replaced Tait as Chairman of the department in 1946. MacLeod had obtained his M.A. at McGill and his Ph.D. at Columbia but had also studied for a time in Germany with Wertheimer, Köhler and Lewin. He stayed only two years at McGill (before becoming chairman of the Department at Cornell) but, during his first year there, obtained funds to re-develop and equip the laboratories and he persuaded D.O. Hebb and George Ferguson to join the staff. When he left for Cornell, Hebb became his successor.

Hebb developed his interest in physiological psychology while a student at McGill. He later studied with Lashley, first at Chicago and then at Harvard where he obtained his Ph.D. In 1937 he returned to Canada to work at the Montreal Neurological Institute with Penfield, but in 1939 accepted an appointment at Queen's. However, in 1942, he went back to the United States to a post at the Yerkes Laboratories of Primate Biology and remained there until his return to McGill. Hebb became for Canada the champion of basic experimental research in psychology and shaped the new image of psychology at McGill which we have today.

At Toronto, for a full decade following the war, there was little change in orientation. The department remained "applied" and focused primarily on the training of clinical students on the scientist-professional model. This was because the pre-war faculty was still there and little new blood was brought in. Furthermore this faculty was aging rapidly and exhausted both from the war effort and the pressures of teaching, with limited resources, the hordes of returning veterans. It was not until Ned Bott finally retired, after more than 30 years as Head, and Roger Myers succeeded him, that any serious attempt to develop a department with a "hard" science research orientation was initiated. It was to Myers' great credit that, being himself a man with applied interests, he was able and willing to carry the department in the direction in which it went, that is into the modern era. Early in the Myers' years Endel Tulving, Abe Amsel, George Mandler, Dan Berlyne, and others were appointed and they brought to Toronto new values. The changes that followed were not welcomed by many of the old Toronto grads. For some years to follow, in the province of Ontario, the professional-scientist schisms were deep and bitter.

Dalhousie began to develop a strong modern department in 1962 when a real psychologist, Henry James, was finally put in charge. Queen's had made a start at developing a strong undergraduate department when Blackburn was appointed in 1948 but did not succeed in developing a stable faculty which could successfully mount and maintain graduate studies until the late fifties when such people as Peter Dodwell, R.W. Payne and James Inglis were appointed. The first Queen's Ph.D. was conferred in 1959. Although Western started offering graduate training as early as the 30's and produced a substantial number of M.A.s and two Ph.D.s in the late forties and mid-fifties, it was largely applied in orientation and did not begin to develop its modern image until the 1960's. When R.B. Liddy retired in 1954 a real psychologist, G.H. Turner succeeded him. Turner was not, however, sympathetic with the trend toward a return to experimental psychology. He was a Toronto graduate with strong humanistic interests. It was not until the early sixties, when Turner resigned as chairman, and Mary Wright assumed responsibility for the department, that any major changes occurred. Wright was also Toronto-trained and had applied interests, but was convinced that the department must, if it was to sustain a first rate graduate program, develop a strong basic research orientation. The appointments in the early sixties of such persons as A.U. Paivio, G. Mogenson, R.C. Gardner, D.N. Jackson, Doreen Kimura and others gave that department its current image. Finally, as was said earlier, McMaster developed into a high quality department which could undertake graduate training very quickly after the appointment of Lynn Newbigging in the late fifties. The first important appointments made there were L.J. Kamin, A.H. Black, W.H. Heron and H.M. Jenkins.

Early in the 1950's the Canadian Social Science Research Council offered to underwrite a survey of Psychology in Canadian Universities. Robert MacLeod, then at Cornell, was selected to undertake this task and his report was published in 1955. He decried what he called the "premature professionalism" of psychology in Canada and made a plea for a return to science. His report sparked the holding of the Opinicon Conference on Research Training in Psychology (Myers, 1958). The conference was held in the spring of 1960 (Bernhardt, 1961) a critical point in time, for it was on the threshold of the period of great expansion for Universities in general and departments of psychology in particular, when new visions could be fulfilled and new goals attained. One of the most influential participants at Opinicon was Don Hebb. It is difficult to assess the impact of Opinicon on the developments which took place in the sixties but in the opinion of the writers it was substantial.

References

Beers, C.W. *A mind that found itself*. Revised (5th) edition. Doubleday-Doran & Co. New York, 1931.

Bernhardt, K.S. (Ed.), *Training for research in psychology. The Canadian Opinicon Conference*. University of Toronto Press, 1961.

Myers, C.R. Professional Psychology in Canada. *The Canadian Psychologist*, 1958, 7, 27–36.

O'Donnnell, J.M. The crisis of experimentalism in the 1920's: E.G. Boring and his uses of history. *American Psychologist*, 1979, 34, 289–295.

Wright, M.J. CPA: The First Ten Years. *The Canadian Psychologist*, 1974, 15, 112–131.

Chapter 1

Psychology at Dalhousie

by

*F. Hilton Page** and *James W. Clark***

I

Dalhousie was founded in 1818 in imitation of the University of Edinburgh and it was only natural that its early instruction should follow the teaching of the Scottish school of philosophy. Yet the actual process by which the Scottish philosophy arrived in Nova Scotia, and ultimately found its way to Dalhousie, is a curious example of the role played by chance, and by purely natural events, in intellectual history.

In 1803 a 27 year old graduate of the University of Glasgow in Arts, Medicine and Theology had been appointed, by the Secession Church in Scotland, to be a missionary to Prince Edward Island. The vessel which bore him across the Atlantic had put in at Pictou Harbour in Nova Scotia. It was then late in the season and ice was already beginning to form in the Northumberland Strait, rendering the remainder of the passage to the Island hazardous. The people of Pictou, taking an immediate liking to the would-be missionary, and fascinated by "the pair of globes" (the symbol of the teacher's craft) that he brought with him, persuaded him to remain and finally to settle in Pictou.[1]

So it came about that while the natives of Prince Edward Island were left to languish in darkness, the Reverend Thomas McCulloch became, a few years later, in 1816, the founder of Pictou Academy. This famous institution was for many years a university in everything but name, and

* Professor Page joined the Faculty of Dalhousie University in 1929 and was the Head of the Department of Psychology there from 1948 to 1962. He is the author of the first three sections of this chapter.

** Professor Clark joined the Faculty of Dalhousie University in 1959 and has been an active member of the Department of Psychology there since that time.

certainly, in those early days, more like a university than either Dalhousie (which was still struggling to get off the ground) or King's College (founded in 1789, at Windsor, N.S., with its Anglican exclusiveness and rather narrow classical tradition).

McCulloch argued that higher education in Nova Scotia must be "adapted to the present state of this province", and "the degree at which the province stands in the scale of civilized society." Nova Scotians needed "mathematical and physical science whose usefulness would immediately become apparent" and also, though he didn't use the word, psychology. He wrote: "... instead of enabling them to display their pedantry by interlarding Latin and Greek phrases with the chit-chat of life, it would be more profitable to give them an acquaintance with the operations of their own minds. ..."[2]

Because of sectarian differences, the bane of educational progress in nineteenth century Nova Scotia, govermental and church support began to waver and the Academy had perforce temporarily to close its doors. It was this reverse that brought McCulloch to Dalhousie College in 1838 as its first Principal and Professor of Mental and Moral Philosophy. Thus it is true to say that the teaching of psychology at Dalhousie is as old as the beginning of the College itself as an actually functioning institution.

A former student has left this account of McCulloch's teaching: "His chief studies had been in what has been called the Scottish school of Philosophy. He had written an outline of both (i.e., of both mental and moral philosophy) on notes which he gave us; and though independent enough to avoid servilely following any master, and acute enough to notice the weak points of each, he in the main followed Reid."[3]

Thomas Reid (1710–1796) was the originator of the Scottish Philosophy of Common Sense, publishing his *Inquiry into the Human Mind on the Principles of Common Sense* in 1763. His *Essay on the Intellectual Powers of Man* (1785) contained his class-room lectures at Aberdeen and Glasgow. He was opposed to a philosophy that is a mere "chamber exercise." On the contrary, he held, there are first principles that are "a part of the human constitution" and they "fall not within the province of reason, but of common sense."[4] Such was the background of McCulloch's teaching.

McCulloch had come to Dalhousie in poor health, prematurely aged, a broken and disappointed man, worn down by the sectarian animosities and social prejudices against which he had had to struggle in his vain attempts to keep his Academy at Pictou solvent. He died after only five years at Dalhousie, in 1843.

Thereafter Dalhousie College promptly collapsed for another twenty years. In 1863 it was revived and reorganized. By 1864 it was calling itself "Dalhousie College and University", and thereafter simply "Dalhousie

University". With its revival the work in psychology was resumed with the appointment of William Lyall to the Chair of Metaphysics, to be renamed the Chair of Psychology and Metaphysics in 1866. It seems probable that Lyall can rightly claim two Canadian "firsts": the first to have the word "psychology" in the title of his chair, and the first to have written in Canada a comprehensive textbook. This is a very substantial volume of 627 pages, entitled *Intellect, the Emotions, and the Moral Nature* (1855). True, it was published in Edinburgh, but it was written in what is now Canada while he was a professor at the Free Church College in Halifax, some eight years before he came to Dalhousie. It almost certainly contains his lectures as he gave them at that time. It is said to have been used as a textbook in several colleges and Lyall himself continued to use it in his classes at Dalhousie until his death in 1890. The class in Logic and Psychology, modelled after the Scottish pattern, which Lyall began was to continue for eighty-four years, until 1948 when Psychology became a department separate from Philosophy.

Lyall, or to give him his full style and title, The Reverend Professor William Lyall, Doctor of Laws, Fellow of the Royal Society of Canada, was a Scot, educated at Glasgow and Edinburgh. The Scottish School had always included a good deal of "straight" psychology in its teaching. A particularly good example is Thomas Brown (1778–1820) whose lectures were posthumously published in 1820 in four volumes. They were enormously popular and went into many later editions. Lyall is said to have been greatly influenced by Brown. Indeed he is said to have been "Brown's" favourite pupil at Edinburgh and to have retained an affectionate reverence for his professor."[5] As Brown died when Lyall was only nine years old this seems a trifle difficult to believe. However, in his book, Lyall does frequently refer to "Dr. Brown", though not always uncritically, and he follows Brown's order of exposition fairly closely.

Brown was an M.D. not, like so many of the other members of the Scottish School, a D.D. He contributed to the development of modern psychology in at least two ways. He was concerned with psychology as a natural science independent of metaphysics and mental philosophy. He thought that Hume's notion of causality, as the invariable sequence of antecedent and consequent, should be applied to mental science as much as to physical. Psychology, he thought, is like physics in so far as it is concerned with "the analysis of what is complex and the arrangement of the various feelings or successive states of mind in regular order of their sequence as causes and effects."[6] He published an unfinished *Physiology of the Mind* (1820), the incomplete first part of a projected textbook for the use of his Edinburgh students. Secondly, he recognized the importance of what he called "muscular" sensations in our exploration of the external world. These kinesthetic sensations had not previously been distinguished from sensations of touch.

On the other hand, Lyall's book, on which successive generations of students at Dalhousie were nurtured in psychology for twenty-seven years, from 1863 to 1890, follows a line quite different from Brown's. It is a charming period-piece in which the psychology is jostled by poetry, piety and philosophy. To savour its distinctive quality one needs to be aware of the conventions and expectations of the time. He did not favour physiological psychology. It was said that "He saw in it the philosophy of mud."[7] He did not like Hume, nor did he later on like Darwin and Herbert Spencer. "Mind", he protests in an eloquent passage, "cannot be an organic product."[8] Admitting that Lyall "may have had some prejudices against some modern types of Philosophy (Spencer and Darwin)", a contributor to the Dalhousie Gazette of 1890 excuses this as a "failing that leaned to virtue's side."[9]

In September 1864 Lyall gave the Inaugural Address at the opening of the 1864–65 session.[10] It took the form of a "simple glance at the different departments of a university course." When he comes to psychology he says "Logic and Psychology are very germane to each other. Logic must be taught separately ... but there ought also to be the Science of Psychology itself. ... The more elementary course, let it be observed, is intended to familiarize the student with the terms and nomenclature of mental science ... it is the sort of grammar of thought and mind. The student is then prepared to enter upon Psychology proper. ... Then all the profounder questions of Being as well as of thinking invite our attention." So almost before we know it we are into metaphysics. "A completer course in metaphysics is more demanded at the present day than ever perhaps previously. It is the counterpoise to the positivism, or materialism of the age." It is not physiology that Lyall finds to be related to psychology, but logic and metaphysics. Yet, curiously for one so much a denizen of the study, the library and the classroom, he excells in his subtle and acute analysis of the complexities of human emotion and motivation. Epistemologically he remains a realist, faithful to the tenets of the Scottish School of Common Sense. He is a G.E. Moore, fifty years ahead of his time, but a G.E. Moore in a Geneva gown.

Lyall's students were prepared to answer questions of a scope that his successors at Dalhousie might well envy: "State the laws of thought, and show what function they perform in mind; dwelling more particularly on the last of the enumeration, and showing its presence in the arrangement of the cosmos." Nor, perhaps, have Lyall's successors matched on their recent course evaluations this irresistible description by a student of 1870: "... the qualities of the non-ego, the states and manifestations of the ego, as well as their relations to the Infinite, are pursued in all their phases as deep as human ken can mine, and as high as winged thought can soar by the lofty mind of Prof. Lyall, LL.D. ..."[11]

II

When Lyall died in 1890, the first International Congress of Psychology had just met in Paris, the new psychology of Wilhelm Wundt was seeping into North America, William James had finally completed his *Principles of Psychology*, and the University of Toronto had appointed one of Wundt's students, James Mark Baldwin, to its first chair of psychology. At Dalhousie the professor of metaphysics took over Lyall's class and the Dalhousie Gazette pleaded with the Governors of Dalhousie "to set all fears at rest concerning the future fate of this highly important professorship in Logic and Psychology." "Psychology is a subject which has made such rapid strides within the last few years that, if the students are to be benefitted by a study of this increasingly important subject, they must have a professor who has made a special study of Psychology. Psychology, now a recognized science, is so far removed from Philosophy, that the professor or student, who has devoted his attention to Mental and Moral Philosophy, can but give the outlines of this subject, that is so rapidly growing, and which, from present appearances, is destined hand in hand with Physiology to give the most satisfactory and definite knowledge of mind and its phenomena." And, as an attempted clincher, the Gazette added this appeal to chauvinism: "Dalhousie will lose prestige among the sister colleges of the Dominion. For a number of years this university was the only institution in Canada that supported two chairs in Philosophy. It is only within the last year that the universities of Toronto and Queens have founded additional chairs in philosophy. If then our Governors suffer this chair to become extinct, the Upper Canada colleges will not be slow to let the world know it."[12]

Despite the eloquence and even prescience of the Gazette, Lyall's chair died with Lyall, and philosophers were to teach psychology at Dalhousie for the next thirty-three years. However, philosophers though they were, they did not ignore the new psychology. James Seth (1890–92, and later Professor of Mental Philosophy at Edinburgh) replaced Lyall's book with James' brand new book and set questions with a more modern ring: "Distinguish carefully between (a) a sensation and a percept, (b) an image and a concept." Walter C. Murray (1892–1908, and later the first president of the University of Saskatchewan) taught educational psychology with Sully's *Teacher's Handbook of Psychology*, used the new texts of Titchener and Baldwin, and offered a master's degree with a course in the psychology of feeling and will (for which "the candidate is expected to consult the writings of Bain, Spencer, James, Baldwin, Ladd, Titchener, Wundt, Külpe, Ribot, Münsterberg, Marshall and Ward on the subject" – a fine list of the psychology of consequence at the turn of the century). In the 1894–95 calendar Murray announced that "experiments will be introduced as much as possible to supply a basis for the theory and for the purpose of illustration", although a member of that class could not later recall any experiments actually being performed. W.D. Tait, who was to achieve the administrative separation of psychology from philosophy at McGill and to become the first head of that illustrious department in 1924, and Robert Magill, who underwent a curious metamorphosis when he resigned his professorship to become Chairman of the Grain Commission of Canada, also taught the psychology class in the early years of this century.

The most brilliant of these, and the one destined to achieve the greatest eminence in the world of philosophy, was John Laird, ultimately Regius Professor of Moral Philosophy at Aberdeen. After an outstanding career at Edinburgh and at Cambridge where he won a First in both parts of the Moral Science Tripos in 1910 and 1911, he came to Dalhousie in 1912. In his contribution to the first volume of Muirhead's *Contemporary British Philosophy* (1924) he mentions his students and colleagues in Nova Scotia as among those who had contributed "through active discussion to the revision and sharpening of my thought." Though primarily a philosopher, Laird wrote extensively on psychological matters in his *Problems of the Self* (1917), *The Ideal of the Soul* (1924) and *Our Minds and their Bodies* (1925). Of all those who have taught psychology at Dalhousie Laird possessed the most searching intellect and the greatest gifts as a writer.

Laird's stay at Dalhousie was brief, but the term of his successor in the George Munro Chair was to be the longest in the history of the university. Herbert Leslie Stewart was professor of philosophy from 1913 to 1947, part-time lecturer until 1951, and Emeritus Professor until his death in September of 1953, a total of forty years. He did his B.A., M.A., and Ph.D. at Belfast, took a Second in "Greats" at Oxford, winning the John Locke Scholarship, studied Divinity at Edinburgh, and in 1912–13 was lecturer at Belfast. In 1912, the year before coming to Dalhousie, he published *Questions of the Day in Philosophy and Psychology*. Five of its nine chapters are devoted to psychological topics. The long first chapter on "The Reform in Psychology" is a measured defence of experimental methods in psychology against the criticism of "experimentation on the mind" voiced by some philosophers of the time. Stewart welcomed the new independence of the science of psychology which "no longer acknowledges a subordinate title of existence held in fee from the metaphysician: it stands by its own right, works by its own methods and announces its own results as free from any overlordship as is physics or chemistry. ... The task of the psychologist is now separated in a more radical fashion than ever before from the task of the metaphysician. ... His own field is now assigned to each of two workers, who in the past wasted much of their time in thwarting and embarrassing each other."[13] Thus it could not have been at Stewart's urgings that Dalhousie continued for another decade to assign both fields to one worker – Stewart – and, when each had at last its own worker, required Stewart, as head of Philosophy, to be psychology's overlord until 1947.

Dr. Stewart ("Herbie" as he was widely known to colleagues and students alike) was a man of strong views, forceful character, immense energy and lively powers of self-expression. He edited the *Dalhousie Review* from its beginning in 1921 until 1947 and for many years gave extremely popular radio broadcasts on Sunday afternoons on world affairs. His method of lecturing was to spend the first quarter hour or so dictating a note to the class, while the time remaining was devoted to elaborating and discussing what he had dictated. His lectures were always carefully prepared and so perfectly expressed that they could often have been sent to the printers without alteration. To the capable and interested student he was an excellent teacher and several of his pupils later went on to become themselves professors of philosophy.

III

In 1923, one-third of a century after the students of Dalhousie had asked for a professor of psychology, they got one. the University of King's College came into association with Dalhousie, established a chair of psychology, and appointed Norman Jellinger Symons to teach the students of both King's and Dalhousie.[14] Symons started a laboratory class and several others including, ominously as it turned out, a class in dynamic psychology. For Symons, who had come innocently enough from the teaching of classics at Queens, became more and more absorbed in psychoanalytic theories and techniques. When he began to solicit accounts of their dreams from his students and then provide them with full-blown Freudian interpretations, carefully written out and suitable for displaying to their parents, the university authorities were seized with alarm. In 1929, after the only really dramatic incident in the otherwise placid history of psychology at Dalhousie, Professor Symons was asked to resign. Dalhousie may have been ready, at last, for psychology taught by a psychologist. It was not yet ready for Freud.[15]

With Symon's departure the senior author (Hilton Page) of this chapter can take up the narrative in the first person. For it was in the fall of

1929 that I first appeared on the scene, blissfully ignorant of what had occurred to create the vacancy I had been invited to fill. In any case I would have been too busy preparing and delivering lectures to have had much time to think about it. In the Faculty of Arts and Science I taught seven classes, four each year. In addition, but without additional remuneration, I lectured in the Faculty of Medicine, in the School of Social Work, and in the Conservatory of Music. Somewhat later I also lectured at Pine Hill Divinity Hall for a modest honorarium. During the war years I lectured in the evenings to members of the armed forces stationed in the area. This made a refreshing change for me. Interest and enthusiasm ran high. I still look back on it with pleasure.

To illustrate how informal, easy-going and carefree were those halcyon days I'll relate an incident that occurred shortly after my arrival. A day or two before classes were to begin I happened to run into the Registrar, who said "Oh! by the way, Page, I meant to tell you, there is a group of girls doing Domestic Science at the Halifax Ladies' College to whom you will have to give a class in child psychology." Child psychology! Terror seized me. Moreover I was shy with girls. I protested that I knew nothing whatever about child psychology, that I had never studied the subject, that it was utterly impossible for me to teach it. "Don't worry", was the reply, "it doesn't matter what you teach them; just keep their minds occupied for a couple of hours a week. Perhaps you could find a book or two in the Library that would help you." I rushed up the stairs to the Library but all I could find there were Kurt Koffka's *Growth of the Mind* and a row of several copies of J.B. Watson's *Psychological Care of Infant and Child*. Fortified by these and aided by a lively imagination I managed somehow to get through the year. The girls were very young and very nice and friendly, and altogether we had rather a pleasant time of it. Later on I made this into a regular second-year Arts class. It turned out to be my most popular class and for a time was the largest second-year class in the whole Faculty of Arts and Science. If I could believe all I have been told, it would appear that about half the population of Halifax had been brought up on the sage precepts, enlightened attitudes and useful information I was fondly credited with having imparted to their parents. I still blush to think of it. Was I not just another of those lucky impostors who somehow manage never to be found out? Or could it possibly be that there really was something sensible, substantial and serviceable in what I had to tell them.

IV

To prevent modesty from introducing further distortions, the junior author must now wrest control of the narrative. For the history of psychology at Dalhousie from 1929 to 1962 is an account of the accomplishments of F. Hilton Page. After two decades of teaching unaided his awesome load of classes, in 1948 Page brought about the separation of psychology from the Philosophy Department and, at the request of the Departments of Health of the four Atlantic provinces for postgraduate work in clinical psychology, established a master's programme which soon contained one-third of the M.A. students at Dalhousie; he expanded the teaching staff to six and trebled the classes; and, when he left psychology in 1962, not to retire but to become head of the Philosophy Department which needed him even more than psychology at that moment, he had laid the groundwork for a Ph.D. programme. If his predecessors had failed to bring Dalhousie's psychology fully into the twentieth century, Professor Page had not.

Although the growth of psychology in the post-war years was continent-wide, the quality of that growth at Dalhousie was a reflection of Page. A scholar of great scope and sympathies rather than an experimenter or clinician, he guided the development of graduate work in clinical and experimental psychology with constant attention to the contribution of psychology to a liberal education. The concept of a liberal education was one with which the new Ph.D.s, brought into the department by Page and often trained in a rawer psychological tradition, soon became familiar. We (for the junior author was among them) were to temper our enthusiasm for the creation of replicas of ourselves with a concern that every undergraduate be given an accurate acquaintance with the operations of his own mind (to use the phrase of Thomas McCulloch again). By example we were made to understand that the freshman was as important as the graduate student and that much was to be expected of both. A thoughtful man of natural dignity and gentleness, Hilton Page represents psychology to generations of Dalhousie students, and the esteem that he earned for psychology among students and faculty continued to benefit the department that he had created long after he left it.

In 1960 the *Canadian Psychologist* printed a paper on psychology at Dalhousie.[16] The bulk of that paper is a description of the department in 1959, with its full-time staff of four housed in three offices, a one-room laboratory, a master's programme in which the emphasis was clinical, research largely restricted to that of the twenty-seven students who had achieved master's degrees in the decade, and a publication record described by the authors as "not over-prolific". Now, from a building constructed for psychology replete with seal tank, laboratory nursery, surgery-histology suites, TV and photographic studios, a couple of hundred laboratory rooms in which one stumbles over computers, and an outlying wolf-pack, the one person who remains of the old faculty of four recalls, with the difficulties of a metempsychotic, both the joys and the frustrations of joining in 1959 an overburdened, ill-equipped, but spirited and developing department. The search for research space may have triumphed only temporarily with permission from the Registrar to use the basement vault in which she kept her files, the sole calculating machine in the Faculty may have been kept locked in the office of the head of Mathematics, and the neighbouring professors of English may have got up a petition against the use of rats for fear that their books would be eaten, but in compensation there was the warmth and enthusiasm of Frances Marshall (1948–61) who would, when pressed, talk about her days as a Ph.D. student in the Chicago of Harvey Carr, the unbounded optimism of H.D. Beach (1957–69) whose multifarious research was not abated by a heavy teaching load, and the patient guidance of Professor Page.

The transformation, begun by Page, was continued by P.H.R. James, head of the department from 1962 to 1968, later Dean of Arts and Science, and more recently Killam Research Professor. Under Henry James experimental psychology at Dalhousie grew and flourished. The department today is an expanded reflection of the department that James planned and built, strong in physiological and developmental psychology, animal behaviour, perception, and information processing, relatively weak in clinical and social psychology, and untouched by many aspects of applied psychology. When James arrived from Queens with an apparatus for imprinting chicks and grand plans for psychology, the department had moved from its few rooms in the formal Arts and Administration Building (most unsuitable for rats) to a war-built temporary-but-thus-far-permanent structure, ideal for experimenters who wanted to cut holes in walls and keep pigeons on the roof and for graduate students who wanted to set up housekeeping in their labs. Within two years James had doubled the size of the department, requiring a move to a large and elegant house whose gardens were soon spoiled by satellite laboratories, and within another two years had trebled it, provoking plans for a building designed to psychology's increasingly specialized needs in research and teaching. The department occupied its building in 1971 where, with its rate of growth abating, it continues to fit comfortably.

In quantity, psychology at Dalhousie has been a mere mild variation on the North American psychological ogive: one (and sometimes no) psychologist from 1838 to 1948, five by 1962, twenty-one by 1968, and thirty in 1980. In content, however, Dalhousie's psychology of the 60's and 70's has been somewhat distinctive.

First, to get them out of the way, the deficiencies in content – at least those to which the department will publicly confess and thus those of which it may be suspected of being less than fully penitent. Clinical psychology, after dominating the graduate work of the department during the later years of Page's chairmanship, declined in relative importance although not in the quality of its teachers. With the thrust of the department elsewhere, the last decade has seen two clinical psychologists coping with large enrollments in their popular classes and few graduate students. The social psychology of humans has obtained no more than a toe-hold at Dalhousie. Although that hold has been occupied by some fine toes, they have shown a disturbing tendency to climb to broader footing elsewhere. The calendar entry for a class in personality, when it has appeared at all, has more often than not been followed by "not offered in 19–". Educational psychology, industrial psychology, counselling psychology, and other applied fields are simply absent, although community psychology is not. Under James the department decided to concentrate in the traditional areas of experimental psychology and, under Charles Brimer (1968–71)[17], John McNulty (1972–74), John Fentress (1974–80) and now Robert Rodger, it has continued to do so, with a spread into neurobiology, and, recently, signs of a return to graduate work in clinical psychology.

Animal behaviour was the first area to be established firmly with seven oppointments in the mid-60's. By the end of the decade the research of the animal behaviourists was attracting attention to Dalhousie and the department was for the first time drawing graduate students in large numbers from beyond the Maritimes. They came not only to work on the central problems of animal learning but also on the navigation of seals, the aggression of lobsters and other watery phenomena appropriate to a department whose windows look out to sea. More recent appointments have brought to Dalhousie laboratories devoted to research on biological rhythms and the control of integrated movement patterns as well as a field research station for the study of social communication in timber wolves.

As some of the investigators of animal learning have moved from associationistic to more cognitive concepts, they have made increasing contact with another sizeable group within the department: the students of human information processing. During much of the 60's three psychologists at Dalhousie were producing important work on memory, and they have been joined by others working on attentional processes and the development of language.

If animal and human learning were the major strengths of the department in the 60's, developmental psychology and perception were well represented, and, toward the end of the decade, after a long search, the department found two physiological psychologists who were able to attract the psychologists and biologists from whom neuroscience has flowered at Dalhousie in the 70's. But textbook areas of psychology are no longer adequate to label the work of psychologists here or elsewhere. The areas are fruitfully intermeshed. At Dalhousie there are developmental investigations of the visual system of insects as well as of the social behaviour of infants, and perception is studied by techniques that include recording from single cells in the cat cortex as well as plotting the paths of buoys towed by human divers swimming to underwater sound sources, just as learning is investigated through changes of synaptic transmission in the rat as well as through generalization gradients of pigeons and the verbal associations of freshmen.

Dalhousie has been a generous home to psychology for two decades. What it asks of psychology in return, it seems to us, can be expressed in the words of our nineteenth-century predecessors: to work hand in hand with physiology to produce a satisfactory knowledge of mind, and to impart this knowledge to students so that they might have an accurate acquaintance with the operations of their own minds.

Notes

[1] John W. Grant. "Thomas McCulloch, Pioneer". *The United Churchman, 47,* 23, December 26, 1962, 15

[2] From a letter quoted by D.C. Harvey in "Dr. Thomas McCulloch and liberal education. *Dalhousie Review,* 1943, 23, 358.

[3] *Dalhousie Gazette,* 1887, 20, 32–33

[4] *The Works of Thomas Reid, D.D.* (Ed.) Sir William Hamilton, Edinburgh, 1863 (6th edition), vol. 1, 110.

[5] *Presbyterian Witness,* Halifax, N.S., 25 January, 1890.

[6] Thomas Brown. *Physiology of the Mind,* Edinburgh, 1820.

[7] *Presbyterian Witness,* Halifax, N.S., 25 January, 1890.

[8] William Lyall. *Intellect, the Emotions, and the Moral Nature.* Edinburgh, 1855, 92–93.

[9] *Dalhousie Gazette,* 1890, 22, 93–94.

[10] Printed in full in the *Presbyterian Witness,* 29 October, 1864.

[11] *Dalhousie Gazette,* 1870, 2, 54.

[12] *Dalhousie Gazette,* 1890, 22, 113.

[13] H.L. Stewart. *Questions of the Day on Philosophy and Psychology,* London, Arnold, 1912, 2, 5

[14] It was in the year of Symon's arrival that the name D.O. Hebb appears in the class list for Logic and Psychology, and, since Dalhousie then published the grades in the calendar for all to see, it can be revealed that the student whom Dalhousie welcomed back as an honorary professor in 1977 ranked somewhat higher in the class than he implied in his contribution to S. Koch (Ed.), *Psychology: A study of a science.* v. 1, New York, McGraw-Hill, 1959.

[15] That Dalhousie may have been ready for Freud thirty years later is suggested by the reply of a distinguished professor to a request for reassurance from a new Ph.D. just arrived

from Queens and unsettled by an account of the Symons incident: "Young man, you may *describe* sex; you must never *advocate* it."

[16] H.D. Beach and F.H. Page. Psychology at Dalhousie. *Canadian Psychologist*, 1960, 1[a], 9–14.

[17] The contribution of Charles Brimer must be singled out. Arriving in 1963 with a McMaster Ph.D. under Leon Kamin, Brimer established an active lab that produced papers of consequence on the role of aversive stimuli in classical conditioning and maintained an even more active office to which students and colleagues flocked in need of anything from advice on the perfect control group to perfect sympathy. His colleagues imposed further on his dedication to their welfare when James became Dean in 1968; as chairman he led the department through the difficult years of planning and adjusting to the new building. Charles Brimer's death in 1971 deprived psychology of a brilliant student; it took from his co-workers at Dalhousie a man they loved.

Further Readings

Anonymous – F. Hilton Page. *The Canadian Psychologist*, 1959, *8*, 68–71.

See also notes in *The Canadian Psychologist*, 1961, *2*, 36; 1962, *3*, 122 and 154; 1963, *4*, 160; 1964, *5*, 259; 1966, *7*, 48.

Chapter 2

Psychology at McGill

by

*George A. Ferguson**

Introduction

The history of a university department is a new genre. Few models exist. The image and reality of a university department consists of the teachers, scientists, and scholars in it. A department is a fabrication of their personalities, relations one with another, standing within the university community, scholarly contribution, reputation within the discipline, and most important of all, their gifts for arousing and shaping the minds of their students. An account of the life of a department is perhaps closer to biography than to history.

This history of the Department of Psychology at McGill University covers in detail roughly the second half of the nineteenth, and the first half of the twentieth centuries, about one hundred years. The intent was to end this history in 1948 when Robert B. MacLeod left for Cornell and Donald O. Hebb assumed the chairmanship. Many individuals have asked that this history be brought "up to date". Because the author has been an involved participant in the affairs of this department for the past third of a century, such an exercise would be more of a subjective memoir than history. As a compromise a brief summary of events from 1948 to 1980 has been added. This summary is as factual as discretion warrants.

A simplistic idea is that the history of Canadian psychology began with the creation of departments of psychology. Obviously this is not true. In some Canadian universities psychology had a long, and not uneventful, association with philosophy before separate departments came into being. The creation of a department of psychology is one

* Professor Ferguson joined the Faculty of McGill University in 1947 and was Chairman of the Department of Psychology there from 1964 to 1975.

episode only, although an important one, in the history of the discipline at McGill.

The earlier philosophers and psychologists did not differ on the nature of the questions asked about the mind, or the areas to explore. Both were concerned with sensation, perception, cognition, affection, and volition, areas that are today the stuff of psychology. The difference was one of method. The philosophers relied on observation and introspection. The psychologists discovered, or thought they had discovered, that the experimental method could be applied in understanding problems of the mind. Their faith in this method was great. They believed that it would lead them far beyond the limits of the philosophical wilderness.

The early history of philosophy and psychology at McGill cannot be grasped without an awareness of the Scottish School of philosophy. Among those identified as members of this School are Thomas Reid, Dugald Stewart, Thomas Brown, James Mill, perhaps John Stewart Mill, Sir William Hamilton, and Alexander Bain. These men, and their contemporaries, carried psychology, as a branch of philosophy, about as far as it could go. They set the shape for its emergence as an experimental discipline. It is as if they mapped a terrain which then required a different, and more sophisticated, methodology for its further exploration. This branch of philosophy, becoming psychology, embellished with the experimental method, reached North America with considerable modification through Germany. It reached McGill directly from the source, unadorned with an experimental approach. The early professors of philosophy at McGill were graduates of the University of Edinburgh. They taught what they had learned. Dugald Stewart loomed large.

In preparing this history of those who made psychology at McGill the question has been clearly kept in mind: What manner of men and women are these? At times it is possible to capture significant aspects of a personality. At other times the picture is cloudy; only crude outlines emerge. All university departments in their journey down the years consist of people both of distinction and mediocrity. Both are important. In writing this history this author has at times felt like Boswell writing the life of Johnson; at other times like Johnson writing the life of Boswell.

The Earliest Years

In 1821 the Board of the Royal Institution for the Advancement of Learning received from the Crown a charter to establish a university. This date is taken as the founding of McGill University. No courses in arts were offered until 1843, when a Faculty of Arts was created with an enrollment of twenty students. Courses in medicine had been taught and medical degrees granted, before that time. At an early date in the life of this faculty, courses were offered in logic, mental science, and moral philosophy. The courses in mental science reflected the philosophically oriented psychology of the period. An early course description, about 1857, reads as follows:

> *Mental Science*: Mental phenomena, different classifications of mental phenomena, unity of the human mind, volition, consciousness, the senses and sensation, perception, understanding, reason, instincts, passions, affections, moral sentiments, reflex sentiments, sentiments of beauty, sublimity, and religion.

Although students were few in number the teaching of mental science, with various modifications, persisted until 1872, when a course called Elementary Psychology was offered to second year students. The teaching of elementary psychology to students in their second year persisted at McGill without interruption for about 100 years.

The offering of a course with the title, Elementary Psychology, coincided with the arrival at McGill of John Clark Murray (1836–1917) who received his education at Glasgow, Edinburgh, Heidelberg and Göttingen. He emigrated from Scotland, taught at Queen's University, and in 1872 became John Frothingham Professor of Mental and Moral Philosophy at McGill University. Murray was a product of the Scottish School of mental philosophy, and was influenced by such men as Dugald Stewart, Sir William Hamilton and Alexander Bain. Murray, although not an experimentalist, was familiar with the work of Wilhelm Wundt, whose influence is reflected in his writings.

In 1885 Murray published an introductory textbook, *A Handbook of Psychology*. This was one of the first books on psychology published by a professor at a Canadian university. It was published in London and later in the United States. The book was highly successful. Between 1885 and 1897 five editions appeared. In 1904 Murray published a sixth revision with a new title, *An Introduction to Psychology*. Murray's textbook was one of the earliest books of its type, and was preceded only by James Sully's *Outline of Psychology* which appeared in 1884. Other texts of the period were John Dewey's *Psychology*, 1886, and George Ladd's *Principles of Psychology*, 1891. James Mark Baldwin's *Hand book of Psychology*, appeared in two volumes, the first in 1889 and the second in 1891. William James' *Principles of Psychology* appeared in 1890, and his *Textbook of Psychology: Briefer Course* in 1892. These books were the direct forerunners of the modern introductory textbooks of psychology.

Murray viewed psychology as the scientific study of the phenomena of mind. This psychology was introspective, elementaristic, and associationistic. Murray had an orderly approach to his discipline. His 1885 *Handbook of Psychology* proceeds in a highly systematic manner. It begins with a study of the elementary constituents of mental phenomena, the sensations of taste, smell, touch, hearing, and sight. It describes the associative processes by which these are combined. It then elaborates the nature of the combinations to which these associative processes give rise, distinguishable by the names cognition, feeling, and volition. Murray emphasized the need for safeguards against error in the introspective process by varying the circumstances under which phenomena are observed. He recognized the importance of physiology. The work of H.L.F. von Helmholtz figures prominently in his text. He recommended that his students read Huxley's *Lessons in Elementary Physiology*. On the importance of physiology he writes, "It may now be accepted as fact that with every phenomena of consciousness a corresponding phenomenon is set up in the nervous system, and it will often be found that a knowledge of the nervous action is the most trustworthy guide to a psychological explanation of the phenomenon in consciousness or the most efficient safeguard against mistakes about its nature." Thus he accepted an isomorphism, and a neurophysiological reductionism as explanation, that is accepted, frequently with no critical scrutiny, by many psychologists today.

The 1885 edition of Murray's *Handbook of Psychology*, although not highly original, was a clearly written, orderly, up to date, and widely accepted presentation of the psychology of the period. Later editions do not adequately reflect the progress of psychology in the intervening years. By 1904 when the sixth edition appeared under a new title, Murray was no longer the authority he had been twenty years before.

Murray was a man of considerable talent. In addition to his *Handbook of Psychology*, he published a number of other books including *An Outline of Sir William Hamilton's Philosophy*, 1870, *An Introduction to Ethics*, 1891, and a *Handbook of Christian Ethics*, 1908. He was a Fellow of the Royal Society of Canada. He wrote and published poetry. He wrote one novel. His wife Margaret Murray achieved a reputation in her own right. She was the founder of the Imperial Order of the Daughters of the Empire.

Murray was neither a great nor a highly original scholar. He was, however, a man of intellectual vigor and lucidity of expression. He would have brought distinction to any university at any period.

Murray retired as Chairman of the Department of Mental and Moral Philosophy in 1903. Under his direction the department was as much a department of psychology as philosophy, although no experimental work had been introduced. About the time of his retirement, a number of courses in psychology were offered to second, third, and fourth year students. James' *Principles of Psychology* was a basic text. Examination papers are available which illustrate the nature of the psychology taught at that time. The examination paper for third year students in psychology, written on 16 April 1902, contained ten questions of which the following are typical.

1. Give some account of the experience of persons born blind and afterwards restored to sight; or explain the stereoscopic effect (a) with double, (b) with single pictures.
2. Explain psychologically the fact that we see the visible world erect, though the retinal image of it is inverted.
3. Describe the principal phenomena of dreaming, or of hypnotism, and indicate how they may be explained psychologically.

Such questions as these would not be inappropriate for an examination in psychology at the present time. The passage of 80 years has not changed the questions. It has changed the answers.

In the spring of 1903, in anticipation of Murray's retirement, William Peterson, then Principal of McGill, wrote to a number of psychologists and philosophers requesting suggestions for a replacement for Murray. Among those to whom he wrote were Hugo Münsterberg and William James at Harvard, J. McKeen Cattell at Columbia, George Ladd at Yale, and E.B. Titchener at Cornell. Among the candidates considered for the position were William Caldwell, W.A. Hammond, William McDougall, and E.B. Titchener.

The correspondence with Titchener is of particular interest. In April 1903, apparently on his own initiative, and before receiving Peterson's letter to him, Titchener wrote to Peterson making enquiries about the position. A passage from his letter reads as follows: "There are persistent rumours here that you propose to separate the department of psychology from that of philosophy proper. If that is true, if there is really to be a chair of psychology with an adequate laboratory on British soil, a thing which as yet does not exist in the Empire, I should naturally like to have a look in myself, and do not want to pass round testimonials for other people!"

In May, following receipt of Peterson's letter Titchener wrote describing the merits of Caldwell and Hammond, and again expressed an interest in the position. He wrote as follows: "I should like now to say a word about myself. It has always been my ambition to be at the head of a department of modern psychology in England, or at least in the Empire somewhere. I am told by Sir John Sanderson that I can have Stout's place at Oxford, but it is little good to go without a laboratory, when one has expatriated oneself to get a laboratory. I have also been invited to stand for Sully's place at University College, but the same difficulty arises. I went in for the Toronto place in 1893 or 1894, but withdrew when I heard that it was not to be a full chair. Cornell has been very good to me. I have had a full salary for the past 7 years ($3000), and I am now only 36, and I have an admirable laboratory. I was rather hoping that some of the McGill benefactors might see fit to found a laboratory for the Department of Mental Philosophy. If that were the case, I should be ready to make certain sacrifices, in order to get into an English environment again. I can get testimonials (whatever they may be worth!) from England, Germany, France, and Switzerland, as well as from America. I can appeal to my books, and their translations into foreign languages. I may also add that an attempt is being made to get me into the Royal Society, and I have heard that I am to be proposed for the American Philosophical Society next year. All this means, I suppose, a certain amount of reputation and influence. But, again, it would be foolish for me to become a candidate for a chair without a laboratory attached. Perhaps even now it may occur to some of your millionaires to give the necessary thousands. At any rate, I hope I have explained my reasons for troubling you in the first instance. No one is quite happy in a foreign country."

Why Titchener was not offered a position at McGill is unknown. Peterson's reply to him is not available. Presumably Peterson was unable, or did not wish, to raise the funds necessary to establish a psychological laboratory. Caldwell was offered, and accepted, Murray's chair. Titchener remained in exile in upstate New York until his death in 1927. Whether Titchener, the displaced Englishman who devoted his life to German psychology on American soil, would have found fulfillment at McGill is clearly debatable. McGill at that time was an academic enclave of tough-minded and tight-fisted Scotsmen from Edinburgh and Nova Scotia.

William Caldwell

William Caldwell (1863–   ) was born in Edinburgh, attended the University of Edinburgh and graduated with a brilliant academic record. He taught logic and metaphysics at Edinburgh. In 1891 he emigrated to the United States, taught at Cornell and Chicago, and from 1894 to 1903 was Professor of Moral and Social Philosophy at North Western University. Caldwell left that post for McGill in 1903. He wrote two books, *Schopenhauer's System in its Philosophical Significance*, 1896, and *Pragmatism and Idealism*, 1913. He published a variety of articles, and while at North

Western engaged in a controversy with Titchener (see W. Caldwell's *Professor Titchener's View of the Self, Psychological Review*, 1898). He was a member of the American Psychological Association. In his later years he received many honours.

Although Caldwell was not a psychologist, he recognized that psychology was an expanding discipline. Within his means and understanding he promoted its interests. He exercised a stewardship over psychology at McGill for over 20 years.

The importance of experimental psychology had clearly impressed itself on the minds of Peterson and Caldwell, because in 1904 Sir William MacDonald was persuaded to give an amount of $6,000 to be used as follows: "To be invested at interest to provide annually $250.00 for Experimental Psychology and fifty dollars annually for the purchase of philosophical literature." This was the origin of the MacDonald Experimental Fund, which, augmented in various ways, has continued to the present time. This fund has on many occasions proved of much assistance to the Chairman of the Department of Psychology.

Following the arrival of Caldwell, much of the teaching of psychology at McGill was done by J.W.A. Hickson, (1872–1957). Hickson was born in Montreal, graduated from McGill, and completed a Ph.D. at the University of Halle in Germany around the turn of the century. It is tempting to speculate that Hickson may have been influenced by Herman Ebbinghaus. It seems more probable that he worked under Alois Riehl who preceded Ebbinghaus at Halle. Whatever these associations were, Hickson was clearly influenced by the German philosophy and psychology of that period. Hickson was appointed a tutor in 1901. In 1905 he was promoted to Assistant Professor of Psychology and Lecturer in Philosophy at a salary of $1000 a year. Hickson was the first person at McGill to be officially designated a professor of psychology. It should be recalled that on his death Hickson left a bequest to establish the Dow-Hickson scholarships awarded to students in their penultimate year in English Literature, Philosophy, and Psychology. He also left a bequest for graduate fellowships in Physics and Theoretical Philosophy.

The course offerings available to students at McGill in 1904 included an Introductory Psychology, which used James' *Psychology, Briefer Course* as a text, an Introduction to Psychophysics in which Wundt's *Outline of Psychology*, and works by Ladd and Külpe were studied, and a General Course in Psychology, Analytic and experimental, for fourth year students, which used James' *Principles of Psychology*, Stout's *Manual of Psychology*, Ebbinghaus' *Grundzuge die Psychologie*, and Titchener's *Manual of Experimental Psychology*. In addition a short series of lectures was offered on what appears to have been social psychology. Also a Psychological

Seminary was introduced for advanced students which met two hours weekly throughout the session.

Honours programs were part of the McGill system in the Faculty of Arts from an early period. In 1904, and perhaps earlier, it was possible for a student to study for an honours degree in psychology. The calendar for that year contains the statement, "Attention is drawn to the fact that it is now possible for students to specialize in Psychology as well as Mental and Moral Philosophy." Apparently about this time consideration was given to graduate work in psychology. The calendar for 1905 contains the statement: "Attention is drawn to the fact that it is now possible for students (graduates and others) to specialize in Psychology as well as Mental and Moral Philosophy." The listing of subjects in which the M.A. degree was offered mentioned philosophy, including psychology. Graduate students in psychology at that period were either nonexistent or few in number. No M.A. in psychology was granted until 1910.

Each year changes were made in the curriculum. In 1908 a course called An Introduction to Experimental Psychology, was introduced which used Judd's *Laboratory Manual*. In the same year a course called Problems of Comparative Psychology, including some lectures on child psychology, appeared. Students were required to read works by Hobhouse, Romanes, and Lloyd Morgan. The recommended reading in child psychology included William Preyer's, *Die Seele des Kindes*, and James Mark Baldwin's *Mental Development in the Child and the Race*. This was the first child psychology taught at McGill.

Obviously this burgeoning psychology curriculum, as well as developments in philosophy, had grown beyond the capabilities of Caldwell, Hickson, and their associates. In the spring of 1909 the decision was reached to add an experimental psychologist to the staff. Peterson wrote to Holt and Münsterberg at Harvard, Holt recommended W.D. Tait. Münsterberg recommended William McDougall. Holt's recommendation on Tait was not without reservation. "I rather think that he finds considerable internal resistance to writing, specially on theoretical matters ... At present I may say that his mind is more sound than brilliant, more critical than original ... I am led to wonder whether he has yet found himself. There will be no trouble, I think, about his getting out experimental papers with due frequency, and whatever he writes will be well considered." For reasons unknown Münsterberg changed his views on McDougall. Three months after his initial letter supporting McDougall he wrote, "He is a weak man with all the ungraspable traits of a second rate personality. There is no spirit of initiative in him, and I have the impression at least that experimental psychology is not the right field for him." That was the end of McDougall's candidature. Münsterberg went on to support the appointment of Tait who became sessional Lecturer in Experimental Psychology in the autumn of 1909. This appointment shaped the image and substance of psychology at McGill for one third of a century.

Interest attaches to a statement by Holt in one letter on Tait's behalf. "I fancy that he has had an uphill road, so far, in life, and that the friendliness of his surroundings may make much difference in the degree to which his nature will continue to expand and grow." This statement contains elements of prophecy unfulfilled. Tait's life was an uphill road.

William Dunlop Tait – The Early Years

William Dunlop Tait (1879–1944) was born in Hopewell, Nova Scotia, the son of John Tait of Edinburgh. He attended New Glasgow High School and Pictou Academy. He taught school for two years before entering Dalhousie University. In 1902 he graduated with high honours in philosophy. He went on to Harvard where he completed his M.A. and Ph.D. degrees. At Harvard he worked under Münsterberg on psychophysical attitudes and memory, and published an article on the subject in 1910.

Tait approached the development of experimental psychology at McGill with considerable vigor. In 1910, one year after his arrival, he established a Psychological Laboratory. This was the second laboratory in Canada. The first was established in the 1890's at Toronto by James Mark Baldwin. It was the custom at McGill at the time to describe the laboratories of the university in the university calendar. The calendar for 1910 contains the following description. "The Psychological Laboratory occupies rooms in the Arts Building. In the main library are found the chief periodicals and works of reference on all branches of the science. Besides this, there has been added during the past year a considerable amount of apparatus so that the laboratory is now equipped for original research work in experimental psychology, physiological psychology, and applied psychology. The same equipment also serves to train students in the methods of experimental psychology, and furnishes material for demonstrations and lectures." In later expanded descriptions the laboratory is said to occupy eighteen rooms in the Arts Building. In 1912 Tait became Assistant Professor of Psychology and Director of the Psychological Laboratories. He carried this latter title for the rest of his career.

Caldwell adopted a highly cooperative attitude towards psychology, an attitude which he maintained throughout all his associations with it.

As a moral philosopher he had no interest in the experimental method, which Tait, and many psychologists of that time, revered with fervour. Caldwell had other gods. Despite this he used his position to help the development of a psychology with a strong experimental emphasis. In 1913 six courses in psychology are described in the university calendar. These are Elementary Psychology, Experimental Psychology, Advanced Psychology, Social Psychology, Advanced Experimental Psychology Seminary, and Psychological Laboratory.

About this time McGill graduated two students in psychology whose subsequent careers were not without distinction. These were J.W. Bridges, B.A. 1911, and A.A. Roback (1890–1965), B.A. 1912. Bridges played a role in the development of psychology in the Faculty of Medicine. Aspects of his career are described elsewhere in this paper. Roback attended Harvard, completed his Ph.D. in 1917, taught briefly at Harvard, Northeastern, M.I.T., and later became head of the Department of Psychology at Emerson College. Roback was a scholar. He had two fields of scholarly interest: psychology and Yiddish literature. Throughout his career he wrote more than thirty books in these two areas. His works on psychology included *Behaviourism and Psychology*, *Personality: in Theory and Practice*, *Freudiana*, and a biography of William James. His best known work was *History of American Psychology*, which first appeared in 1952. He wrote a number of books in Yiddish the latest being *Der Folksgaist in der Uidisher Shprakh* (The Genius of the Yiddish Language). Roback's life and work deserve detailed attention.

The routine of academic life at McGill was seriously disrupted by the Great War of 1914–18. In 1916 the No. 6 (McGill) Overseas Battery, subsequently the No. 7 Canadian Siege Battery, was recruited at McGill with a strength of 150 men. W.D. Tait, then 36, became commanding officer, and Cyrus Macmillan, Associate Professor of English, was second-in-command. The Battery served with distinction at Lens, Hill 70, Passchendale, Arras, Valenciennes and Mons, some of the severest battles of the war. Tait relinquished his command in February 1918. Anecdotal evidence suggests that Tait's war experience seriously affected his personality, and also his interest in psychology. He was no longer the same man.

Despite the interruption of the war, psychology continued to flourish. In 1920 seven courses were offered, including abnormal and educational psychology. In 1921 Tait was promoted to Associate Professor. He retained his title, Director of the Psychological Laboratory. He taught in the Extension Department, and also in the Department of Psychiatry which was organized in 1922. One of the early lecturers in psychiatry was C.M. Hincks, (1885–1964) subsequently creator of the Canadian National Committee for Mental Hygiene.

In 1922 a lecturer, Harvey R. DeSilva was added to the staff. DeSilva had an M.A. from Harvard. He remained at McGill for two years, and returned to Harvard to complete his Ph.D. He wrote a number of papers on apparent visual movement, binocular perception, and equipment design. In later life he occupied a number of senior government positions in Washington.

A McGill graduate of that period, later to achieve much distinction in psychology, was Otto Klineberg (1899–), who graduated in 1919 with first class honours and the Prince of Wales Gold Medal. Klineberg was influenced by Hickson. Tait at the time was in the Army. In his autobiography Klineberg writes: "My honours course was in philosophy and psychology, but all the courses were taught by a philosopher, and J.W.A. Hickson, a brilliant teacher, was my professor of psychology. His knowledge in this field was limited; he read long passages from William James in the introductory course and from Margaret Washburn in the course on comparative psychology. In the field of philosophy, however, he was a real scholar, who wrote very little but read a great deal, and he was the first to acquaint me with what a life of scholarship might have to offer." Klineberg with Hickson's help obtained a scholarship to study at Harvard, and completed an M.A. there in 1920. He returned to McGill to study medicine, graduating in 1925. His first love, however, was psychology; and immediately on graduation in medicine he enrolled as a psychology student at Columbia University, completing his Ph.D. in 1927. Klineberg became professor of psychology at Columbia University, served for a period as Director of the Division of Applied Social Science in UNESCO, and in 1960 became a professor of social psychology at the University of Paris. He has written a number of important books on social psychology. On June 6, 1969, fifty years almost to the day following Klineberg's graduation with a B.A. degree, he was awarded an honorary D.Sc. degree by McGill University.

As the years passed the relations between philosophy and psychology at McGill became less harmonious, although Caldwell at no time failed to represent psychology's interests. Tait was allowed much autonomy. Further, the number of students in psychology was increasing more rapidly than in philosophy. In June 1922 Tait wrote: "The number of students taking logic, ethics, metaphysics and the history of philosophy is 117. The number taking psychology, excluding extension lectures, is 253. If these are included the total will be 353. There is twice as much teaching in psychology as philosophy." Tait held the view, that statistical arguments based on student enrolment might serve as a basis for rational administrative decision. For many reasons a consideration of the separation of philosophy and psychology could no longer be delayed. In the end the reasons for separation were personal rather than statistical.

A Department of Psychology

Apart from substantive reasons for the separation of psychology and philosophy, Caldwell, Tait and Hickson were incompatible personalities, and reached a point where they could no longer coexist within the same department. Caldwell was scholarly, contemplative, religious, a believer in free will. His letters display indecision and a tendency to discursive, ambivalent, introspective analyses. He was disturbed by many aspects of psychology, including Freud's discussions of sex. Tait was unproductive as a scholar, aggressive, materialistic, irreligious, a believer in determinism. He missed no opportunity to decisively promote the interests of psychology as an applied, rather than a theoretical, discipline. He was crudely objective, lacking in apparent tact and sensitivity. Caldwell, obviously biased, viewed him as: "difficult to get along with, brusque, headstrong, domineering, unreasoning, ready to take offence." Caldwell and Tait had nothing in common with each other or with Hickson, who had a dual interest in philosophy and psychology. Hickson felt threatened both by Caldwell and Tait. His career at McGill was not a success. He was required to teach subjects that he did not wish to teach. He was passed over for promotion. His salary was low. He made no original scholarly contribution, although in his latter years at McGill he developed an interest in the philosophy of science. Hickson had independent means. He was a son of Sir Joseph Hickson, President of the Grand Trunk Railroad. With the passing of time he became more frustrated with his position and his relations with his colleagues. In the spring of 1923 he submitted his resignation, not to Caldwell, but to Sir Arthur Currie. This event precipitated the creation of a separate department of psychology.

Caldwell saw Hickson's resignation, he was in England at the time, as an opportunity for reorganizing his own position and being rid of the tribulations and the bondage that he felt in his association with his two colleagues. He wrote a highly discursive letter to Currie recommending the creation of a separate department of psychology. "Psychology is a perfectly definite thing," he wrote, "and a man can and should be a professor of psychology just as he might be a professor of anatomy or physiology ... The Psychologists resent the interference of the philosophers as they would resent priestly or scholarly interference. Neither set of men wholly approves of the other. The separation has come about at many places through a life-long quarrel. To the psychologist the philosophers are dealing with another world with values and ideals. To the philosophers the psychologists have gone too far and their science is a bundle of tendencies. But one word cannot be said against the idea that it is for psychologists to say what psychology is, and no theory of philosophy or religion should influence this ... Dr. Tait is now entitled to a seat on the Faculty of Arts, and psychology, this tremendous subject, should be represented by a man who speaks for it. Now that Dr. Hickson is leaving, and that Hickson's partial proprietorship is gone, psychology should be absolutely independent, and I for my part intend to fight for this all along the way ... Step in, Sir, in your fine strong way and free us all, and make us all remain friends for the sake of the University."

Sir Arthur Currie did step in. A separate department of psychology was created in 1924. Tait became Professor of Psychology and Director of the Psychological Laboratory. Tait was granted permission to appoint an additional professor in psychology. Among the candidates considered were Chester Kellogg, Gordon Allport, Paul Young, and George Humphrey who was then an associate professor at Wesleyan University. Herbert Langfeld at Harvard was consulted. Of Kellogg he wrote, "He is very clever and a hard worker. He is very strong in theoretical psychology but he has no more than average ability as regards laboratory technique. I have heard that he is better in the more advanced courses than he is in elementary work. I have always liked Kellogg, but I am aware that he does not make an entirely pleasing impression at first due to a slight hesitation in manner and jerkiness of speech. I do not want to exaggerate his idiosyncracies because they are after all very slight, and I have never heard anyone complain of them." Kellogg, who was then at Acadia University, was offered and accepted the appointment of associate professor.

Chester E. Kellogg (1888–1948) was a graduate of Bowdoin, obtained a Ph.D. from Harvard in 1914, worked as a psychologist on testing problems during the war, became Professor of Psychology and Education at Acadia University, and left his appointment there to join the staff at McGill in 1924. Kellogg's research interests were in psychological testing, particularly the testing of illiterates, test construction, statistical method, aesthetics, and, in his later years, parapsychology. He had broad interests and supervised research on a wide range of topics. He exerted a substantial influence on the work of the Department of Psychology for 23 years.

In its first year of independent operation the Department offered nine undergraduate courses in psychology and three graduate courses. Tait and Kellogg were busy men. At that time, although classes were small, teaching responsibilities were onerous, and tended to preclude much opportunity for research. At one point Tait wrote: "At present I am teaching nineteen hours per week. This includes lectures in the Faculty of Arts, laboratory periods in the same Faculty, lectures in the Faculty of

Medicine, Department of Social Service, and the School of Physical Education. I also conduct a clinic in mental deficiency at the Royal Victoria Hospital, two hours per week. At this clinic medical students, nurses, social workers, and even physicians attend for instruction. This makes a total of twenty-one hours per week." In addition Tait had interests outside the university. He was an active policy maker in the War Veterans Association. Clearly neither Tait nor Kellogg had much time for individual research.

Tait did not lack vision about a future of promise for psychology. His vision was that of the applied scientist. He saw flourishing application for psychology in education, medicine, business, social work, physical education, and human relations. He showed little concern for psychology as a scientific discipline. In a letter written in 1920 on the application of psychology to education he wrote: "Educational psychology demands more attention because psychology forms the basis of nearly all educational method. Courses in genetic psychology, child psychology, and the practical applications in the schoolroom should be available for the teaching profession as also graduate courses for teachers desiring higher degrees." In the same letter on applications in medicine he wrote: "Psychology is rapidly becoming of vital importance to all physicians, nurses, social workers, and those specializing in mental disease and mental deficit. If a psychopathic hospital is arranged for, another psychologist will be absolutely necessary for this aspect of the work alone." Tait was also fully aware of the contribution of psychology to McGill's role in the community. Here he wrote: "There is almost unlimited opportunity for bringing McGill in closer touch with the community by means of extension lectures on the psychology of history, art, nationality, and business." Under Tait's chairmanship psychology at McGill developed an applied direction. This direction, was characteristic of the period, and was related to the break with philosophy. Philosophy was the antithesis of the utilitarian. Having separated from it psychology must now show that it could serve society in many practical ways.

In 1925, concerned as it was with education, the Department of Psychology announced the establishment of a School Service Bureau with the following description: "Its purpose is to furnish aid and advice with regard to intelligence tests, classification of pupils, remedial treatment, standardized tests and measurements, and other psychological aspects of education. As far as time and equipment permits this service is at the disposal of superintendents, principals, teachers, parents, and others interested in education." This service existed for some years. Nothing is known regarding its success.

About the time the Department of Psychology was established in the

Faculty of Arts certain developments of interest to psychology occurred in the Faculty of Medicine. Psychology has a separate history in that Faculty.

Psychology in the Faculty of Medicine

Psychology at times prospered in the Faculty of Medicine as a separate department and in association with neurology and psychiatry. The first psychologist to hold an appointment in the Faculty of Medicine at McGill was J.W. Bridges, who became Associate Professor in 1924. This appointment was the result of the action of Clare M. Hincks, who founded the Canadian National Committee for Mental Hygiene. Hincks obtained funds from the Rockefeller Foundation in support of Bridges' appointment.

James Winfred Bridges (1885–1980) was born in Prince Edward Island, worked as a school teacher for several years, and later attended McGill University, where he graduated with a B.A. in 1911. He was one of W.D. Tait's first students in experimental psychology. With Tait's help he obtained a scholarship at Harvard and completed his Ph.D. in 1915. Bridges was influenced by Münsterberg, Langfeld, Holt, and Yerkes (Bridges 1966). In 1913 he was appointed a psychological intern in the Psychopathic Hospital in Boston. The belief is that he was the first psychologist to hold a clinical appointment as part of his training. In 1915 he accepted an appointment at Ohio State, and later served as a civilian with Yerkes on psychological test development in the United States Army. Following the war Bridges returned to Ohio State where he wrote his book, published in 1919, *An Outline of Abnormal Psychology*. This was one of the earlier attempts at a systematic organization of psychological abnormalities. In 1921 he accepted an appointment at Toronto, and in 1924 arrived in the Medical Faculty at McGill. This was the same year in which the Department of Psychology in the Faculty of Arts was established.

Bridges taught both normal and abnormal psychology. These subjects were viewed at that time as part of the training of medical students. A separate Department of Abnormal Psychology was created. In 1929 Bridges was joined by his wife Katherine M. Banham Bridges, (1897–   ) a graduate in psychology of Manchester and Toronto. In 1931 this Department offered four courses to medical students; a basic course in normal and abnormal psychology directed towards all students of medicine, a course on mental measurement designed for students of psychiatry, a course in child psychology for students specializing in pediatrics, and a course on psychology in industry intended for students in industrial medicine.

During this period J.W. Bridges and K.M. Banham Bridges were actively engaged in research. In 1925 the McGill University Nursery School (Northway 1973) was created under the direction of Dr. A.B. Chandler, a pediatrician, with K.M. Banham Bridges responsible for research, and J.W. Bridges acting in an advisory capacity. A number of studies were published on child development, juvenile delinquency, and various aspects of abnormal psychology.

Psychology flourished in the Faculty of Medicine at that time and was considered an important subject by the Dean of Medicine. These years were the most productive in J.W. Bridges' career. In 1930, he wrote a textbook, *Psychology, Normal and Abnormal*, and in 1932 he published *Personality, Many and One*, a book concerned with personality variables, and their integration. In 1935 his book, *The Meaning and Varieties of Love*, appeared. Bridges was clearly the most productive psychologist at McGill. His work was valued and respected. The Dean spoke highly of it in his annual report. In 1929 he was promoted to full professorship in the Faculty of Medicine.

These propitious beginnings in the Faculty of Medicine did not evolve to more lasting stature. Financial problems arose. The Department of Abnormal Psychology had been supported largely by funds from the Rockefeller Foundation. These funds came to an end. Also a new dean, less favourable to psychology, was appointed. Tait in the Department of Psychology in the Faculty of Arts and Science thought that medical students should pursue their studies in the Faculty of Arts and Science. In 1935, for a variety of reasons, mostly financial, the Department of Abnormal Psychology ceased to exist. J.W. Bridges and K.M. Banham Bridges found themselves without academic appointments. J.W. Bridges later established himself at Sir George Williams University where he remained from 1940 to 1963. He was a stimulating and informed teacher. Many students chose careers in psychology because of his influence. K.M. Banham Bridges spent many of her later academic years in the field of child development at Duke University in North Carolina.

Psychology was active in other branches of the Faculty of Medicine at different times. In 1937 D.O. Hebb and Molly R. Harrower were appointed as research fellows in the Montreal Neurological Institute. Hebb's work during that period is discussed elsewhere. Molly Harrower remained there until 1941 and did extensive research on personality changes accompanying cerebral lesions, epilepsy, and on the diagnostic value of the group Rorschach test. The research initiated at the Montreal Neurological Institute by Hebb and Harrower in 1937 has achieved continuity in the work of Dr. Brenda Milner. No substantial association of psychology with psychiatry occurred at McGill until 1945 when Robert B. Malmo was appointed.

The above is a digression on psychology in the Faculty of Medicine. Let us now return to the work of Tait's Department of Psychology.

Graduate Training and Research

Although some provision for training at the Master's level was made in 1905, no master's degrees in psychology were granted until 1910. In that year two master's degrees were awarded for theses on the span of attention and inhibition. Only five such degrees were awarded between 1910 and 1924.

After the Department of Psychology became a reality in 1924, Tait and Kellogg proceeded rapidly with the development of graduate work. In 1928 a Ph.D program was introduced. Five graduate courses were offered. The calendar for that year lists the regulations governing the award of the Ph.D degree. The requirements for the degree were not dissimilar from those that existed for many years. Students were required to have some knowledge of advanced statistical method. Some ability in shopwork, enough at least to show that the candidate was capable of designing and constructing simple apparatus, was considered important. Comprehensive examinations were required on the history of psychology, principles of psychology, experimental and physiological psychology, statistical method, and contemporary psychology. Between 1924 and 1946, the year in which Robert B. MacLeod became chairman of the Department, about 40 master's degrees in psychology were granted. The first Ph.D. was awarded in 1933. Four such degrees were granted between 1933 and 1946.

A report prepared by Tait in 1930 describes the typical research interests of the time. The list of topics actively under research reads as follows: relation of reaction time to physiognomy, race, and sex; the study of humidity as it affects work in cooperation with the Department of Industrial Medicine; correlation between Allport A-S Reaction Test and intelligence; psychological survey of Rushbrook school with special reference to grading, mental hygiene, and curriculum; psychology of journalism with reference to make-up, headlines, etc.; the study of the fatigue of school children at three levels of intelligence; the psychology of applause; study of rythm and time; a new type of paper image allowing for visual cues. This is clearly a creditable list of research topics for a small department, and reflects largely applied interests. The vigor with which these topics were pursued is unknown.

The reader should bear in mind that the research climate in Canada at that time in psychology, and other disciplines, was not invigorating. Professors were overworked and underpaid. Research funds were limited or nonexistent. Scholarships for the support of graduate students were few and available to students of only the highest scholarly attainments, and no travel funds to attend meetings were provided. Departments usually had no telephone, typewriter, or secretarial assistance. No community of scholarship among the few psychologists in Canada existed. The Canadian Psychological Association was not organized until 1939. No forum or journal for the presentation or publication of scientific work existed. Given this catalogue of negative circumstances it is, indeed, remarkable that the early psychologists at McGill, and elsewhere in Canada, were able to maintain a creative dedication to their discipline, and support some of the elements of a stimulating environment for their students.

In the early 1930's some funds for psychological research became available. These had their origins in an unusual source – the Great Depression. A high level of unemployment was an important national problem. McGill received a five year grant, beginning in 1930, of $15,000 a year to support research on unemployment and employment. This was known as the Social Science Research Project. This project was such as to permit a number of studies all related to the central subject of unemployment and employment to proceed simultaneously in a number of fields of specialized knowledge. Seven departments, including psychology, cooperated. For several years this project determined in part the pattern of research in the Psychology Department. Among the topics investigated were these: the qualitative character and industrial aptitudes of unemployed as compared with employed groups; vocational guidance and juvenile placement in Montreal; occupational abilities of female clerical workers; the permanence of the effect of school teaching and its relevance to employability. Several graduate students received financial support under this project, and completed doctoral degrees in this field of enquiry.

The recipient of the first Ph.D. in psychology at McGill, granted in 1933, was Nelson Whitman Morton (1910–1976) who worked under the direction of Kellogg. Morton became a lecturer in psychology in 1932, and was promoted to Assistant Professor in 1939. His Ph.D. thesis research resulted in a book, *Occupational Abilities*, published by the Oxford University Press in 1936. Much of the research of the period was conducted by Kellogg and Morton. Kellogg's interests were in statistics, aesthetic abilities, psychological testing, and extra-sensory perception. He published a variety of papers in these areas. Morton's interests were largely in psychological testing and industrial psychology.

An event of interest to psychologists was the revision of the U.S. Army Beta Examination by Kellogg and Morton. During Kellogg's career in the U.S. Army he had been concerned with the development of the

Army Beta. The revised test was published by the Psychological Corporation, in 1935, and has been widely used since that time. An episode associated with the publication of this test illustrates attitudes of the period toward psychology. Kellogg and Morton initially described the test as the McGill University Revision. Objections were raised to this. The good name of McGill was thought not to be enhanced by its association with an intelligence test. In July 1933 Sir Arthur Currie wrote to Tait: "There is no doubt in my mind that the Department of Psychology is unjustified in calling printed intelligence tests 'McGill University Tests,' and I would like steps taken to correct this." Steps were taken.

Tait was not infrequently in trouble with the university authorities, and others, because at times the actions or opinions of psychologists seemed to offend current morality. This is a common experience of chairmen of psychology departments. On one occasion he was criticized because he had the audacity to conduct an enquiry into attitudes toward prohibition. On another occasion, referring to a statement by Knight Dunlop that, "The psychoanalysts have already shown that the 'sense of sin' is but a psychophysical attribute of adolescent sentimental development." Currie wrote: "I sometimes find it difficult to understand just what a psychologist is talking about. Just what does this mean, and are there no simple words in the English language that psychologists might use to make their meaning clear." Tait was in trouble with Currie on more substantive issues. He quarrelled with Currie over the promotion of Kellogg to the rank of full professor. Despite a productive and devoted career Kellogg was not promoted to a full professorship until 1947, shortly before his death in 1948. He had spent 23 years as an associate professor.

Despite limited resources, an environment that was not always congenial, some research was done, papers were published, and students were trained. Some of these achieved eminence in psychology.

Students of Eminence

University departments, and professors, nurture their reputations on the achievement of their students. The Department of Psychology in its early years graduated a number of students who subsequently achieved stature in psychology. One of these was Robert B. MacLeod.

Robert B. MacLeod (1907–1972) was born in Glengarry County, Ontario, where his father was a Presbyterian minister. The family moved to Montreal in 1918 where MacLeod attended Montreal High School. Later at the age of 15 he entered McGill University, where he graduated with a B.A. in 1926. In an unfinished autobiography MacLeod describes his experiences at McGill during that period. "McGill was a wonderful experience – great teachers, fascinating subjects; I don't think I was ever bored by anything I studied. My first love was mathematics and physics, for which I won a prize in high school; but during my freshman year I took a course in logic from J.W.A. Hickson. This seemed to go beyond mathematics, and since I was destined for theology, I switched from mathematics to philosophy. Philosophy at that time included psychology, and I took the elementary course with W.D. Tait. Tait was not a great psychologist, nor a great teacher, but he was a warm human being, and he conveyed the conviction that one could be scientific about human problems. By that time, largely through an intensive study of the synoptic gospels that left me with a good deal of scepticism, but also because of my father's obvious discomfort with many of the trivial concerns among his pastoral responsibilities, I had given up the thought of the church as a career. Psychology seemed like a possibility: not psychology as it was but psychology as it might be. The problems of logic lead inevitably to the psychology of thinking. How do people actually think?" (Myers 1974)

MacLeod pursued studies at the master's level at McGill and completed a thesis in 1927 on: "Recent tendencies in the interpretation of instinct." On graduation he was awarded a Moyse Travelling Scholarship for study in Germany and spent periods of time at Frieburg, Rostock, Frankfurt, and Berlin. His experiences at the Psychological Institute in Berlin brought him in touch with Max Wertheimer, Wolfgang Köhler, and Kurt Lewin. These men greatly influenced his subsequent thinking. He also played a role in their migration to the United States when their life in Nazi Germany became no longer tolerable.

When in Germany MacLeod kept in touch with the McGill Department of Psychology. In March 1929 he wrote to Tait: "You asked me in one of your letters how my McGill preparation fitted me for the requirements of the German university with a view to possible improvements in the McGill curriculum. That is a hard question to answer, because the German requirements are so indefinite. However, judging from the subject matter in the lectures, the discussions in the colloquium, and many conversations with students, I don't think you need fear any comparisons. I think I can say, without assuming any credit for myself, that my general knowledge of psychology will stand up pretty well against that of any of the German students who are getting their degrees now. In fact I have been going through a slow process of disillusionment with reference to German academic standards, and though I'm still impressed by German scholarship and German devotion to science, I can't see that the University standard is any higher than our own. When working in the Berlin Institute one cannot escape the impression that psychology is still first and foremost an experimental science with most of its experiments still lying in the future. It is tremendously stimulating to feel oneself actually in the presence of creative work, to have unsolved problems stated in the classroom, and see them being investigated in the laboratory. If I could suggest anything for McGill it would be a greater emphasis on systematic investigation, if necessary, at the expense of some of the teaching."

MacLeod subsequently completed a Ph.D. at Columbia, taught at Columbia and Swarthmore, where he became Chairman of the Department, and came to McGill in 1946 as Chairman of Psychology. His research interests were in the experimental psychology of perception, language, thinking, cross-cultural psychology, history and theory, and phenomenology. In 1955 he published a survey, conducted under the auspices of the Social Science Research Council, *Psychology in Canadian Universities and Colleges*. MacLeod left McGill in 1948 to become Chairman of Psychology at Cornell. One of the attractions of that position was the prestige which attached to psychology at Cornell because of the work of E.B. Titchener, who had expressed a desire to come to McGill about half a century before.

Another early graduate of the Department of Psychology, who made substantial contributions to psychology, was Kenneth W. Spence, (1907–1966). Spence was born in Chicago, attended West Hill High School in Montreal, and later McGill University where he received a B.A. in 1929. On graduation he was honoured with the Prince of Wales Gold Medal in Mental Sciences. In 1930 he was awarded an M.A. for a thesis titled: "An experimental study of the maze with special reference to its reliability." This research was done under the direction of C.E. Kellogg. Spence received the Governor General's Medal for Research. He completed his Ph.D. at Yale in 1933, and after holding positions at Yale and the University of Virginia, he was appointed in 1942 Professor and Head of the Department of Psychology at the State University of Iowa. He remained at Iowa for most of his life, moving to Texas shortly before his death. Spence made substantial contributions to the formulation and testing of theories of discrimination learning, classical and instrumental conditioned-response learning; and the relation of motivation to learning. He had an interest in mathematical formulations of learning phenomenon. In 1956 he published an important work, *Behaviour Theory and Conditioning*. Also in 1956 he received the American Psychological Association's distinguished scientific contribution award.

Another student at McGill around 1930, who was destined to play an important role in the history of the Department of Psychology was Donald Olding Hebb (1904–   ). Hebb was born in Chester, Nova Scotia, the son of a country physician, attended school in Chester, and later became a student at Dalhousie University where he graduated with a B.A. in 1925.

At that time psychology was not well-established at Dalhousie. Hebb's early intentions were to become a novelist. In 1925 he accepted a teaching position in Montreal with the idea of devoting his spare time to literary pursuits. His interest in the writing of novels waned. In 1928 he enrolled as a part-time student in psychology. Hebb's academic record was, indeed, dismal. His admission to McGill, he claims, came about because Tait was a classmate of his mother's, a most fortunate connection. Hebb quickly developed an interest in physiological psychology, a field in which the Department of Psychology had little to offer. For a time he worked in the Department of Physiology with Leonid Andreye, a collaborator of Pavlov's. Pavlov's *Lectures on Conditioned Reflexes* was published in English in 1928. Hebb mastered, and was greatly influenced, by this work. In 1929 he was admitted as a graduate student in psychology. He studied experimental psychology under the direction of Spence who was then an assistant in the Department. Spence always referred to him as "my first student." In 1932 he received a master's degree for a thesis entitled: "Conditioned and unconditioned reflexes and inhibitions." In 1934 Hebb was accepted for further graduate studies at the University of Chicago. When Lashley moved to Harvard in 1935 Hebb followed, and completed his Ph.D. at Harvard in 1936. Lashley played a formative role in Hebb's thinking about physiological psychology. In 1937 he returned to McGill, and for two years worked as a research fellow in the Montreal Neurological Institute under the direction of Wilder Penfield. Hebb quickly appreciated that the behavioural study of brain damaged patients held some importance for psychology. He published a number of papers based on his work in the Neurological Institute. These papers were concerned with the effect on intelligence in man of large removals of left frontal lobe tissue, and with the effects on intelligence of early and late brain injury. Some of the ideas subsequently presented in the important theoretical work, *The Organization of Behaviour*, published in 1949, found their geneses in this period of research in the Montreal Neurological Institute. In 1939 Hebb went to Queen's University where he remained until 1942. In that year he accepted a position at the Yerkes Laboratories of Primate Biology, where he remained until his return to the Department of Psychology at McGill in 1947.

The First Doctoral Graduates

Prior to the second world war McGill awarded Ph.D.'s in psychology to N.W. Morton, E.C. Webster, J.S.A. Bois, and K.E. Norris. These men had interesting careers.

N.W. Morton, McGill's first Ph.D. in psychology, became a member of the staff of the Department of Psychology. Some aspects of his work are described elsewhere in this historical account. In 1941 he joined the Canadian Army, and became a Lieutenant Colonel in the Directorate of Personnel Selection. This organization was initially under the direction of Brock Chisholm, and later William Line. Morton played an important role in psychological work in the Canadian Army. Following the war he spent some time in India. He later joined the Defence Research Board in Ottawa and contributed substantially to the development of psychology within that organization. He held a number of senior positions in the public service. He served as President of the Canadian Psychological Association in 1952.

E.C. Webster (1909–) was born in North Battleford, Saskatchewan, came to Montreal in the late 1920's with an interest in Y.M.C.A. work, enrolled as a student at McGill and graduated with a B.A. in psychology in 1931. He continued as a graduate student and in 1936 was awarded the Ph.D. degree for a thesis entitled: "Vocational guidance in relation to school training and the distribution of mental abilities." Webster's interests were in industrial psychology. In 1936 in collaboration with J.S.A. Bois he established the Psychological Institute. This Institute was concerned with the applications of psychology and had the full support of W.D. Tait. Webster's interest in public opinion led to the creation of Opinion Surveys Limited in 1938. He occupied the position of President. Also, between 1936 and 1940 he lectured in psychology at Sir George Williams College. Because of the war the Psychological Institute and Opinion Surveys Limited had a short life. In 1942 Webster joined the Canadian Army as a Major and worked on problems of morale and information. In 1946 he returned to Montreal, obtained a part-time appointment in the Department of Psychology, and continued his active interests in industrial psychology. Webster played a highly important role in the post-war history of the Department of Psychology, and served as Chairman from 1958–1964. He made substantial contributions to applied psychology. He became Director of the Centre of Continuing Education at McGill in 1967 and retired in 1972 to devote his later years to industrial practice.

J.S.A. Bois was one of the more vital personalities to be associated with psychology at McGill. Bois graduated from Laval University in 1910 and for about twenty years pursued a successful career in the priesthood. Seized by elements of doubt, he enrolled as a student of psychology at McGill and received an M.A. in 1935. In 1936 he was awarded a Ph.D. for a thesis titled: "Graphic signs of introversion-extraversion." He collaborated with Webster in the founding of the Psychological Institute and Opinion Surveys Limited. Although Bois worked as an industrial psychologist, he was a gifted clinician, much possessed of the therapeutic urge. He served in the Canadian Army during the war as a Lieutenant Colonel. He later established a firm in Montreal concerned with industrial selection at the executive level and management training. In his later years he developed enthusiasm for the general semantics of Alfred Korsybski, perhaps as an antidote against his early training in Thomistic philosophy. He wrote several books on the subject, and became one of the leading gurus of the general semantics movement in North America.

Another McGill graduate in psychology of some prominence was Kenneth E. Norris, who completed his Ph.D. in 1939. Norris had a long standing interest in YMCA work. He served as Principal of Sir George Williams University during its formative period.

Although in its early years the Department of Psychology was small, and suffered from various forms of scholarly and financial malnutrition, credit must attach to Tait and Kellogg for arousing the interest, and fostering the careers, of such men as MacLeod, Spence, Hebb, Morton, Webster, Bois, and Norris. This role is not without honour.

The War Years

At the outbreak of war in 1939 Tait, Kellogg, Morton, and a demonstrator, Alfred B. Udow, comprised the Department of Psychology. At that time psychologists in Canada were much concerned about the possible contribution of psychology to the war effort. One focus of attention was psychological testing and selection and there McGill's contribution was substantial. Early in the war the newly formed Canadian Psychological Association created a committee charged with the development of a test that would have wide application for a variety of selection purposes within the Armed Services. Funds were obtained first from two insurance companies and later from the National Research Council. The writer is uncertain about the original membership of the committee, but at one meeting held at the University of Toronto in April 1941, the following attended: Liddy, Humphrey, Long, Howard, Line, Penrose, Myers, Morton, Hebb, and Ferguson. This enterprise resulted in a test known as Revised Examination M. Much of the work involved in the preparation of this test was done by N.W. Morton at McGill who relied heavily on his previous work with Kellogg on the Revised Army Beta Examination. Revised Examination M consisted of eight subtests, four nonverbal, two mechanical, and two verbal. The nonverbal subtests were modifications of subtests in the Army Beta examination. Revised Examination M, and its revisions, was one of the most widely used psychological tests ever developed in Canada. During and after the war this test was administered to over one million Canadians. It had many applications, extending from the selection of illiterates for courses in remedial education to the selection of officers. The test had high construct validity. It correlated with a wide variety of criteria. It served admirably the purposes for which it was designed.

A small mystery has always attached to the name, Revised Examination M. The question is frequently asked: What does M stand for? The most plausible theory is that M stands for McGill. The use of M rather than McGill was clearly subterfuge. The constructors of the test remembered clearly, and perhaps with resentment, the umbrage taken by Sir Arthur Currie in 1933 at the association of McGill's good name with a published test of intelligence.

An event of importance to psychology occurred at McGill in 1940. This was the first annual meeting of the Canadian Psychological Association, which at that time had about 110 members. The President was E.A. Bott, the Secretary, George Humphrey, and the Treasurer R.B. Liddy. The annual fee was $2.00. The meeting at McGill was held on December 30 and 31, 1940, and was attended by 26 members. One of the items of business was the adoption of a constitution for the Association. The first day was devoted to the presentation of scientific papers. Papers were presented by H.W. Wright, Magda B. Arnold, D.O. Hebb, Elizabeth Gifford and C.R. Myers, Leola Neal and L.S. Penrose, E.C. Webster, Mary D. Salter (now Ainsworth), Alfred B. Udow, and others. The second day was occupied with round table discussions chaired by H.W. Wright, W.D. Tait, K.E. Norris, J.S.A. Bois, and Douglas J. Wilson. These discussions were concerned with psychological problems in post-war rehabilitation, and with the status of psychology as a profession within and without the university. At seven o'clock on the second day of the meeting, New Year's Eve, the members assembled for drinks, dinner, discussion, and perhaps celebration, at that welcoming harbour of good fellowship, the McGill Faculty Club.

Psychology at McGill did not prosper during the war years. Tait and Kellogg were growing old. Their energies and enthusiasms had waned. Both men were in poor health. Morton left for the war in 1941. Francis Alexander, a clinical psychologist, was appointed sessional lecturer in 1942, and Assistant Professor in 1945. M.C. De Jersey was appointed sessional lecturer in 1944, and lecturer in 1945. Among the students receiving master's degrees during this period were Verity Mitchell Ross, Gerald Shane, Donald Spearman, Douglas Burns Clark, and Alfred B. Udow. Clark became Vice-Principal of Sir George Williams University.

Udow went on to complete a Ph.D. at Columbia and pursued a career in New York in the public opinion motivation research fields.

W.D. Tait died in 1944 after 35 years at McGill. C.E. Kellogg became acting chairman of the Department. He remained in that position until the arrival of Robert B. MacLeod in 1946.

The Chairmanship of Robert B. MacLeod

MacLeod arrived at McGill in 1946 following war service with the Office of Strategic Service in the United States and Europe. The Department of Psychology was in a debilitated state, and was viewed with low esteem within the University. His primary task was to initiate action that would ensure a more promising future for psychology at McGill.

MacLeod made changes in the curriculum, fostered the expansion of graduate work, and emphasized the teaching of experimental psychology which had been neglected for some years. He himself taught the course in introductory psychology. On his arrival the Department was housed in the Arts Building in the space where Tait had established a psychology laboratory in 1910. Much of the original equipment was still there, and available for use. MacLeod took steps to re-equip the laboratory, and expand the physical facilities of the Department. He arranged for the long overdue promotion of C.E. Kellogg to full professor.

MacLeod was an outstanding teacher, respected by his students and dedicated to their interests. He portrayed psychology as a great adventure, a quest, an exploration into the unknown. He was well grounded in the history of his discipline, and the philosophical context which was its genesis. He knew what the important problems of psychology were, and sensed where solutions might be found. Although a strong advocate of experimentation, he had distrust for highly complex experimental methodology and design, an attitude shared by many of the important psychologists of this century. He was an advocate of the phenomenological method in psychology. The minds of MacLeod's students were readily captured, and stimulated, by his sense of adventure. Many students at McGill, and elsewhere, were attracted to psychology because of his teaching. Although a kindly and competent administrator, he found fulfillment largely in his relations with his students. Among the students who came under MacLeod's influence during his two years at McGill were Gordon McMurray, Gerald Mahoney, Herbert Dörken, Brenda Milner, Peter Milner, Abram Amsel, Herbert Lansdell, Robert Wake, and Sam Rabinovitch.

An important role of the chairman of any department, and more particularly a small one, is to project an image of his discipline within the university. MacLeod was admirably suited for this role. He enjoyed a wide scholarly reputation in the United States and Canada. As a man of substance he was greatly esteemed by colleagues in all disciplines at McGill. His positive and kindly personality lent itself to non-abrasive administrative decisions. He served psychology well, and added to its stature within the University.

Shortly before MacLeod's arrival an event occurred of importance for McGill psychology. Steps were taken to organize a Department of Psychology at the Allan Memorial Institute. This Institute is not only the Department of Psychiatry within the Faculty of Medicine but also is an active psychiatric treatment centre for the Royal Victoria Hospital. The person chosen to create this department was Robert B. Malmo. He arrived at McGill in 1945. Robert B. Malmo was born in Panama in 1912, completed his B.A. and M.A. at the University of Missouri, and received his Ph.D. from Yale in 1940. At Yale he worked in Yerkes Laboratory with C.F. Jacobson, H.W. Nissen, and Yerkes himself. He acquired a broad knowledge of neuropsychology and animal research. He worked subsequently as a clinical research psychologist, at Norwich State Hospital, and later joined the staff of the National Institute of Health at Bethesda. After his arrival at McGill in 1945 he established a psychophysiological laboratory at the Allan Memorial Institute. The work of this laboratory combined clinical observation with the techniques of experimental psychology and physiology. The early work of this laboratory was concerned with autonomic nervous system functions. Later work was concerned with brain mechanisms related to need state, arousal functions, and cardiovascular functions. Malmo held an appointment in the Department of Psychology in the Faculty of Arts and Science. Over the years many doctoral students in psychology completed their research in his laboratory. His most recent contribution to psychology is his book, published in 1975, *On Emotion, Needs, and our Archaic Brain*.

The decision, taken by MacLeod, with the most far-reaching consequences for psychology at McGill was the appointment of Donald O. Hebb and George A. Ferguson. Edward C. Webster had been appointed, part-time, by Kellogg before MacLeod's arrival. Brief and early biographical accounts of Hebb and Webster have already been presented. Some comment on Ferguson's early career may be not without interest.

George Andrew Ferguson (Bernhardt 1958) was born in 1914 in New Glasgow, Pictou County, Nova Scotia, a few miles from the birthplace of W.D. Tait. His ethnic origin requires no comment. He attended the Halifax Academy where he learned mathematics from a superb teacher,

S.A. Morton, an uncle of N.W. Morton. Under the influence of Joshua Logan, an outstanding teacher of classics dedicated to the greatness of Rome, he proceeded to Dalhousie University where he obtained a B.A. in 1936 with Great Distinction in Latin and classical philology. He contemplated further studies in classical philology, but this avenue was closed because of his lack of a knowledge of Greek, a subject he had overlooked. At that time the depression was in full swing; penury was the order of the day. He studied to become a school teacher. A career as a rural teacher in Nova Scotia seemed the only realistic possibility. Chance and the Imperial Order of the Daughters of the Empire, decreed otherwise. This latter organization, the creation of the wife of John Clark Murray, awarded him an overseas fellowship of $1500 for study at the University of Edinburgh, the source of McGill's early psychology. Transported from penury to affluence by this event he proceeded to Edinburgh, where he studied under Sir Godfrey Thomson, James Drever, Mary Collins, W.G. Emmett, Boris Semonoff, and Alexander Mowat. He completed an M.Ed. in 1938, and a Ph.D. in 1940. His thesis, written under Thomson's direction, was on the reliability of mental measurement. Thomson required him to commit the Lord's Prayer in German to memory, a useful skill. Ferguson was enrolled initially as an education student. Education at that time at Edinburgh was largely psychology with a strong emphasis on psychological measurement and statistics. Ferguson acquired his long interest in human intelligence and statistics from Thomson. This latter interest stood him in good stead. His book, *Statistical Analysis in Psychology and Education*, is now in its fifth edition. Ferguson returned to Canada in 1940, and worked as a research associate under Peter Sandiford in the Department of Educational Research at the University of Toronto. In 1941 he produced a book, *The Reliability of Mental Tests*, published by the University of London Press. In that same year he collaborated with R.W.B. Jackson on the writing of a monograph, *Studies in the Reliability of Tests*. These two works contain some of the early ideas involved in psychological test theory. Ferguson collaborated with Jackson on other projects. Theirs was a worthwhile cooperative arrangement. In 1941, clearly a busy year, Ferguson joined the Army, serving as a Major both in Canada and abroad, under Brock Chisholm, William Line and J.W. Howard in the Directorate of Personnel Selection, and later in the RCAMC. Following the war he worked for two years as an industrial psychologist before being invited by Robert MacLeod to join McGill in 1947.

Hebb and Ferguson arrived at McGill on the same day, 1 September 1947. On that day they equipped the laboratory by purchasing saws, hammers, screwdrivers, electric motors, and other useful psychological instruments from Eaton's hardware department. The first major task of

Hebb and Ferguson was to organize the teaching of experimental psychology. An approach was used in which each student conducted an original research project. This approach proved successful and persists to the present time. During this year MacLeod and Hebb laid plans for the development of the animal and physiological laboratories, which became available for use in the Donner Building in the autumn of 1948. Hebb arrived at McGill from the Yerkes Laboratories with a draft of the book, *The Organization of Behaviour* in his briefcase. During that first year he found time to revise it and seek a publisher.

MacLeod's chairmanship was a period of transition. The arrival of Hebb, Webster, and Ferguson changed the history of psychology at McGill. In 1948 MacLeod accepted the Chairmanship of psychology at Cornell. Hebb became Chairman of the McGill Department. A new era for psychology at McGill began to unfold.

Thirty Years Growth

In 1946–48, MacLeod's second year as Chairman, the Department offered 10 undergraduate courses with about 1300 registrations. Approximately half of these were in the introductory course. About 40 students were registered at the graduate level. Some were qualifying students. These student numbers are large for that time. University enrolment was inflated because of the return of war veterans. These students were taught by four full-time staff members, R.B. MacLeod, D.O. Hebb, C.E. Kellogg, and George A. Ferguson, and two part-time staff members, E.C. Webster and Frances Alexander. Several graduate students also taught undergraduate courses. Hebb's chairmanship began in 1948. It initiated a period of growth in terms of undergraduate and graduate enrolment, staff size, research productivity, and the reputation of the Department both within and beyond the university.

Growth, as reflected in undergraduate enrolment, reached a peak in the mid 1970's when enrolment in psychology was the equivalent of about 1000 full-time students. About this time the Department had 90 full-time graduate students enrolled in Ph.D. programs.

The physical facilities available to the Department continued to expand. In 1948 a laboratory for research and training in physiological and comparative psychology was opened in the Donner Building. In later years parts of the Department were housed in about five different locations on or near the McGill campus. This circumstance detracted from a sense of departmental unity. In 1964 all branches of the Department were brought together, and integrated as a unified department in the Stewart Biological Sciences Building.

Since MacLeod's departure in 1948 the Department has had five chairmen: D.O. Hebb (1948–1958), Webster (1958–1964), George A. Ferguson (1964–1975), Dalbir Bindra (1975–1980), and Peter Milner (1980–   ). Since its official founding in 1924 the Department has had seven chairmen.

Before the second world war four Ph.D.'s were awarded. In the post war years graduate education flourished. From 1949 to 1980 the Department graduated 20 Ph.D.'s in psychology. From about 1950 to 1970 more Ph.D.'s in psychology were produced by McGill than by most other departments of psychology in Canadian universities. After about 1970 with the rapid development of many active psychology departments this situation changed.

Research funds to support graduate training and research were very limited in 1948. Precise amounts are unknown. In the mid 1970's research grants available to members of the Department varied, but were roughly of the order of $600,000 a year.

Apart from teaching and research members of the McGill Department have been occupied over the years with a wide range of activities. These include holding office in psychological associations, serving on research committees, promoting research funding, reviewing research grants and publications, planning programs for scientific meetings, and serving on the editorial boards of journals. Six members of the Department have served as Presidents of the Canadian Psychological Association. These are D.O. Hebb (1953), George A. Ferguson (1956), Dalbir Bindra (1959), R.B. Malmo (1962), W.E. Lambert (1970), and Virginia Douglas (1971). D.O. Hebb served as President of the American Psychological Association in 1960. Three staff members have served as Honorary Presidents of the Canadian Psychological Association, D.O. Hebb (1966–1967), E.C. Webster (1969–1970), and George A. Ferguson (1976–1978).

Five members of the Department have been elected Fellow of the Royal Society of Canada. These with the dates of their election are as follows: D.O. Hebb (1959), George A. Ferguson (1962), Dalbir Bindra (1973), W.E. Lambert (1972), and Brenda Milner (1976). D.O. Hebb served as Chancellor of McGill University from 1970–1974. D.O. Hebb and Brenda Milner were elected Fellows of the Royal Society of London. Honors and awards held by members of the Department in the post-war years have been numerous.

Applied Psychology: Graduate Training and Research

In its earlier years under W.D. Tait the Department of Psychology had an applied orientation. The first four Ph.D.'s were in applied areas.

After 1948 the perpetuation of an applied tradition became in large part the responsibility of E.C. Webster. Sustenance for applied psychology presented difficulties. Despite outstanding practical contributions by Canadian psychologists to the war effort post-war psychology in Canada tended to develop a rigorously scientific rather than an applied orientation. Few funds were available to support training in such fields as clinical, industrial, and counselling psychology. In 1948 a grant was received from the Department of Health and Welfare for the training of clinical psychologists. A.S. Luchins was employed under that grant. This grant was of limited duration and was terminated a few year later.

In 1953 a semi-autonomous administrative unit, the Applied Psychology Center, was created under the direction of E.C. Webster. The purpose of this Center was to provide training and conduct research in clinical, industrial, and counselling psychology. A further purpose was to provide short intensive courses for individuals outside the university in such areas as human relations, personnel appraisal, supervisory methods, and related topics. The staff of the Center initially consisted of E.C. Webster, W.N. McBain, and E.G. Poser. Part time lecturers were D. Dörken, G. Dufresne and Blossom Wigdor.

The Applied Psychology Center was the principal agency for training and research in clinical, industrial, and counselling psychology from 1953 to 1965. The relations between applied psychology and more basic scientific psychology were not harmonious. In general the dichotomy between scientific and applied psychology was ideologically divisive. Also the concept of a semi-autonomous unit, the Applied Psychology Center, within the Department of Psychology, was in principle administratively unsound. Despite its valuable contribution as the guardian of applied psychology at McGill for well over a decade the Center ceased to exist in 1965. Its training and research responsibilities were merged with those of the Department as a whole.

Many individuals have contributed to the growth of applied psychology at McGill. Among the full time staff members are E.C. Webster, Ernest G. Poser, Virginia I. Douglas, Sam Rabinovitch, Robert O. Pihl, William Piper, and Irv Binik. The clinical program has also used to advantage the services of many part-time members.

Basic Research

During the past third of a century the Department of Psychology has explored many research areas. Among them are comparative and physiological psychology, general experimental including perception, cognition and learning, social psychology, psycholinguistics, child psychology, measurement, and quantitative methodology. This research has resulted in about 2000 publications. Obviously an adequate review is not possible here. Any commentary must be deficient in many respects.

In 1947 when D.O. Hebb arrived at McGill he brought with him a draft of a book, *The Organization of Behavior*, published in 1949. This book was timely and an immediate success. For years physiological psychology had been in the doldrums. Hebb's book brought new interest to the classic problem of the neural correlates of behavior. It opened new avenues of research. One of Hebb's ideas was that perception and thinking are affected by learning, and learning had its effect by promoting the development of neuronal connections in the brain. These were called cell assemblies. Hebb's ideas had both theoretical and practical implications. Although some of his theoretical constructions can no longer be sustained, his general approach has, rather successfully, weathered the passage of time.

Research on sensory deprivation emerged from Hebb's ideas. Experiments on this topic were initiated in the 1950's. The idea underlying these experiments was that a variable sensory environment was necessary for normal brain functioning. The first experiments were done on human subjects under the direction of Woodburn Heron assisted by W.H. Bexton and T.H. Scott. Following a period of sensory deprivation subjects experienced perceptual distortion, impaired cognitive processing, and hallucinatory activity. This was pioneer research. It began a course of exploration that was later followed by investigators with much more sophisticated technology than existed at that time at McGill.

Another series of experiments, begun in the early 1950's, involved rearing animals in variable environments, enriched and restricted, and relating variation in the environment to subsequent behavior. In many of these experiments so-called animal "intelligence" or problem-solving ability was measured using the Hebb-Williams maze test. Among those conducting such experiments were John Zubek, Roderick Cooper, Donald and Janet Forgays, Ronald Melzack, W.R. Thomson, Sam Rabinovitch, Woodburn Heron, and others. These experiments using experimental animals showed that early experience, whether enriched or deprived, had an effect not only on problem-solving ability but also on emotional behavior.

One day in the summer of 1954 large headlines appeared in the Montreal Star, MCGILL SCIENTISTS OPEN GREAT NEW FIELD OF RESEARCH. This referred to the work of Peter Milner and James Olds who, working collaboratively, discovered that electrical stimulation of "so-called" pleasure centers were rewarding in rats. This opened a research field of fundamental importance. The technology of electrical stimulation used in these experiments had been developed by Peter Milner, who had followed a career in electrical engineering before becoming a psychologist. This discovery prompted a variety of studies throughout the world on the emotional and motivational mechanisms of the brain. The method itself became important in investigating the workings of the brain. James Olds (1922–1976) devoted his entire research career to this field of research and achieved distinction.

Research contributions by psychologists at McGill in the 1960's and 1970's have been made in many areas. Ronald Melzack's research and theory on the experience of pain has been widely recognized. Dalbir Bindra's work on motivation and on the relation between brain processes and behavior has been extensive. Wallace E. Lambert's contribution to psycholinguistics has continued for about 25 years. He and his colleagues and students have made McGill a recognized centre in this field. In the classic areas of experimental psychology contributions have been made by Don C. Donderi, Albert S. Bregman, and Michael C. Corballis. Research in clinical and child psychology has grown rapidly. Virginia I. Douglas initiated an extensive program of research in hyperactivity in children. Sam Rabinovitch's work on learning disabilities led in 1970 to the creation of the McGill-Montreal Children's Hospital Learning Center. Sam Rabinovitch was a great teacher of child psychology. McGill has had a lengthy history of research in quantitative methodology. Among those who have contributed to this field are George A. Ferguson, Michael Corballis, James Ramsay, Anthony Marley, Charles Olson, and Y. Takane. Ferguson's *Statistical Analysis in Psychology and Education*, McGraw-Hill, which first appeared in 1959, is now in its 5th edition.

This very brief summary of research at McGill is grossly inadequate. The rich mosaic of research at McGill over the past third of a century cannot be clearly brought into focus in a few words. Discussion of major contributions by psychologists whose primary appointment is in the Faculty of Medicine, such as Robert B. Malmo (Bernhardt 1958) and Brenda Milner, has been omitted. Their work has received outstanding recognition and deserves more than cursory treatment. Reference to the work of many other contributors has also been omitted. The author offers sincere apologies for his sins of omission. These are both numerous and gross.

On the whole research in psychology at McGill over the past third of a century has been richly textured. Students who have lived a few years of their lives in the McGill milieu, and have absorbed its perspectives, perpetuate the McGill tradition in psychology in many universities in Canada and the United States.

Note on Source Material

Much of the source material used in the preparation of this history was obtained by search in the McGill University Archives. An important source was correspondence relating to psychology by Sir William Peterson, principal from 1895–1919, and by Sir Arthur Currie, principal from 1919–1935. Use was also made of early university calendars, year books, and departmental correspondence. Oral histories were available for a number of psychologists associated with McGill, including Dalbir Bindra, George A. Ferguson, D.O. Hebb, Robert Malmo, E.C. Webster, and others. The earlier issues of the *Bulletin of the Canadian Psychological Association*, 1941–1946, also provided information. In addition departmental records and correspondence were available for the period 1947 until the present.

References

Bernhardt, K.S. Five new Fellows of the C.P.A. (Professors George A. Ferguson and Robert Beverley Malmo). *The Canadian Psychologist*, 1958, *7*, 96–98.

Bridges, J.W. Professional autobiography with comments on teachers and associates. *The Canadian Psychologist*, 1966, *7a*, 399–406.

Myers, C.R. R.B. MacLeod (1907–1972) talks about psychology in Canada. *The Canadian Psychologist*, 1974, *15*, 105–111.

Northway, M.L. Child study in Canada: a casual history. In Lois Brockman, John Whiteley & John Zubek (Eds) *Child Development: Selected Readings*. Toronto. McClelland & Stewart Ltd 1973 Pp 11–46

Further Readings

Anonymous – Quebec, McGill University. *The Canadian Psychologist*, 1961, *2*, 34.
– Award of Centennial Medals, 1967 (Donald Olding Hebb). *The Canadian Psychologist*, 1968, *9*, 227–229.
– Citation: Wallace E. Lambert. *The Canadian Psychologist*, 1965, *6a*, 296.
– Award of Centennial Medals, 1967 (Robert B. Malmo). *The Canadian Psychologist*, 1968, *9*, 231.
– Robert B. Malmo. *The Canadian Psychologist*, 1971, *12*, 96–98.
– E.C. Webster. *The Canadian Psychologist*, 1959, *8*, 70–71.

Douglas, V.I. Student attitudes toward formal requirements in graduate training. *The Canadian Psychologist*, 1961, *2*, 14–19.

Frost, S.B. *The history of McGill in relation to Montreal and Quebec*, study commissioned by Commission D'etude sur les Universités, 1979.

Hebb, D.O. D.O. Hebb. In Gardner Murphy (Ed). *A History of Psychology in Autobiography*. Volume 7. San Francisco: Freeman 1980 Pp 272–303

Krech, David (Ed.). *The MacLeod Symposium*. Department of Psychology, Cornell University, Ithaca, New York, 1973.

Levin, V. and Zagolin, L. *History of the Department of Philosophy, McGill University*, unpublished manuscript, 1975.

MacLennan, Hugh (Ed.). *McGill, the story of a university*. London: George Allen and Unwin Ltd., 1960.

Murray, J.C. *Handbook of psychology*. London: Gardner, 1885.

Chapter 3

Psychology at Toronto

by

*C. Roger Myers**

Outline

Psychology as part of Philosophy: 1850–1889
  –Reverend James Beaven (1850–1871)
  –Reverend George Paxton Young (1871–1889)
The "New" Psychology from Germany: 1889–1915
  –Controversy: Baldwin vs. Hume (1889)
  –James Mark Baldwin (1889–1893)
  –August Kirschmann (1893–1909)
  –Edward Alexander Bott (1909–1915)
Psychology Goes "Applied": 1916–1956
  –Edward Alexander Bott (1916–1956)
Psychology Goes "Scientific": 1956–
Chairs Since 1968

Acknowledgments

This sketch of the history of the Department of Psychology at the University of Toronto was to have been done by Glenn Macdonald.[1] Glenn had begun to collect the relevant documents for this history before the onset of his long and painfull illness which led eventually to his death in 1978. Accordingly, in what follows, I am indebted to him at several points in the early history of the Department for copies of these documents which were turned over to me after his death. On the other hand, if any errors have been made in the interpretation of these documents, I must take full responsibility for them.

* Professor Myers joined the Faculty of the University of Toronto in 1927 and was the Chairman of the Department of Psychology there from 1956 to 1968.

There are several others who have helped greatly in the writing of this sketch: Professor Mary Jean Wright of the University of Western Ontario, my co-editor, has read carefully and critically every one of a long series of versions of this sketch; Tory Hoff of Carleton University, my research assistant during the summer of 1979, whose thesis work on the Baldwin years has been invaluable to me; and Professor Endel Tulving, the present Chairman of the Department at Toronto, who has somehow managed to find the time to read with care a late version of this sketch, and who has made many helpful suggestions for both correction and clarification.

May 1979   C.R.M.

Psychology as part of Philosophy: 1850–1889

Although the University of Toronto dates its beginning from 1827 when a Royal Charter was granted to King's College for the establishment of a University at the city of York (later renamed Toronto), it did not in fact open its doors for students until 1843. It was not uncommon in those days for there to be a long delay between the granting of a charter and having the building and staff required to teach students, and what we now call philosophy was then commonly referred to as "metaphysics".[2] The first Professor of Metaphysics at Toronto was the Reverend James Beaven. He had been Oxford-trained in the Classics, and was first appointed to the staff of King's College in 1843 as Professor of Theology (Campbell, 1902, p. 68–72). When the University was reorganized in 1850 on a non-sectarian basis as the Provincial University of Ontario, the Chair in Theology was necessarily abolished. It became the Chair in Metaphysics and Ethics in the University, and Beaven assumed the duties of the new Chair. The change from theology to metaphysics was probably difficult for Beaven. It required him to undertake a serious study of new fields of learning, including the works of the Scottish "realists" since the Scottish "common sense" school of psychology was then much in vogue elsewhere in Canada. The texts prescribed for his students were Francis Wayland's *Moral Science*, Thomas Reid's *Intellectual Powers* and Dugald Stewart's *Moral and Active Powers* (U of T Calendar, 1857–58, p. 18 – the earliest Calendar available).

So, from 1850 on and for the next 39 years, pre-scientific psychology was taught at the University of Toronto as an important part of philosophy. But Beaven was not at all popular with his students who played many pranks on him. He was described by one of his professorial colleagues as "a dry old stick". He was finally asked to resign, and did so in 1871. He was replaced by another clergyman, the Reverend George Paxton Young. Unlike Beaven, Young was a very effective, charismatic lecturer, and he had a most influential 18-year career at Toronto as a teacher of philosophy (Hume, 1927, p. 21–22). Indeed, many Toronto graduates practically worshipped the man. This fact became particularly important later, at the time of the selection of his successor.

Young had been trained at Edinburgh under the great Sir William Hamilton, and so was thoroughly familiar with the "common sense" empiricism of the Scottish "realists". But he came into increasing disagreement with that school of thought and, even before his appointment in Toronto, he had espoused German idealism in preference to Scottish empiricism. Thus, in 1872, he was already offering his systematic comparison of Hamiltonian and Kantian philosophy – no doubt to the disadvantage of the former, since Kant's *Critique of Pure Reason* was prescribed for this course (U of T Calendar, 1872–73, p. 34). By 1885, Young at Toronto and Watson at Queen's were among the foremost exponents of British idealism on this continent. Green's *Prolegomena to Ethics* was prescribed for honour students in philosophy at Toronto (U of T Calendar, 1885–86, p. 35). Young's sudden death in February, 1889, made it possible for the University of Toronto to consider importing the "new" psychology which had been flourishing in Germany ever since Wundt had established his famous psychological laboratory at Leipzig ten years earlier.

The "New" Psychology from Germany: 1889–1915

Controversy: Baldwin vs. Hume (1889)

The "new" psychology from Germany was brought to Canada by James Mark Baldwin, a young American, when he was appointed Professor of Logic, Metaphysics and Ethics at Toronto in 1889. But, before this was accomplished, there was a lively local controversy, since there was another strongly-supported candidate for the vacant Chair, James Gibson Hume, one of Professor Young's prize pupils. Bringing such a person as Baldwin to Canada at that time was a truly remarkable achievement. The main credit for this must go to the man who was then the President of the University of Toronto, Sir Daniel Wilson. But the difficulty he had in securing Baldwin's appointment can only be understood in the light of the following historical facts. First, University affairs at Toronto were completely dominated by the provincial government.

Among other things, all appointments to the staff of the provincial University were made, at that time, by the Ontario Cabinet and announced by the provincial Minister of Education, sometimes without any prior consultation with the President of the University. Second, Victorian Toronto was then under the strong political influence of the "nativists" who believed not only that Canada should be reserved for Canadians but also that all University appointments at Toronto should be reserved for graduates of the University of Toronto. Third, Professor George Paxton Young had built up enormous prestige at Toronto, and his espousal of idealism had created widespread suspicion of, if not antagonism to, the "new" psychology.

President Wilson had been striving for excellence in University appointment but, in doing so, had to struggle against not only the extreme Canadian nationalism – which is not unfamiliar to us today – but against the even more narrow view that only Toronto graduates should be considered for University appointments – a form of parochialism which was not, at that time, peculiar to Toronto. Wilson's efforts to secure the "best" men for vacant chairs were not always successful. But even when they were, as in the cases of Hutton, an Englishman appointed to the Chair in Classics, and Alexander, a London-trained Canadian appointed to the Chair in English Literature, these appointments produced a public outcry and caused the Edinburgh-trained Wilson to be suspected of being against the appointment of both Canadians and also Toronto graduates. Langton says that Wilson's private journal "... is full of indignant reference to the provincial and short-sighted self-interest which would exclude highly trained specialists merely because they were trained elsewhere than in Toronto". (Langton, 1929, p. 154).

We do not really know why Wilson was so determined to secure the appointment of Baldwin, but there were probably many factors which influenced him. For one thing, Baldwin's appointment was supported by the Principals of two of the theological colleges closely affiliated with the University of Toronto (Caven of Knox and Sheraton of Wycliffe) – and opposed, of course, by the "nativists". The "nativists" were led, on the faculty, by James Loudon, of whom Wilson was deeply suspicious and who, in his private journal, Wilson called "the Mole". In the Ontario cabinet, the "nativists" were supported by some powerful Ministers, including the Hon. Col. Gibson, Provincial Secretary, and the Hon. G.W. Ross, Minister of Education. The candidate of the "nativists" was Hume, who was not only a native-born Canadian and a Toronto graduate, but also a devoted disciple of the late much-revered Professor Young. On the other hand, Hume had not even finished his training at that time and was, in Wilson's view, a "raw, inexperienced youth" and so was patently unfit to head such an important department. Other factors may also have influenced Wilson to favour Baldwin's appointment. Wilson had close personal ties with Princeton, the President of which was one of Wilson's former students, and with his Edinburgh training, Wilson was more sympathetic to Scottish realism than either Professor Young or the "nativists". Then, there was, between Wilson and Baldwin, a shared interest in hand preference. Wilson had been left-handed, was now ambidextrous, and would author a scholarly book on the subject, (Wilson, 1891), whereas Baldwin made hand preference the object of his first direct observation of his infant daughter. Also, the fact that they had both attended the Annual Meeting of the American Association for the Advancement of Science held at the University of Toronto in August, 1889, suggests that Wilson had probably interviewed Baldwin at that time, and had been much impressed by him.

Wilson was in the habit, in University matters, of appealing directly to the Premier of the Province, Oliver Mowat, whom he knew personally, over the head of the Minister of Education, for whom he had little use. Of Mowat, Wilson wrote in his journal on September 26, 1889, "He urged a compromise today and assured me that his experience taught him that compromises were often the wisest course. In politics they may be; but in University patronage they mean MEDIOCRITY" (Langton, 1929, p. 165).

It was not until October 19, 1889, long after the academic session had begun, that the conflicting views of Wilson and the government were settled. Wilson recorded in his journal on that date what he clearly regarded as his success: "The agony is over; and Professor Baldwin of Princeton takes the Metaphysical Chair ... after endless vacillations and vexatious worry he [Mowat] sent for me to tell me that I had practically secured my point. Baldwin assumes duty forthwith ..." (Langton, 1929, p. 168). What Mowat probably meant by using the word "practically" was that he had managed to achieve one of his political compromises. Since the "nativists" would consider that the decision to appoint Baldwin was a decision not to appoint Hume, and since Mowat's Liberal government had been threatened with "the whole weight of graduate opposition" at the next (upcoming) general election in Ontario unless Hume were appointed, it was clearly time for a compromise. So it was decided that, at the University of Toronto, following the example set earlier at Queen's, the Chair in Philosophy would be divided into two, thus making it possible for the government to appoint two Professors, *both* Baldwin and Hume. James Mark Baldwin was appointed Professor of Logic, Metaphysics and Ethics in 1889. James Gibson Hume received an "advance appointment", a practice not so very much unusual in those days. He immediately resumed his studies at Harvard, and then went to the

University of Freiburg in Germany. It was not until 1891 that he assumed active duties as Professor of the History of Philosophy in the University of Toronto (and Professor of Ethics in University College) (U of T Calendars, 1889–90, p. 22 and 1891–92, p. 27).

James Mark Baldwin (1889–1893)

There can be little doubt that Baldwin was the first "modern" psychologist in Canada. In his Murchison autobiography, Baldwin recalled that, as an undergraduate at Princeton, he had been much impressed by the courses he had taken from President McCosh. Baldwin wrote that McCosh "had seized upon the project of scientific psychology as announced in Wundt's *Physiologische Psychologie*, then just out, ..." (Murchison, 1961, p. 2). When Baldwin graduated from Princeton in 1884, he won a "Mental Science Fellowship" and went to Germany for his graduate work. At Leipzig, he found that "Wundt was the rage" and that his laboratory and lectures were crowded. In retrospect, he said that the principal"... result of the German visit was a sort of apostolic call to the 'new psychology' " (Murchison, 1961, p. 2). Upon returning to Princeton he entered theology, but could not shake off the Leipzig virus. He then accepted an invitation to teach philosophy and psychology at Lake Forest University in Illinois. What Baldwin called his "pedagogical need" there for an exposition of general psychology, " motivated the first volume of my *Handbook of Psychology, Senses and Intellect* ..." (Murchison, 1961, p. 3). But in his much longer book of memoirs, which was published a quarter of a century earlier, he said that he wrote it in the hope of getting a better position (Baldwin, 1926, p. 40). Whatever the reason may have been, he then had his "call" to Toronto.

Baldwin described his Toronto appointment as follows: "At this time I was given the means to found the laboratory of psychology in the University of Toronto – the first anywhere on British soil" (Murchison, 1961, p. 3). Baldwin arrived in Toronto and was introduced to his classes by President Wilson in November, 1889. On January 11, 1890, he delivered his "Inaugural Address" which, in the fashion of those days, he was required to give before the assembled faculty and the public. In it, after paying a graceful tribute to his predecessor, Professor Young, he went on to say that, in his view, a philosopher must now also be a scientist, and that "Comparative and experimental psychology are the direct outgrowth of the modern scientific spirit, and it is to the merit of contemporary philosophy that the new work is receiving its hearty endorsement" (Baldwin, 1890, p. 13). We now know, as his audience doubtless knew then, how lacking in heartiness the "endorsement" was at that time in Toronto. The controversy stirred up by his appointment was certainly not over. It was said that Baldwin was one of the "Scotch School of Philosophy" and that he was "a mere psychophysicist and little better than a materialist". Being called "a materialist" was next thing to being called "an atheist" and would not do, at that time, in "Toronto, the Good".

And yet the record shows that Baldwin's "Inaugural" words were not without effect at Toronto. Later in 1890, a survey called "Psychology in American Colleges and Universities" was published with detailed descriptions of the situation at ten of these: Wisconsin, Nebraska, New York Teacher's College, Columbia, Harvard, Yale, Pennsylvania, Indiana, Clark and Toronto. Baldwin reported for Toronto that the Senate had now ratified a new curriculum for students in psychology, providing for more "special and advanced courses and opportunity for research". He wrote that, although the recent fire had postponed equipping the psychological laboratory, the plans for restoration provided even more ample accommodation. He described a suite of four rooms (with an area of about 2,000 square feet) which were to be devoted to this purpose (*American Journal of Psychology*, 1890, p. 285–6). The "recent fire" to which Baldwin makes reference took place on February 14, 1890, and destroyed a large portion of the Main Building, which is now University College.

By 1891, Baldwin was recommending that his students read the works of Locke, Berkeley, Hume, Ward, Spencer, Bain and James. The Calendar for that session also states: "Good facilities are now offered for laboratory work in Experimental Psychology. Students in the third and fourth years may apply to Professor Baldwin ..." (U of T Calendar, 1891–92, p. 120). Also in 1891, the "Department of Psychology" was granted an appropriation of $1,451 for laboratory "fittings and apparatus" (Senate's *Standing Committee on Finance*, 1891, p. 30). This was a very large sum in those days and, especially in view of the financial consequences of the fire, it provides further evidence of Baldwin's influence at Toronto. The establishment of a psychological laboratory within a department of philosophy was not at all unusual at that time. It had been done by Wundt at Leipzig. Such a laboratory was sometimes called a "Department", especially in financial reports presumably because of the expense entailed in buying equipment for it.

In 1892, Balwin from Canada was one of the founding members of the American Psychological Association (APA), and was made a member of APA's first Council on which he served for the next five years until he was elected to be APA's sixth President in 1897 (APA's *Biographical Directory*, 1975, p. 12). Since Baldwin was, at least initially, from outside the USA, this not only gave APA a somewhat "continental" flavour, but also served to enhance the international standing of the University of Toronto.[3] Just as there were many factors which influenced Wilson's determination to secure Baldwin's appointment at Toronto in 1889, there probably were many factors which influenced Baldwin's decision to leave for Princeton in 1893 after only four short, but very effective, years at Toronto. For one thing, Baldwin's chief champion at Toronto, Sir Daniel Wilson, had died in 1892 and was succeeded in the Presidency of the University by "the Mole", James Loudon, who, as noted earlier, had been prominent among the "nativists" in opposing Baldwin's original appointment. For another thing, Baldwin had been trying unsuccessfully for two years to get someone to help him supervise the increasing numbers of students who wanted to work in the psychological laboratory. Finally, Princeton's offer was said to be "very liberal" and the prospect of returning to his Alma Mater to establish there another "first" psychological laboratory must have been very appealing.

Before leaving Toronto, however, Baldwin saw to it that his laboratory would survive his departure and wanted to make sure that it would be supervised by a Leipzig-trained psychologist, so he sought advice from Wundt. Wundt strongly recommended one of his students, August Kirschmann. But there was a long delay in offering Kirschmann an appointment. One reason for the delay was that Baldwin was in Europe in the summer of 1892, which made communication with the government in Ontario slow and difficult. By the time an offer was actually made to Kirschmann, he had left on a tour of South America, and could not be located. Another reason for the delay was that Hume, who was now back "in harness" at Toronto, wanted the appointment to go to a man named Frederick Tracy, a Toronto graduate and former pupil of Professor Young's, who had taught philosophy at Toronto during Hume's absence. But when Baldwin returned, he managed somehow to persuade Hume to change his mind about Tracy and to join him in recommending that the Minister of Education offer a lecturership to Kirschmann. Baldwin may have managed this, at least partly, through his efforts to get Tracy accepted as a graduate student at Harvard or Clark. In 1892, Tracy left Toronto to do a Ph.D. with G. Stanley Hall at Clark on a topic that, he says, was suggested to him by Baldwin (Tracy, 1893, p. 90 footnote). His thesis, when completed, was immediately published in book form as *The Psychology of Childhood* and was hailed by a world hungry for knowledge about children. It went through at least seven editions and was translated into several foreign languages. This book did much to add to the international reputation of the Department of Philosophy at the University of Toronto, to which Tracy[4] returned in 1894.

When Baldwin finally made a firm decision to leave Toronto for

Princeton in 1893, his Chair was advertised by the government. Among the applications received, was one from Titchener, who had been appointed the year before as Assistant Professor of Psychology at Cornell University. The testimonials attached to his application included enthusiastic letters of support from J.G. Schurman, the President of Cornell, Creighton of the Philosophy Department at Cornell, Ladd of Yale, Angell of Stanford, Stout of Cambridge, and three of Titchener's former tutors at Oxford (Evans, 1970). Why did Titchener apply for Baldwin's Chair at Toronto? Earlier, the present writer thought and wrote that it was because "At Toronto, Baldwin had broken the academic ground and had prepared a laboratory nest ..." (Myers, 1965, p. 9). But it has since been learned that the same had been done for Titchener at Cornell. However, it was not until reading an early version of George Ferguson's history of the Psychology Department at McGill, that it was discovered that Titchener, a decade later, had sought an appointment at McGill. Furthermore, Ferguson quoted from a letter that Titchener wrote to the Principal of McGill at that time (1903): "It has always been my ambition to be at the head of a department of modern psychology in England, or at least in the Empire somewhere." Accordingly, it must now be concluded that Titchener was such an incorrigible Englishman that he simply wanted to move himself and his family onto British soil.

As things turned out, neither Titchener nor anyone else was appointed to the Chair being vacated by Baldwin. On September 14, 1893, the Minister of Education wrote a brief note to Titchener, returning his testimonials, and pleading unforeseen financial difficulties as the reason for the government's decision not to appoint anyone to the vacant Chair for which he had applied (Copy in possession of writer). It is of interest to note that, before the government had decided to leave the Chair vacant, Baldwin had supported Titchener's appointment, even to the point of saying that, if Kirschmann on his arrival should be upset by it, Kirschmann should be "let go".

August Kirschmann (1893–1909)

Kirschmann, the missing world traveller, finally turned up and was duly appointed "Lecturer and Demonstrator in Philosophy" in 1893, even though his knowledge of English was not suficient to permit him to lecture in the session 1893–94. On his arrival, he was surprised to find that Baldwin, the man he had been appointed to assist, was leaving but, since he was put in sole charge of the psychological laboratory, he decided to stay. According to the Calendar in the first session in which Kirschmann taught, the study of philosophy embraced. "... Logic, Psychology, Ethics,

History of Philosophy and Metaphysics ..." (U of T Calendar, 1894–95, p. 90–91). Three years later, the Calendar stated: "The Psychological Laboratory ... is stituated in the West Wing of the Main University Building in close proximity to the Physical [Physics] Laboratory, the apparatus of which is available for some of the work in Psychology. The Laboratory is well equipped for investigations in Psychophysics, Psychological Optics, and the time relations of mental phenomena ... On account of the increased number of undergraduates and graduates ... and especially to facilitate the independent research of graduates, it has been found necessary to extend the Psychological Laboratory by addition of the rooms adjoining the Ethnological Museum..." (U of T Calendar, 1897–98, p. 32). The pressure of increasing numbers of students evidently continued because, in 1900, the psychological laboratory had to be extended again. It then comprised 16 rooms on the first and second floors of the Main Building (See floor plan at the end of U of T Studies, Psychological Series, Vol. I., No. 4, 1900).

That the work done in this laboratory, under Kirschmann's supervision, was closely modelled on the German (Leipzig) pattern is shown by a glance at the titles of the first psychological papers to appear in the University of Toronto Studies which began publication in 1898. The psychological papers were edited by "Dr. A. Kirschmann". The first article in the Psychological Series was entitled "Space-Threshold of Colours and its Dependence on Contrast Phenomena" by W.B. Lane.[5] The second article in this series is entitled "A Case of Abnormal Colour-Sense with Special Reference to the Space-Threshold of Colours" by J.W. Baird[6] and R.J. Richardson[7]. In the fourth paragraph of this article, the authors state that "The experiments which furnished the data for this paper were conducted in the psychological laboratory of the University of Toronto at the request of Dr. Kirschmann, director of the laboratory ..." (U of T Studies, Vol. I., No. 1, 1898, p. 87).[8] Readers should note, in the foregoing quotation, the German flavour of "at the request of" – students in the laboratory did what the Director instructed them to do.

Boring lists Kirschmann as the fifth of the German students to train in Wundt's laboratory, and has this to say about his work: "The psychology of vision prospered in the 90's ... Kirschmann ... published important works on color contrast" and "worked out the laws that are still current in the textbooks" (Boring, 1929, p. 627). However, in the first decade of the new century while at Toronto, Kirschmann was publishing articles on more subjects than "color contrast". His non-psychological publications included such improbable topics as "Artificial Glaciation", "The Alaska Boundary Dispute" (Kirschmann, 1903) and, in 1904, a gem called "The Decimal System of Notation – A Relic of Savagery" in which he demonstrated conclusively to his own satisfaction, but without any help from psychology, that the number 12 is vastly superior to the number 10 as a basis for a rational system of notation (Kirschmann, 1904, p. 224–28).

Among the Titchener Papers in the Cornell Archives are several letters from Kirschmann to Titchener whom he addressed as his "old friend" because they had been together as students of Wundt in Leipzig. The first of these letters is handwritten from Toronto in 1901 and merely expresses Kirschmann's appreciation of being "among the five to whom the book is dedicated".[9] The second letter from Kirschmann is dated January 19, 1904, and is one of a number of letters Titchener received from those of his colleagues to whom he had written, expressing his dissatisfaction with APA as having become too applied, and proposing the formation of a new society to be called "The American Society of Experimental Psychology". In his reply, Kirschmann wrote that he heartily approved of "… your plan of founding a new society limited to that part of psychology which is accessible to exact experiment, thus keeping out of its proceedings hypnotism, pedagogy, folklore, and everything that is not truly experimental…". But Kirschmann begged Titchener not to call it "American" since some English and Canadian psychologists might wish to join (Titchener Papers, Cornell Archives, 1904). The third letter from Kirschmann is a short typewritten note dated March 5, 1904. It is of more than ordinary interest because it was written on University of Toronto letterhead with the University's crest in red at the top, and "DEPARTMENT OF PSYCHOLOGY" in bold, black, embossed, capital letters at the top left of the page. Although this might be taken as evidence that there was, as early as 1904, a "Department of Psychology" at Toronto, it is clear that it was still administratively within the Department of Philosophy. In this third note, it is also of interest that the German, Kirschmann, tells his "old friend" the Englishman, Titchener, that "I find it a little hard on ladies who take an interest in experimental psychology, if we exclude them altogether …" (Titchener Papers, Cornell Archives, 1904). Subsequent developments suggest that, although Titchener seems to have accepted Kirschmann's first suggestion since he dropped the "American" and called his new society simply the Society of Experimental Psychology (SEP), Titchener could never bring himself to accept the suggestion about "ladies who take an interest in experimental psychology" since it is reported that women were excluded from membership in SEP as long as it remained Titchener's private club – which it did until his death in 1927.

Kirschmann achieved considerable power and prestige at Toronto. In the summer of 1909, he withdrew his accumulated pension reserve (of nearly $4,000), left for Germany and never came back. This seems to have had almost no effect on either the University or the psychological laboratory. He was shown as being on "sick leave" – so the University went on paying him a salary: one year at full salary; then two years at half salary; and then three more years at quarter salary. Indeed, Canada had been at war with Germany for nearly a year when, in June, 1915, a Toronto newspaper found out that the University was still paying Kirschmann (through Switzerland) and created such a fuss about it that his appointment had to be terminated (*Toronto Telegram*, 1915). Meanwhile, everyone in the Philosophy Department kept looking for Kirschmann's return, and his spirit continued to preside over the psychological laboratory. [10]

George Sidney Brett

At this point we must digress long enough to take note of a man who, although primarily a philosopher, had earned a name in psychology and who, later, played an important role in the formal establishment of a Department of Psychology at Toronto. Brett had been appointed to the staff of Trinity College in 1908 as "Lecturer in Classics and Ethics". After his Oxford training and his five-year exposure to Eastern philosophies at the University of Punjab in India, he was busily engaged in the writing of his scholarly three-volume *History of Pscyhology*, the first volume of which was published in 1912 (Brett, 1912). This bright and gifted scholar was promptly (1909) invited over to the University's Philosophy Department to help fill the gap left by Kirschmann's departure. In University Calendars, he was first shown, in 1910, as "Class Assistant in Psychology"; then, in 1911, as "Assistant in Logic and History of Philosophy"; then, in 1912, as "Lecturer in Greek Philosophy" which he remained until, in 1917, Brett suddenly is shown as "Professor of Philosophy" (U of T Calendars, 1910–11, 1911–12, 1912–13 and 1917–18). Long before becoming "Head of the Department of Philosophy", which was not made official until 1927, he was largely instrumental, as we shall see, in establishing an independent Department of Psychology separate from philosophy. But even more important than his distinguished career in philosophy, it should be noted that Brett became a very powerful figure in the general affairs of the University of Toronto. He had much to do with the organization of an effective School of Graduate Studies at Toronto of which he later became Dean. He had great organizational abilities which made him a close advisor and confidant of the President, and this gave him an influence in University affairs which went far beyond the confines of the Department of Philosophy.

Edward Alexander Bott

Bott was the man who not only created an independent Department of Psychology at Toronto but determined the direction it would take during the thirty-year period when he was its official "Head"

Edward Alexander Bott: 1887–1974

(1926–1956).[11] In the fall of 1909, after Kirschmann had left for Germany, Bott entered the "Sophomore-Freshman" year in honour philosophy at Toronto so that he could get his degree in three years, but in fact he thus began a career of almost half a century at the University. Of his undergraduate years, Bott says that Kirschmann "… was a very live tradition around the place …" and that "a great rivalry" had developed among the junior members of the faculty (Abbott, Smith and Robinson) as to who would become the "effective understudy" to Kirschmann and who would direct his laboratory (Bott, 1962, p. 15). However, all of these juniors disappeared at various times and in various ways,[12] thus leaving the field clear for Bott.

By the time Bott graduated in 1912, he had clearly been much influenced by Kirschmann's ghost. Although he immediately became a Ph.D candidate in philosophy, it is evident from his reminiscences that most of his interests and work were in the psychological laboratory. Of his graduate work, Bott says: "I had no really serious training. As a matter of fact, by the time I graduated in 1912, I was carrying on most of the instrumental work that was done in the laboratory" (Bott, 1962, p. 15). Another sign of the Kirschmann-Leipzig influence occurs later when Bott says: "I had that whole room rigged up. The windows were blacked out. I had lights in tin cans with pin holes – a whole visual experimental setup" (Bott, 1962, p. 16).

Bott's doctoral thesis was on the thoroughly philosophical subject of the emergence of Western "scientific method" in early Greek thought, part of which he later published as a journal article (Bott, 1923). This was a subject in which he continued to be interested for the rest of his life and which later became the basis for his famous seminar in "Systematic Psychology" (Myers, 1974). But Bott was never granted a Ph.D. degree at Toronto. The junior members of the psychology staff (Cosgrave, Bernhardt, Wilson and Myers) were told, and believed, the plausible story that Bott's Ph.D. degree had been blocked by Brett on the grounds that no one should be allowed to do a thesis on early Greek thought who could not read Greek in the original. However Bott, in his reminiscences, says that he never heard of any obstacle of that kind. He claims that his thesis was mislaid while circulating through the philosophy staff, and says that "It was my own fault that that thing went fallow because I was so diverted into war activities" (Bott, 1962, p. 27).

Psychology Goes "Applied": 1916–1956

The World War of 1914–18 completely changed the orientation of psychology at Toronto. Early in the war, Bott (like others) attempted to enlist for active service in the Canadian Army, but was rejected because of poor eyesight. So he promptly plunged into civilian war work: the rehabilitation of war-injured soldiers. For this work, Bott first used the Kirschmann-style psychological laboratory and transformed it into a rehabilitation clinic. The laboratory which had had to be enlarged several times because of increasing numbers of students, had to be enlarged again in 1915–16 because of the increasingly large number of soldier-casualties that now streamed up from the General Hospital. Bott opened up the whole second floor above the "Cloisters" in the West Wing of what is now University College, by making a passage-way in the cross partitions. But this was not enough. Bott's rehabilitation clinic grew so large that, in the Spring of 1917, it had to be transferred to the newly-constructed Hart House, where this work on the muscular re-education of wounded veterans brought Bott into close contact with members of the Medical Faculty of the University.

In his Annual Report for the session 1916–17, the President of the

University, Sir Robert Falconer, wrote: "Last winter an extremely promising piece of work was begun under the direction of Dr. [sic] E.A. Bott of the Psychology Department [sic] in the way of the re-education of disabled soldiers. The work has expanded rapidly and has been taken over by the Dominion Hospitals Commission with Dr. Bott still in charge but with assistance from members of the Medical Faculty and others. In the Spring, it was transferred to much larger quarters in Hart House ..." (President's *Annual Report*, 1916–17, p. 15). It is evident from this quotation that Bott did not really need a doctorate since everyone at Toronto, from the President down, was already referring to him as "Dr. Bott", and that there was a "Psychology Department" at Toronto, referred to as such, at least a decade before it was officially declared to be a new department separate from philosophy in 1926.

Although a non-medical man, Bott's services in Hart House were recognized medically by his appointment as Honorary Captain in the Royal Canadian Medical Corps. In cases of muscle injury, paralysis or hysteria, Bott concentrated on the motivational aspects of therapy. He insisted on treating the whole man and on making him an active and confident participant in the treatment of his disability. To this end, he invented an impressive collection of gadgets designed to intrigue, amuse and challenge the best efforts of the injured man to regain the use of his limbs.

By the end of the war, the *de facto* Department of Psychology had grown to an intolerable size. In terms of the number of staff and students, the space requirements and the size and complexity of the budget, this "upstart" had grown quite beyond the control of the unfortunate philosophers who were supposed to administer it. Although Bott had been dealing directly with the President on financial matters for some years, he was still only a "Lecturer" and so did not have the academic rank required for the Headship of an independent department. Then there was also the desire to capitalize on the prestige of the medical connection that had been established in Hart House. So, in 1920, Dr. C.K. Clarke, the retired Dean of Medicine, was made "Director of the Psychological Laboratory." In the Calendar for that session, Philosophy and Psychology are shown separately for the first time in terms of both staff and courses (U of T Calendar, 1920–21, p. 192 and p. 195).

By this time, according to Bott, Brett had become "nominal Head" of the Philosophy Department and was advising the President on what to do. The old Department of Philosophy was breaking up. Psychology had more students than all of the rest of philosophy combined. So the question was who would head up psychology and whether there would be a new department. Brett asked Bott if he wished to specialize in psychology rather than philosophy, and Bott said "Yes". Bott recalls that when Brett "... asked me what my feeling about it was, it was the beginning of forming psychology into a separate department by itself. It wasn't formally done until 1926 but it was in the making long before that" (Bott, 1962, p. 26).

Throughout the 1920's, Bott was already acting like the head of a new department. He devised, and obtained approval for, a four-year honour course in psychology in 1921 which produced its first graduates in May, 1925. In 1921 also, he recruited Win Bridges from Ohio State and Katharine Banham from Cambridge. Bridges, with his Harvard Ph.D., had taught for one year (1914–15) at the University of Alberta where he developed his permanent interest in abnormal psychology, before going to Ohio State. Banham was a developmental psychologist who obtained her Ph.D. from Toronto. Between them, they kept the department at Toronto "applied" through the first half of the 1920s. But they stayed at Toronto for only three years before moving to Montreal. In 1924, Bott brought in Earle MacPhee from Alberta and Bill Blatz, with his brand new Chicago Ph.D., to replace them. MacPhee was "applied" because he had taught educational, medical and legal psychology at Alberta. Blatz was brought in to head up the new Nursery School Project at Toronto which later became the Institute of Child Study. So Toronto stayed "applied" through the latter half of the 1920's.

Further evidence of just how "applied" it was can be gleaned from the staff publications and research listed in the President's *Annual Reports* for that period. Growing out of his work in Hart House during the First World War, Bott had published, mostly in medical journals, his "Mechanotherapy" (Bott, 1918), and his "Training for Lay Workers in Functional Restoration" (Bott, 1919a) and his "The Mentality of Convalescence" (Bott, 1919b). In 1920, he published locally his "Juvenile Employment in Relation to Public Schools and Industries in Toronto" (Bott, 1920). After a return to philosophy with his "Criticism and Ways of Inquiry" (Bott, 1923a), and to his war work with "Some Characteristics of Reciprocal Wrist Action" (Bott, 1923b), and later (with Raymond Dodge) their "Antagonistic Muscle Action in Voluntary Flexion and Extension" (Dodge and Bott,1928), Bott turned to the current scene at Toronto with his "Principles of Mental Hygiene Research" (Bott, 1929). The other members of his staff were similarly "applied" in their interests. Bridges published his "Theories of Temperament: An Attempt at Reconciliation" in 1923 (Bridges, 1923). In 1926, MacPhee was reported to be doing research on the "Learning of Modern Languages" and "Practical Methods for the Classification of Public School Pupils", and published his "Psychology in the Clinic" (MacPhee, 1927) and his "Pychology of Adver-

tising" (MacPhee, 1928). Blatz was reported to be studying "young delin-
quents" in 1926 and, in 1927, was doing research on the "behaviour of
public school children" and the "treatment of eneuresis." In 1928, he was
doing research on "methods of solving problem situations by preschool
age children" and published with Bott's wife, Mrs. Helen Bott, the first of
their two books entitled *Parents and the Pre-school Child* (Blatz and Bott,
1928). In the latter half of the 1920's, Chant who had become a Lecturer,
and Ketchum who was first appointed as a "Class Assistant for Medical
Students", begin to appear on the staff list for psychology. In 1926, Chant
was reported to be doing research on a "rating scale for clerical staff" and,
in 1927, on the "selection of taxi-cab drivers". In 1928, Ketchum was doing
research on "boy gangs and companionships in a selected urban
neighbourhood" and one of his graduate students, Myers, did an MA
thesis on "The Child and the Comic Strip" in the same neighbourhood
(President's *Annual Reports*, 1920–29).

The session 1926–27 was the time when the University of Toronto
finally admitted officially that Bott was Head of the new Department of
Psychology that he had created. By the end of the 1920's, the senior staff of
the new Department were: Bott "Professor and Director of the Psychological Laboratory"; MacPhee and Blatz, Associate Professors; and Chant
and Ketchum, Lecturers. With William Line replacing MacPhee when the
latter resigned in 1929 to go into business, these men composed the senior
staff of the Department through the 1930's. Indeed, with the single
exception of Chant who moved to UBC after World War II, they continued
to be the senior staff of the Department through the 1940's and 1950's until
they died or were retired. The number of graduate students in the
Department had steadily increased and some of them, including Gerald
Cosgrave, Karl Bernhardt, Douglas Wilson and Roger Myers, became
junior members of the staff in the late 1920's. The Department of
Psychology at Toronto which had "gone applied" under the stress of
World War I, and had stayed "applied" during the 1920's, was forced to
stay "applied" following the stock market crash of 1929. During the
"Depression Years", the only way to afford the luxury of teaching at
University was to get a part-time job outside and show that your training
in psychology was actually worth something. (The writer managed to get
himself a half-time job with the Provincial Department of Health.) During
this period, everyone's concern at the University was not how much their
salary for next year might be raised, but rather by how much it might be
cut. The records show that in May, 1933, President Cody announced that
University salaries for the next year would be cut on a graded basis: 5% on
salaries under $1,000 but ranging upwards to 20% on salaries over $6,000.
(The writer's salary was cut by 10%.) Although there were rumours and

fears of cuts in other years, this seems to have been the only year that a cut in salary was actually made.

When Clifford Beers published the story of his mental illness in *A Mind that Found Itself: an Autobiography* (Beers, 1908), he started a flourishing movement in the United States called "Mental Hygiene". Clarence Hincks, a young Canadian physician who had once (1918–20) worked with Bott in the psychological laboratory at the University, founded, and later became the Director of, The Canadian National Committee for Mental Hygiene. Hincks proved to be an inspired fund-raiser, and all of the senior staff in psychology, Bott, Blatz, Line, Chant, and Ketchum, were subsidized from the funds of this committee for doing research related to mental health. Bott kept alive his early philosophical interest in the origin of the scientific method through his seminar in "Systematic Psychology", and took sporadic dives into visual experimentation when required to do so by graduate student interest, but most of his work was in arranging things with Hincks so that his staff could be engaged in research on mental health problems. Hincks had suggested that Bott should recruit MacPhee from Alberta, and MacPhee promptly became active, with Blatz, in studying the mental health of children in the elementary grades of school called the Regal Road Project. MacPhee also worked closely with his friend, Dr. Bernard T. McGhie, who had recently been appointed the Superintendent of the Orillia Hospital for the Feebleminded, and who was trying hard to improve the treatment of subnormals in Ontario. One of the last publications of MacPhee before he left academia to enter business,[13] was *Training and Research in a Hospital for Subnormals* (McGhie and MacPhee, 1930), which had been ghost-written for him by a couple of graduate students (Cosgrave and Myers) who were the first "psychological interns" to be employed in the Ontario Hospital Service.

But more should be said about certain other members of the senior staff during the 1930's:

Wilhelm Emet Blatz

Blatz was probably the brightest member of the staff, and during his long career of almost forty years in the Department of Psychology from 1925 until his death in 1964, he was the most colourful and controversial lecturer in the Department. His rapier-like wit gained him notoriety among not only his students but the general public of Toronto. His views on child training, which then seemed radical, resulted in many headlines in the newspapers of the time, and he thoroughly enjoyed the controversies he started. He liked to say shocking things as a way to induce what we would now call "cognitive dissonance", and therefore fresh inquiry. As Mary Northway says correctly in the introduction to Blatz's last book: "He taught, not so much to instruct, as to provoke. In this he was very successful ..." (Northway in Blatz, 1966, p. ix). With the later popularity of Nathan Cohen's "Fighting Words" on TV in the 1950s, the people of Canada as a whole were involved in controversies over "that man Blatz". As the first Director of the Institute of Child Study at Toronto, Blatz was unquestionably the founder and leader of child study in Canada, – a fact that is well described and documented by Mary Northway in the second chapter of *Child Development: Selected Readings* (Northway in Brockman et al., 1973, p. 11–46). At the Annual Meeting of the CPA held in Victoria, B.C. in 1973, Mary Wright, currently a leader in developmental psychology in Canada, urged that field to "rediscover Blatz"[14] (Wright, 1974b, p. 140–4).

William Line

In the 1930's, Line was the humanist on the staff of the Department. As a bright young and extremely promising Ph.D. of Spearman's, he had been brought in to repace MacPhee and may have been Bott's first abortive attempt to change the direction of the Department toward science. In his first years at Toronto, Line taught graduate students all about Spearman's "g" and "s's" but, being a humanist, he quickly succumbed to the applied mental hygiene atmosphere of the Department, and never did live up to his early scientific promise. He often bewildered some of his students because, after one of his lectures (usually delivered from notes hastily scribbled on the outside of a cigarette package), they could never remember what he had said that so inspired them. But inspire them he did, and became perhaps the most admired and beloved member of the faculty throughout his entire career at Toronto.

Sperrin Noah Fulton Chant

In the 1930's, Chant was the statistician of the Department. He, like Blatz before him and later Ketchum and Bernhardt, went to Chicago for his graduate training, but never did complete the requirements for a degree there. (Blatz and Bernhardt were the only ones to earn a Ph.D. from Chicago.) Chant took summer courses with Louis Thurstone at Chicago, and his liking and admiration for Thurstone are very evident in his reminiscences many years later (Chant, 1970, p. 19).[15] Chant was very popular with graduate students, partly because he was able to help them with the statistics required for their theses, but mostly because of the breadth of his interests.

John Davidson Ketchum

In the 1930's, Ketchum was the musical satirist of the Department. While studying music in Germany in 1914, he had been caught by the outbreak of World War I, and interned with 4,000 other Britishers for four years in Ruhleben, an abandoned racetrack near Berlin hastily transformed into a prison camp. His imagination had been caught by the manner in which a complete and complex human society had been created by these men, and ever afterwards tried to write about it. Like Chant, he spent several summers at the University of Chicago but did not complete a thesis, and so did not earn a degree there. For Ketchum[16] was a perfectionist in his writing, and everything he heard or read in social psychology or sociology caused him to revise again something he had written. His book, *Ruhleben: A Prison Camp Society*, was completed at his request by his long-time friend, R.B. MacLeod of Cornell, who wrote the Foreword and the Postscript. It also contains a biographical sketch of Ketchum by D.O. Hebb of McGill (Ketchum, 1965). Ketchum was also meticulous in assessing the efforts of his students. Hebb quotes from a resolution presented in the U of T Senate (moved by Myers and Bernhardt) that says that, for many years, "… he taught them to be skeptical of the cliché, to question assumptions, to cherish clarity and to write plainly …" The resolution also says: "As a lecturer, he was always stimulating … He presented his material with the artistry of a composer and the dramatic skill of an accomplished actor." (Hebb in Ketchum, 1965, p. 382). After one of his lectures, a chuckling student was overheard to say: "That man should not be lecturing – he should be on the vaudeville stage!"

But perhaps the most memorable contribution of Ketchum to the life of the Department was in the area of music. Every time there was some special occasion in the Department, Dave would compose a song or parody to commemorate it. When invited (as he always was), he would remove his jacket, sit at the piano, and perform his latest composition which was invariably an hilarious "spoof". It was always the highlight of the evening. His humour was always timely, never cruel, and served to make both staff and students feel that they belonged to a happy family. His "Hymn to Free Enterprise" and "The Uses of Statistics" have been widely quoted. On the occasion when the Rockefeller grant came to an end, Dave composed and delivered, in his inimitable style, a "Mental Health Requiem" in what he called "an ecclesiastical monotone with appropriate cadences" while the staff, as pall-bearers, led by Clare Hincks, dressed in widow's weeds, buried the staff's hopes of further financial help from this source. On a later occasion when nearly all of the staff were leaving for World War II, Dave composed and delivered the hilarious "What a dirty trick to play on Hitler ... Who will break the news to Hitler" that "Bott and all his brainy boys" are "hurrying off to war", which was sung to the tune of "John Brown's Body" and is quoted in full by Myers (Myers, 1974, p. 292–302).

The Canadian Psychological Association 1938–

Toward the end of the 1930's, war clouds were forming over Europe, and Bott, together with some fifty other psychologists in Canada, became convinced that Canada would need its own national organization to represent psychology in Canada. By this time, it was evident that Canada would be involved in the war long before the United States, and that if Canadian psychologists were going to contribute to the war effort as they should, they would need a national association of their own. Ever since Baldwin from Canada had participated in the founding of APA in 1892, Canadian psychologists had joined APA and found in it all they needed in the way of professional affiliation. But now, for the first time, they would need their own association to speak authoritatively for them to the Canadian government. So Bott of Toronto, supported by Humphrey of Queen's, Liddy of Western, Morton of McGill and MacEachran of Alberta, set about the formation of The Canadian Psychological Association (CPA). This development has been well described by Mary Wright in her "CPA: The First Ten Years" (Wright, 1974a).

World War II: 1939–1945

Upon the outbreak of the war, Bott immediately became involved in research for the Royal Canadian Air Force (RCAF). He and his staff co-operated with Morton of McGill, Penrose of Western, and many other psychologists across Canada, in the standardization of the "M Test" for the Canadian Army. By the Fall of 1941, Line had left to join Chisholm in the Personnel Selection Branch of the Canadian Army, Bott and Myers were leaving to become "Training Advisors" for the Royal Air Force (RAF) in the United Kingdom, and Chant was leaving to head up Personnel Selection for the RCAF in Ottawa. In 1942, Blatz was to leave for England with a team of five young ladies (Margaret Fletcher, Ann Harris, Dorothy Millichamp, Mary Wright and Mary MacFarland) to establish the Garrison Lane Nursery Training Centre in the slums of Birmingham for the training of the many nursery school teachers required to free mothers in the UK for war work. Ketchum would also leave for service in Canada's War Information Board in Ottawa. This general exodus of the staff for war service left only Karl Bernhardt who, with the able support of Mary

Northway and Magda Arnold, "kept the home-fires burning" in the Department of Psychology. Mary Salter also helped, until she was called away to take charge of Personnel Selection for the Canadian Women's Army Corps (CWAC). With these ladies, Bernhardt, as "Acting Chairman", did an excellent job of keeping the Department going during the absence of virtually all of the regular staff. About the war work of the staff, it should be said that most of them, plunged suddenly into strange situations and working on problems with which they had had no experience, were surprised at the power of the method in which they had been trained to solve practical problems.

After World War II

The war was followed, at all Universities, by what came to be known as the "veteran bulge". Canada's provision of educational credits for veterans meant the abrupt soaring of University enrolments. This was a particularly challenging time for all University teachers because veteran-students were more mature than their counterparts direct from high school and more determined to get the best out of their University experience. There followed the Federal Mental Health Grants. These not only provided Mental Health Bursaries (with "return-of-service" agreements) which added greatly to graduate student enrolment in clinical courses, but provided funds for the necessary expansion of staff. This made it possible for Bott to attract Carl Williams from Manitoba to help with the expanded graduate program at Toronto. Williams[17] was well known at Toronto, having obtained his Ph.D. there in 1941, and was a very welcome addition to the staff. After the war, Bott seems to have made some further abortive attempts to bring his "applied" Department up-to-date scientifically. For instance, in 1946, he recruited Hess Haagen, a young American with an Iowa Ph.D., but he only stayed three years before returning to the United States. Then, in 1950, Bott recruited one American (Everett Bovard Jr) with a Columbia Ph.D., and one Canadian (Alfred Shephard) with an Iowa Ph.D. Bovard did not stay long, but Shephard[18] who did, says that, coming fresh from Kenneth Spence's Department, he felt that he had landed in a scientific wilderness and that the Department of Psychology at Toronto though filled with kindly, well-meaning people, was "medieval" as far as modern scientific method was concerned (Shephard, 1972, p. 43).

The End of an Era

Bott retired in 1956. By this time, he was generally recognized as the Dean of Canadian psychology and the chief architect of its development.

His major contribution had been in putting psychology to work to serve the needs of Canadians. At the end of her "CPA: The First Ten Years", Mary Wright says: "The 'great man' of the period was clearly Ned Bott. As first president of the Association and first Chairman of every major committee that the Association established during this entire period he was the recognized leader of the flock". (Wright, 1974a, p. 130). Long before that, Bott had been the first Canadian to teach psychology in a Faculty of Medicine. He had selected, and sponsored the graduate training of, the first Director (Blatz) of what later became the Institute of Child Study at Toronto, and promoted the development of that Institute into an autonomous administrative unit in the University. He had served early as psychological consultant to the Toronto Family and Juvenile Court – a position he later bequeathed to Blatz. He had a hand in establishing the course in Physiotherapy and the School of Social Work at Toronto. In collaboration with the Professor of Medicine (Dr. Farquarson) and the Superintendent of the Toronto General Hospital (Dr. Sharpe), he arranged for the appointment of the first clinical psychologist (Morgan Wright) to be attached to the ward staff of a General Hospital. He was invited to become the first Head of the Institute of Human Relations at Yale University, but declined the offer, preferring to remain in his native land. He was awarded an OBE for his service in World War II, and given an Honorary Doctor of Science Degree by McGill University in 1954.

Psychology Goes "Scientific": 1956–

It was in 1956, the year that Bott retired, that two things happened at Toronto that were destined to change the direction of psychology there. The first of these was that Endel Tulving joined the staff, fresh from his brilliant record of graduate studies at Harvard. He had originally come to Canada after the war from Estonia, but later became a distinguished graduate of the honour course in psychology at Toronto, and went on to obtain his Ph.D. from Harvard University. The second was that the President of this University (Sidney Smith) announced a new, and much improved, salary scale for Toronto which, although it did not add to his popularity at other Canadian Universities, suddenly made this University competitive with Universities in the USA.

Another thing that happened in 1956 was that, much to his own surprise (and everyone else's), the writer was appointed to be the new Chairman of the Department of Psychology succeeding Bott. Karl Bernhardt had done such a magnificent job of keeping the Department going when most of the staff went off to war, that everyone in the

Department took it for granted that Bernhardt would succeed Bott when the time came for the latter to retire. Karl must have been deeply disappointed that he did not receive the appointment but, like the solid citizen and perfect gentleman that he was, he never gave the writer the slightest inkling of his disappointment and behaved with unswerving loyalty to the Department.[19] The day after Myers' appointment was announced, Dave Ketchum, his former teacher and later his colleague and friend, came into his office ostensibly to congratulate him. But, after discussing the enormous expansion that everyone anticipated in the 1960s, what he said was: "Well, Roger, you can look forward to being Chairman of the largest invisible Department of Psychology in the World!" The Department *was* scientifically "invisible", so the new Chairman made it his primary goal to recruit scientists who would make the Department visible. Endel Tulving represented a good start. Next, in 1957, he managed to recruit Richard Walters from Stanford. During the six years Walters was at Toronto, he was unbelievably productive of publications. (In 1963, he left Toronto to become Chairman of Psychology at the new University of Waterloo, Ontario.) In 1960, the Department managed to recruit Abram Amsel from Iowa and George Mandler from Harvard, both of whom proved to be productive scientists. In 1961, John Arrowood from Minnesota was added, and, in 1962, the Department managed to stop the "rolling stone", Daniel Berlyne, from rolling any further. (After joining the staff, "Dan" stayed at Toronto for 16 years, until his premature death in 1978.) In 1965, Ben Murdock from Missouri was added and, in 1967, John Furedy from Sydney, Australia. All of these have contributed much to the scientific visibility of the Department.

In 1960 and 1965, CPA organized and held two conferences which were important in the development of psychology in Toronto (and elsewhere) because they were the first occasions when psychologists from all across Canada were given the opportunity to meet together to discuss the future of their science and profession. The first of these conferences was held, in the Spring of 1960, near Lake Opinicon, north of Kingston, Ontario. The Opinicon Conference served to strengthen the writer's resolve to have the Department of Psychology at Toronto go "scientific". Both the conference itself, and the subsequent publication of the Report edited by Karl Bernhardt (Bernhardt, 1961), were supported by grants from the National Research Council and The Canada Council ($5,000 each) on condition that the conference would be concerned exclusively with the standards of psychological research and research training in Canada. In dealing with the "background" of the Opinicon Conference, Bernhardt wrote: "... problems of Canadian psychology were brought to a sharp focus by the MacLeod Report ... he pointed out some serious weaknesses ..." (Bernhardt, 1961, p. 4–5). R.B. MacLeod, the Chairman of Psychology at Cornell and former Chairman at McGill, had been invited by the Social Science Research Council of Canada to make a survey of the state of psychology in Canada and his Report, which was published in 1955, came to the conclusion that psychology in Canada was suffering from "premature professionalism" (MacLeod, 1955). Bernhardt continued: "In April, 1958, an article by C.R. Myers in the *Canadian Psychologist* raised the question again ... (Myers, 1958). This article brought an immediate response from C.P.A. members" (Bernhardt, 1961, p. 5).

The Opinicon Conference was seen to have been organized for, and dominated by, academics, as a consequence of the condition attached to the grants. So the pendulum swung to the other extreme, and CPA was required to organize and hold another conference which would, this time, be dominated by applied psychologists. This conference came to be known as the "Couchiching Conference" because it was held at the Geneva Park Convention Centre on Lake Couchiching, north of Toronto, Ontario. The editor of the Report of this conference was Ed Webster of McGill, who wrote: "Opinicon angered professionals. They felt that they had not been fairly treated ..." (Webster, 1967, p. 117). He also stated: "... in Canada neither the Federal nor Provincial governments appear interested ..." in supplying funds for training programs in professional psychology (Webster, 1967, p. 123). The truth of this statement is illustrated by the fact that, despite vigorous efforts, no grant support for this conference or the publication of this Report could be found, and the cost of both well nigh bankrupted the CPA. The discussion at this conference did nothing to weaken the writer's resolution to have Toronto go "scientific".

It should be understood why the present writer chooses to draw the fine line between "history" and "current events" and stop this sketch at the termination of his Chairmanship in 1968.

Chairs and Acting Chairs since 1968

1968–69: Glenn E. Macdonald (Acting)
1969–70: Glenn E. Macdonald; Joan E. Foley (Acting)
1970–74: Glenn E. Macdonald
1974–75: Endel Tulving (Acting)
1975–76: Endel Tulving
1976–77: Endel Tulving; Fergus Craik (Acting)
1977–78: Endel Tulving; Robert Lockhart (Acting)
1978–80: Endel Tulving
1980–   Jonathon Freedman

Notes

[1] Glenn Macdonald addressed the Institute for the History and Philosophy of Science and Technology at the University of Toronto on this subject on October 15, 1976. The manuscript of his address (if there was one) has not been found. On March 16, 1977, he also addressed a "staff seminar" in the Department of Psychology on the announced topic: "From Baldwin to Craik" (Craik was the Acting Chairman for that session). This talk was taped – but the tape has, so far, not been found.

[2] Fowler has this to say about the word "metaphysics" and "metaphysical": They are "... often used as quasi-learned and vaguely deprocatory substitutes for ... philosophy and philosophic ... – [but] an appeal to its etymology – will not serve. It is agreed that *Metaphysics* owes its name to the accident that the part of Aristotle's works that treated of metaphysical questions ... stood after (*meta*) the part concerned with physics ... and that the word's etymology is therefore devoid of significance ... Metaphysics is the branch of philosophy that deals with the ultimate nature of things ..." (Fowler, 1950, p. 353).

[3] James Mark Baldwin was one of the most outstanding psychologists on this continent in the 1890s and at the turn of the century. In 1903, Cattell used his "order of merit" ranking method to determine the relative eminence of scientists (including psychologists) in North America. The names of the six most eminent psychologists in 1903 (when revealed later in 1929) were: William James, J. McKeen Cattell, Hugo Munsterberg, G. Stanley Hall, J. Mark Baldwin and Edward B. Titchener – in that order (Watson, 1968, p. 383–384).

[4] In 1917, Tracy finally succeeded Hume as Professor of Ethics in University College. He still held that position in 1927 and almost prevented the writer from graduating. In his final year of Philosophy (English or History option), the writer decided that he preferred billiards in Hart House to Green's *Prolegomena to Ethics* which Tracy was teaching, – so decided to skip Tracy's lectures, unaware that Tracy, who was a sensitive man, would be deeply offended by this. Tracy threatened to prevent the writer from trying his final examination in ethics, but after a humble apology, Tracy, who was also a kindly man and very gentle person, agreed to let him write. The writer managed to pass, and so was allowed to graduate after all.

[5] Lane obtained his B.A. in 1893 and his M.A. in 1894 (both degrees from Toronto). Later he went on to earn a Ph.D. from Wisconsin, and held teaching positions at Chicago and Virginia before returning to finish his career as Professor of Ethics in Victoria College, Toronto.

[6] J.W. Baird obtained his B.A. from Toronto in 1897, and is reported to have studied later in "Leipzig and Cornell" (Morgan, 1912, p. 51). He earned his Ph.D. with Titchener in 1902, and there is an interesting reference to him in Kirschmann's first (1901) letter to Titchener: "How are you satisfied with your new assistant? I was very glad to hear that he got a position in your laboratory. Mr. Baird is a peculiar fellow whose outside appearance might sometimes be a little against him ... I hope he has succeeded in getting a permanent position in Cornell" (Titchener Papers, Cornell Archives, 1901). It appears that Baird was not successful in getting a "permanent position" at Cornell, because he taught at the University of Illinois in Urbana before being appointed to the staff at Clark University. There is also, in the Titchener Papers, a letter from Baird to Titchener from Urbana in 1907 in which he thanks Titchener for telling him of an opening in California, but says the thing does not appeal to him because he has "... no desire to go further from civilization than I am now". The fact that Baird wrote the following to Titchener may, perhaps, throw some light on the attitude of Titchener toward Kirschmann. Of the situation in California, Baird wrote: "... the presence of another Toronto man, Wrinch, a weakling and a Kirschmannite, complicates things." (Titchener Papers, Cornell Archives, 1907).

[7] Like Baird, Richardson also obtained his B.A. from Toronto in 1987. He is reported to

have been "… educated in Germany and at Clark University", and was later, in 1906, appointed as Professor of Philosophy at the University of Manitoba in Winnipeg (Morgan, 1912, p. 839).

[8] Other studies published later in the *Psychological Series*, and all edited by "Dr. A. Kirschmann", were: No. 2: "A Contribution to the Psychology of Time" by M.A. Shaw and F.S. Wrinch; No. 3: "Experiments on Time Relations of Poetical Metres" by A.S. Hurst and John McKay. Both of these studies were published in 1899. In 1900, there appeared No. 4 which included: "Conceptions and Laws in Aesthetic" by A. Kirschmann; "Experiments on the Aesthetic of Light and Colour" by Emma S. Baker; and "Experiments with School Children on Colour Combinations" by W.J. Dobbie. In 1902, Vol. II., No. 1, included an Invited Address given at Toronto by Professor Oswald Külpe (from Würzburg) on "The Conception and Classification of Art from a Psychological Standpoint"; "Spectrally Pure Colours in Binary Combinations" by Emma S. Baker; "On Colour Photometry and the phenomenon of Purkinje" by R.J. Wilson; "Experiments on the Function of Slit-Form Pupils" by W.J. Abbott. In 1904, Vol. II., No. 2 included "Combinations of Colours and Uncoloured Light" by Susie A. Chown; "The Complementary Relations of Some Systems of Coloured Papers" by W.G. Smith; and "Stereoscopic Vision and Intensity" by T.R. Robinson. It is of interest to know what happened to these authors after the publication of their studies out of the psychological laboratory in the *Psychological Series*. Apart from Kirschmann and Külpe, who had obtained their Ph.D.s earlier from Wundt at Leipzig, there were 15 local authors (counting Lane, Baird and Richardson), all of whom obtained their B.A.s from Toronto between 1896 and 1904. Most of them also obtained their M.A.s from Toronto. Nine of them (60%) seem to have gone on to earn Ph.D.s: Lane (Wisconsin), Baird (Cornell), Richardson (Clark?), Wrinch (Leipzig), Shaw (Harvard), Baker (Toronto), Dix (Toronto), Smith (Toronto) and Robinson (Toronto?). Wrinch became Professor of Psychology at the University of California, but later left psychology to go into fruit farming. Shaw became Professor of English in Iowa City. Baker was appointed to the staff of the Women's College of Maryland. Dix chose to study theology and later became a prominent Presbyterian minister in Saskatoon. Smith and Robinson were on the staff in philosophy at Toronto. Like Dix, three others chose to study theology: McKay, Wilson and McGregor. Wilson and McGregor later became prominent protagonists in the controversy over Church Union. Two of the authors chose medicine and later became specialists: Dobbie (Tuberculosis), and Abbott (Eye, Ear, Nose and Throat). The latter was clearly not the same Abbott who was on the staff in philosophy. Nothing much is known about Susie Chown, except that she obtained her B.A. from Victoria College (Toronto) in 1899, and seems to have died by 1920. The only one about whom nothing can be found is Hurst.

[9] "The book" to which Kirschmann refers was probably a first edition of Titchener's *Experimental Psychology: A Manual of Laboratory Practice*, first published in 1901, since a later edition, not published until 1918, is still dedicated: "To my friends: Frank Angell, Max von Frey, August Kirschmann, Oswald Külpe and Ernst Meumann (Titchener, 1918, Dedication Page).

[10] Bott had heard that Kirschmann was seeking a Chair somewhere in Germany. It is now evident that he did not get one, but Wundt took him back as a research assistant in the psychological laboratory at Leipzig. There is a letter from Kirschmann in the "Robert Falconer Papers" in the U of T Archives, dated December 8, 1919, and addressed to "The Authorities of the University of Toronto", in which he wrote: "… I am standing now before my complete financial ruin. My state of health, though somewhat better, is not so that I could take up full work again. I have tried to do some assistant work in the Leipzig Laboratory but the present Government is not willing to continue even the little payment for this. Being in my sixtieth year now there is absolutely no prospect for me to get a call to any position …",

and ends his letter with an appeal to be granted "a pension out of the Carnegie superannuation fund" (Robert Falconer Papers, 1919). In view of the known fact that, a decade earlier, he had withdrawn his pension reserve, this letter sounds like a cry of desperation. The President replied to his letter on March 12, 1920, stating on behalf of the Board, that there was not much likelihood that the Carnegie Foundation would offer Kirschmann relief, and adding: "I regret that I am unable to hold out any expectation of help from the University of Toronto" (Robert Falconer Papers, 1920). However Bott, who had never laid eyes on Kirschmann while the latter was in Toronto, looked him up in Germany after the war was over. He said that Kirschmann, like everyone else in Germany, was suffering greatly from the post-war inflation there, and that he was able to help Kirschmann by supplying some very welcome "hard" currency.

[11] Bott was born in 1887 near Ingersoll in southwestern Ontario. It seems that, while teaching school, he attended an Extension lecture in Woodstock, which led him to decide to enter philosophy at the University of Toronto.

[12] The ways in which Bott's "rivals" disappeared were as follows: In 1919, Abbott appears to have slipped on a spiritualistic "banana peel" called the "Twentieth Plane" when he started to investigate, and later came under the influence of, a local medium by the name of Louis Benjamin, who claimed to have had conversations with several famous, but long-dead, scholars. When Benjamin proved to be a fake, this caused something of a local scandal, and Abbott was promptly dropped from the staff of the University. Smith tried hard to become the successor to Kirschmann but, according to Bott, he had no aptitude for laboratory work. He seems to have been a quarrelsome person. As a result of one quarrel, he resigned from the staff at Toronto in 1921 to become Head of the Philosophy Department at Wesley College in Winnipeg. From this position he was dismissed in 1922, presumably as a result of another quarrel.

Robinson stayed at Toronto, but wisely decided to make his career in philosophy rather than in psychology.

[13] MacPhee's later career in business was remarkably successful. He left academia in 1929, first to become a "trouble-shooter" for Wood-Gundy in the manufacture of women's lingerie. Later he became world-wide General Manager for Dent's Gloves. During World War II, he was Production Manager in Short's Aircraft Company in the United Kingdom for the manufacture of Stirling Bombers for the Royal Air Force. Finally, after the war, he became Vice-President for Finance at UBC.

[14] Blatz was born in 1895 in Hamilton, Ontario, the youngest of nine children. He said that, after his rejection for active service with the Canadian Army in 1917, he met "... by chance, a man who was to have a large part in my future career, Professor E.A. Bott ..." (Blatz, 1966, p. 4). Bott liked to tell the story of how he met this young medical student wandering disconsolately across the campus because he had been turned back at the gangplank of a troopship in Halifax Harbour due to his German-sounding name. Blatz became interested in the work Bott was doing with wounded soldiers, and for a time, became part of the "Hart House re-education team". When the war was over, Blatz returned to the U of T Medical School where he completed the last year of his clinical work, and obtained his MB in 1921. Then, "sponsored by Bott", he was awarded a scholarship in he Department of Psychology at the University of Chicago. He received his Ph.D. in psychology from the University of Chicago in 1924, with a thesis on the physiological changes produced by emotion which he evoked in the laboratory there by inventing a "collapsing chair". Then he was appointed to the staff in psychology at Toronto.

It was the dynamic Dr. Clare Hincks who persuaded the Laura Spelman Rockefeller Memorial Foundation to make a grant to the University of Toronto to found a child study centre, and to appoint Blatz to direct it. The St. George's Nursery School which began in

January, 1926, in a remodelled house at 47 St. George Street, was moved five years later to more ample quarters at 96–98 St. George Street to be nearer the Department of Psychology with which it and its staff were closely associated. In 1938, it became the Institute of Child Study at Toronto, an autonomous administrative unit of the University. It moved again in 1953 to Walmer Road where, combined with Windy Ridge School, it could offer training up to Grade 6. Blatz remained Director of the Institute until 1960, and was succeeded in the Directorship by Karl Bernhardt.

[15] Chant was born in 1899 in St. Thomas, Ontario. After World War II, during which he had been Head of Personnel Selection for the RCAF, and toward the end of which he had directed Canada's rehabilitation program for veterans, he moved to the staff at the University of British Columbia (UBC). The improved climate of Vancouver may have appealed to him, but his earlier friendship with the President of UBC, Larry MacKenzie, probably had most to do with his move. He went first as Chairman of Psychology, but soon was also appointed Dean, and ultimately became a very influential figure, not only at UBC, but also in the general educational affairs of the province.

[16] Ketchum was born in 1893 in Cobourg, Ontario. After two years in Political Science at Trinity College (Toronto), he decided to make his career in music and left Toronto to study piano in England and Germany. In the Preface to his book, *Ruhleben: A Prison Camp Society*, he says: "When the war began in August, 1914, I was a naive youth of 21, studying piano in Berlin under Joseph Lhevine ... [I was] transferred to stables in a suburban race course at Ruhleben ... In this community of exiles, I lived until November 24, 1918 ..." (Ketchum, 1965, p. xvi). After his return to Toronto, he completed his B.A. with two years in English and History. After graduation, Ketchum rode two horses: music (as teacher and choirmaster) and social psychology (because he had been "hooked" by his experience at Ruhleben). As he says in the Preface to his book: "This book might be called an excursion into social psychology through the gates of a prison camp ... this camp provides the fullest picture known to me of the actual growth of a human society, from its origin in a miscellaneous collection of individuals to its culmination in a complex social order" (Ketchum, 1965, p. xvii). So Ketchum undertook graduate training at both Toronto and Chicago, and spent the rest of his life trying to complete his book, which had to be finished for him after his death by his old friend "Robbie" MacLeod of Cornell.

[17] Carl Williams later became Director of Extension at Toronto, and then Vice-President and Principal of the newly-established Scarborough College. Then he was appointed President of the University of Western Ontario. After his retirement from that position, he was made Chairman of Ontario's Royal Commission on "Freedom of Information and Individual Privacy".

[18] After 12 years at Toronto, Alf Shephard left in 1962 to become Chairman of the Department of Psychology at the University of Manitoba.

[19] Karl Bernhardt was born in 1901 in Toronto, but his family soon moved to Orillia where Karl went to school. He attended Victoria College at Toronto, and became Don of one of the Men's Residences there. Although his original intention had been to enter the Methodist ministry, he joined the staff in psychology in the late 1920's, and spent the rest of his life in that form of service to humanity. He did his graduate training at the University of Chicago, and obtained his Ph.D. there in 1933. He became the "comparative" psychologist of the Department, running the rat laboratory, and, in the 1930's when the Nursery School moved up the street to be nearer the Department of Psychology, became active in the school assisting Mrs. Helen Bott with the Parent Education programme. He succeeded her as Director of that programme in 1938 when the Institute of Child Study was established. In 1960, when Blatz retired as Director, Bernhardt became the second Director of the Institute of Child Study at Toronto. However, ill health forced his retirement four years later.

Manuscripts

Bott, Edward Alexander. Oral History Transcript. Public Archives of Canada, Ottawa, 1962.

Chant, Sperrin Noah Fulton. Oral History Transcript. Public Archives of Canada, Ottawa, 1970.

Evans, Rand. Copies of the "testimonials" attached to Titchener's application to Toronto in 1893. Personal Communication from Evans, University of New Hampshire, 1970.

Robert Falconer Papers. In the University of Toronto Archives, 1919 and 1920.

Shephard, Alfred. Oral History Transcript. Public Archives of Canada, Ottawa, 1972

Titchener Papers. Cornell University Archives, Olin Library, Ithaca, 1901 to 1907.

References

Baldwin, James Mark. "Philosophy: Its Relation to Life and Education.: Toronto: University Press, 1890.

Baldwin, James Mark. "Psychology at the University of Toronto.", *American Journal of Psychology*, 3, 285–6, 1890.

Baldwin, James Mark. *Between Two Wars: 1861–1921*, Vol. I., Boston: Stratford Co., 1926.

Beers, Clifford. *A Mind That Found Itself: an Autobiogrphy*. New York: Longmans, Green & Co., 1908.

Bernhardt, Karl S. (Ed.) *Training for Research in Psychology*. (Report of the Opinicon Conference) Toronto: University of Toronto Press, 1961.

Biographical Directory of the American Psychological Association. (1975 Edition) Washington: American Psychological Association, 1975.

Blatz, William E. and Bott, Helen. *Parents and the Preschool Child*. London & Toronto: J.M. Dent & Sons, 1928.

Blatz, William Emet. *Human Security: Some Reflections*. Toronto: University of Toronto Press, 1966.

Boring, Edmund G. *A History of Experimental Psychology*. New York: The Century Co., 1929.

Bott, Edward Alexander. "Mechanotherapy", *American Journal of Orthopedic Surgery*, 16, 441–6, 1918.

Bott, Edward Alexander. "Training for Lay Workers in Functional Restoration". *Medical Record*, 95, 856–8, 1919a.

Bott, Edward Alexander. "The Mentality of Convalescence". *Chicago Institute of Medicine*, 2, 218–30, 1919b.

Bott, Edward Alexander. "Juvenile Employment in Relation to Public Schools and Industries in Toronto." *University of Toronto Studies, Psychological Series*, Vol. 4. Toronto: The University Librarian, 1920.

Bott, Edward Alexander. "Criticism and Ways of Inquiry." *Journal of Philosophy*, 10, 253–271, 1923a.

Bott, Edward Alexander. "Some Characteristics of Reciprocal Wrist Action." *British Journal of Psychology*, General Section, 14, 1–14, 1923b.

Bott, Edward Alexander. "Some Principles of Mental Hygiene Research." (Abstract) *Psychological Bulletin*, 26, 10–11, 1929.

Brett, George Sidney. *A History of Psychology*. Vol. I., London: G. Allen Ltd., 1912.

Bridges, Win. "Theories of Temperament: an attempt at Reconciliation." *Psychological Review*, 30, 36–44, 1923.

Brockman, L.M., Whiteley, J.H., and Zubek, J.P. (Eds.) *Child Development: Selected Readings*. Toronto: McClelland and Stewart, 1973.

Calendars for the University of Toronto in the U of T Archives: For sessions 1857–58 up to 1919–20: Toronto: Rowsell & Hutchison. For the Sessions 1920–21 and later: Toronto: The University of Toronto Press.

Campbell, John. "The Rev. Prof. James Beaven, D.D., M.A." *University of Toronto Monthly, 3*, 68–72, 1902.

Dodge, Raymond, and Bott, Edward A. "Antagonistic Muscle Action in Voluntary Flexion and Extension." *Psychological Review, 34*, 247–273, 1927.

Fowler, H.W. *A Dictionary of Modern English Usage*, Second Edition, New York and Oxford: Oxford University Press, 1965.

Hume, James Gibson. "Professor George Paxton Young." *University of Toronto Monthly, 28*, 21–22, 1927.

Ketchum, John Davidson. *Ruhleben: A Prison Camp Society*. Toronto: University of Toronto Press, 1965.

Kirschmann, August. "On Parallel Curves (And consequently on the Alaska Boundary Dispute). *University of Toronto Monthly, 4*, 46–50, 1903.

Kirschmann, August. "The Decimal System of Notation – A Relic of Savagery." *University of Toronto Monthly, 4*, 224–228, 1904.

Langton, Hugh Hornby. *Sir Daniel Wilson, a memoir*. Edinburgh/Toronto: Thomas Nelson & Sons, 1929.

MacLeod, Robert B. *Psychology in Canadian Universities and Colleges*. Ottawa: Canadian Social Science Research Council, 1955.

MacPhee, Earle D. "Psychology in the Clinic." *Canada Lancet and Practitioner*, 80, 47–52, 1928.

MacPhee, Earle D. "Psychology of Advertising." *Proceedings of the Association of Canadian Advertisers*, 1928.

MacPhee, Earle D. "The Values of the Classics." *School* (Toronto), *16*, 110–120, 1927.

McGhie, Bernard T., and MacPhee, Earle D. *Training and Research in a Hospital for Subnormals*, Vol. I. Toronto: Provincial Department of Health, 1930.

Morgan, Henry James (Ed.) *The Canadian Men and Women of the time*, 2nd Edition. Toronto: William Briggs, 1912.

Myers, C. Roger. "Professional Psychology in Canada", *The Canadian Psychologist, 7*, 27–36, 1958.

Myers, C. Roger. "Notes on the History of Psychology in Canada." *The Canadian Psychologist, 6a*, 4–19, 1965.

Myers, C. Roger. "Edward Alexander Bott (1887–1974)." *The Canadian Psychologist, 15*, 292–302, 1974.

Murchison, Carl (Ed.) *A history of Psychology in Autobiography*. Vol. I., New York: Russell & Russell, 1961.

Northway, Marty L. "Child Study in Canada: A Casual History." Chapter 2 in *Child Development: Selected Readings*. Edited by Brockman et al. (see above), Toronto: McClelland and Stewart, 11–46, 1973.

Titchener, Edward Bradford. *Experimental psychology: A Manual of Laboratory Practice*, Vol. I., *Qualitative Methods*, Part 2, *Instructor's Manual*. New York: MacMillan Co., 1918.

Toronto Telegram. June 9 and 11, 1915.

Tracy, Frederick. The Psychology of Childhood. First Edition. Boston: D.C. Heath Co., 1893.

University of Toronto. Report of the Senate's *Standing Committee on Finance*. Toronto: Warwick & Sons, 1891.

University of Toronto. Office of the President. *Annual Reports* in the U of T Archives for the session 1916–17, and each session in the 1920s.

Watson, Robert I. *The Great Psychologists, from Aristotle to Freud*, 2nd ed. Philadelphia: J.B. Lippincott, 1968.

Webster, Edward C. (Ed.) *The Couchiching Conference on Professional Psychology*. Montreal: The Eagle Publishing Co., 1967.

Wilson, Daniel. *The Right Hand: Left Handedness*. New York & London: MacMillan & Co., 1891.

Wright, Mary J. "CPA: The First Ten Years" *The Canadian Psychologist, 15*, 112–131, 1974.

Wright, Mary J. "Should We Rediscover Blatz?" *The Canadian Psychologist, 15*, 140–144, 1974b.

Further Readings

Anonymous – Citation: Dr. A. Amsel. *The Canadian Psychologist*, 1965, *6a*, 294–295.
      – Citation: Dr. Daniel Berlyne. *The Canadian Psychologist*, 1965, *6a*, 295–296.
      – Award of Centennial Medals, 1967 (Edward Alexander Bott). *The Canadian Psychologist*, 1968, *9*, 226–227.
      – William Line. *The Canadian Psychologist*, 1964, *5a*, 154–155.
      – Award of Centennial Medals, 1967 (Charles Roger Myers). *The Canadian Psychologist*, 1968, *9* 231–233.
      – C. Roger Myers: LLD Citation. *The Canadian Psychologist*, 1971, *12*, 97–98.

Babarick, P. William Line. *The Ontario Psychologist*, 1976, *8*, 57–62.

Bernhardt, K.S. Dr. William E. Blatz. *The Canadian Psychologist*, 1965, *6a*, 1–3.

Day, H.I. Daniel Ellis Berlyne. *Canadian Psychological Review*, 1977, *18*, 276–277.

Furedy, J.J. Berlyne as a disinterested critic. A colleague's account of some academic interactions. *Canadian Psychological Review*, 1979, *20*, 95–98.

Griffin, J.W. William Line, 1897–1963: An appreciation. *The O.P.A. Quarterly*, 1964, *17*, 43–44.

Myers, C.R. Karl Schofield Bernhardt. *The Canadian psychologist*, 1968, *9*, 95.

Tulving, E. Glenn Ewen Macdonald (1925–1978). *Canadian Psychological Review*, 1979, *20*, 79–81.

Wright, Mary J. William Emet Blatz (1895–1964). *The O.P.A. Quarterly*, 1964, *17*, 87–88.

Wright, Mary J. Psychologists in Profile: Charles Roger Myers. *The Ontario Psychologist*, 1977, *9*, 55–58.

See also a note in *The Canadian Psychologist* (1960, *1*, 103).

Chapter 4

Psychology at Queen's

by

*James Inglis**

The Department of Psychology first appears as a separate entity in the Queen's University Calendar for 1949–50 which names its three members of faculty as Professor J.M. Blackburn, Assistant Professor E.I. Signori and Instructor J.A. Easterbrook. We must, however, turn back further than that particular page in its history in order to trace the details of the development of psychology at Queen's; perhaps it is best to begin at the beginning.

In the 1830's, the devout members of the Synod of the Presbyterian Church in Canada began to feel the need for a ministry trained within their own country. The offshore supply of ministers from their natural, native source, Scotland, was now inadequate and tended (as one Report succinctly put it) rather, "To show the extent of the want than to meet the want" (Calvin, 1941, p. 21). It then seemed that graduates produced by a new Canadian university might serve the need.

Many impatient and impious words were exchanged by many pious and patient men before the actual foundation was agreed upon, but on October 16th, 1841, a Royal Charter was issued by Her Majesty, Queen Victoria, for the establishment of Queen's College at Kingston in Upper Canada. Its founders were as prudent as they were pious, and they imported the Royal Charter and their first Principal, the Reverend Thomas Liddell (formerly Minister of Lady Glenorchy's Church in Edinburgh) both on the same ship. The College Agent in London, Alexander Gillespie, cannily penned a note to William Morris, Chairman of the Board of Trustees, to say, "I send the present by the Rev. Principal Liddell, to

---

* Professor Inglis joined the Faculty of Queen's University in 1959 and, except for a 3 year period during which he taught at Temple University in Philadelphia, has been an active member of the Department of Psychology there since that time.

whose care I have committed the charter of Queen's College and I sincerely hope that both Principal and Charter may reach Kingston in safety; to protect the College from loss I shall however insure the latter". (Calvin, 1941, p. 47). The Charter had, after all, cost the College nearly six hundred pounds (Neatby, 1978), whereas the Principal was not so expensive, being, on arrival, expected to go out to canvass the countryside for some part of his own funds.

For the first years of its existence the College faculty was small and the students but few. Two or three professors gave, and a dozen or so students attended, six hours of lectures a day, six days a week. Even from those early days we have a record of professorial protest against the layman's view that the academic life is one of slothful ease. The Presbyterians of Wolfe Island had no minister of their own and they wanted the Sunday services of those teachers at Queen's College who were ordained ministers and had but light duties, with no Sabbath commitments at all. Thomas Liddell sprang to the defence of his staff, "Would", he asked, "from 4 to 6 hours lecturing and examining each day on 4 or 5 different and unconnected subjects during 6 days in the week and for 8 months in the year be deemed at all an approximation to heavy duties?". As for work on Sunday, "I trust", he said, "there would be in them Christian fortitude and practical orthodoxy sufficient to enable them to (obey) the Divine Commandment, 'Six days shalt thou labour and do all thy work; but the seventh is the Sabbath of the Lord thy God.'" (Gundy, 1971, p. 23). The curriculum of that time certainly seems rather heavy today; it included Greek, Latin, Hebrew, Church History, Theology, Logic, Mathematics and Natural History.

Some six years after the foundation of the College there newly appears in the curriculum, Moral Philosophy, the mother-discipline of psychology at Queen's, then taught by the Reverend George Romanes, who was also Professor of Greek. He was the father of George John Romanes, FRS, born in Kingston on May 20th, 1848, who himself later made significant contributions to the study of problems in psychobiology (Hearnshaw 1964), and was a friend of Charles Darwin.

A later occupant of the Chair of Mental and Moral Philosophy was the Reverend James George, who held this position from 1853 to 1862. As Gundy laconically notes, "When he came to Queen's, he was in his fifties, a tall, rather florid man with a shock of grey hair which had turned white before he left" (1955, p. 23). An early victim of academic in-fighting, he was accused by his colleague, the Reverend George Weir, Professor of Classical Literature, of having fathered an illegitimate child by Weir's sister. Weir made the accusation in writing, alleging that, "What I learned in Scotland was that my sister bore a child in March 1855 – a son – at this moment a living image of yourself ... of which she has uniformly and solemnly affirmed that you are the father". (Report of the Court of Error and Appeal for Upper Canada, 1865). He repeated this charge, among other libels, in a set of very bad verse, sixteen cantos long, entitled, "The no-conscience theory in practice – a new and startling discovery by the most profound of modern philosophers". Although the embarrassed Professor of Moral Philosophy indignantly denied the charge, he soon resigned his beleaguered chair for the sanctuary of a Presbyterian pulpit in Stratford, Ontario. His immediate successor as Professor of Philosophy was the Reverend John Clarke Murray.

The modern era, however, began in 1872 when a young graduate of Glasgow University was appointed to the Chair of Mental and Moral Philosophy. He may have been encouraged by the praise of Kingston recorded in the University Calendar of that year (praise which, expressed in the same terms nowadays, would be almost certain to astonish our colleagues from, say, British Columbia) which claimed that, "Kingston is easily accessible on account of its central location and is one of the healthiest locations in Western Canada".

John Watson, MA, was 25 years old when he came to Queen's and gave his Inaugural Address on the "Relationship of Philosophy to Science" in Queen's Convocation Hall on October 16th, 1872. He was made Emeritus Professor when he retired in 1924, some 52 years later. It was during his long reign that the first rudiments of psychology at Queen's began to evolve.

In the description of the third year course in Metaphysics in the early days of Watson's tenure, it was already announced that, "The course will comprise 1. A critical account of the main philosophical systems of Greece. 2. Lectures on (a) Psychology (b) Pure Metaphysics, and (c) The relation of philosophy to consciousness and the special senses". Questions from the examination papers in Metaphysics stand in stark contrast to the contemporary questions then asked in Medicine. The young philosopher might, for example, be asked, "How does immediate sensation become perception?", or, "Distinguish between remembrance and imagination". The medical student's problem was more likely to be phrased thus, "In the case of a child twelve months old suffering from Diarrhoea, write a prescription for a mixture containing Laudanum, Subnitrate of Bismuth, Pepsin, Syrup of Ginger and Cinnamon Water. Give directions for using". The psychological questions might, with but little modification, be asked today; the prescription for physic would perhaps not now be in much demand. Perhaps we should be modest and ask, were we really so far in advance then, or has medicine now left us so far behind?

In 1887 Professor Watson was using Dewey's newly published

Psychology as one of the texts for his courses in Mental and Moral Philosophy. Two years later Dr. S.W. Dyde, a Queen's graduate (Gold Medallist in both Classics and Philosophy) who had briefly served at the University of New Brunswick, was appointed Professor of Mental Philosophy in Watson's department. In 1892, Dyde offered his Junior Class a "Critical study of James's *Psychology* (American Science Series, Briefer Course). Tuesday, attendance voluntary".

The closer specification of psychological studies within the Department of Philosophy was not, however, undertaken until graduate work began at Queen's in 1889. In that year, regulations for the Ph.D. and the D.Sc. were formally adopted. For the Ph.D. in Mental and Moral Philosophy both course work and a thesis were required. As part of the course work the student might choose to study the Principles of Psychology, general reference being made to the writings of James Mill, John Stuart Mill, Bain, Wundt, Sully, Ladd and Lotze.

Calvin (1941) has pointed out that just after the turn of the century, a Committee of the Board of Trustees of the University began to discuss with Government the creation of a Faculty of Education at Queen's. This may explain the appearance, in 1903, of a Special Course for Teachers under the Ph.D. regulations, that enabled those candidates to concentrate much more of their efforts on the study of psychology, as well as upon the history and science of education. By 1905, the recommended reading for these latter topics included Wundt's *Physiological Psychology*, James's *Principles of Psychology*, Ward's chapter on 'Psychology' in the *Encyclopedia Britannica*, Stout's *Manual of Psychology* and his *Analytical Psychology*, Adamson's *Lectures on Psychology* (Works, Vol. II), Harris's *Psychologic Foundations of Education*, Münsterberg's *Psychology and Life* and Dewey's *School and Society*.

The Faculty of Education was duly established in 1907, with the Officers of Instruction then listed as one Dean (Cecil F. Lavell, MA, Professor of the History of Education), and one Associate Professor (J.J. Stevenson, MA, D.Paed.). In that same year the Special Course for Teachers in the regulations for the Ph.D. had apparently changed into studies for both the Bachelor's and the Doctoral degree in Paedagogy.

As the interest in psychology began to wax in the new Faculty of Education, so it seemed partly to wane in the Department of Philosophy. For his undergraduates in Mental Philosophy in 1906, Professor Dyde recommended Stout's *Manual of Psychology*, but in the next year he changed to Bosanquet's *Philosophy of the Moral Self*, a work perhaps less in the mainstream of the development of modern psychology. In 1910, A.D. Ferguson, BA, was appointed in the Philosophy Department as Assistant Professor of Philosophy and Lecturer in Psychology and Logic. The text he used was Stout's *Groundwork of Psychology*; it would seem, despite the bulk of Stout, that these were rather lean times for psychology in that department!

The Faculty of Education, meanwhile, had established examinations at both the general and the advanced levels in "Psychology; principles and general method". A specimen question from one examination, for example, reads, "Under what conditions are habits formed? Point out the practical value to the individual of the formation of fixed habits of work. 'Habit is the enormous flywheel of society, its most precious conservative agent.' Explain. State some simple rules for forming new habits and breaking off old ones."

By 1915 when the only psychological text mentioned by the philosophers was Stout's *Analytical Psychology*, the roll-call of authors recommended by the educators began to have quite a modern ring. Among those mentioned were Baldwin, Galton, Hall, Hobhouse, James, Judd, Ladd and Woodworth, McDougall, Münsterberg, Myers, Thorndike and Whipple.

The very existence of the Faculty of Education at Queen's came to an end in 1920, because the Government of the time decided to extend the scope of the Normal Schools and to create, in Toronto, the Ontario College for Teachers (a new Faculty of Education was later established at Queen's in 1968). During the dozen years of its initial existence it would certainly seem, both from the studies prescribed and from the examinations set, that the real stronghold of the teaching of psychology at Queen's was to be found in its Faculty of Education.

Watson's long tenure in the Department of Philosophy was at that time drawing to a close. To take his place, in 1924, came a psychologist in philosopher's clothing, or at least one bearing a philosopher's sheepskin, Professor George Humphrey.

George Humphrey was born in Boughton, England in 1889, and took his degree in Greats in Oxford in 1912. He then studied psychology at Leipzig in Wundt's laboratory as a Cassel Scholar. After that he came to Canada and spent two years as Professor of Classics at St. Francis Xavier University. He then went on to Harvard as Townsend Scholar and gained his Ph.D. there in 1920. After his doctorate he went on to work with Raymond Dodge at Wesleyan University in Middletown, Connecticut. While he was still at Wesleyan he published his first book, the *Story of Man's Mind* (1923), which was a popular psychology text; its contents were described on its dust cover as, "The psychology of business, home and school, with its thousand uses and applications explained for everyone."

Humphrey's name first appears in the Queen's University Calendar for 1925–26 as Charlton Professor of Philosophy in the Department of

George Humphrey: 1889–1966

Mental and Moral Philosophy; his only colleague in that Department for the next three years being H. Reid MacCallum. Humphrey was, as later described by Bartlett (1966),"A man above normal height, neat, active, very friendly; but also on occasion, unyielding, and a good companion." He is now portrayed in a place of honour in Humphrey Hall, the present home of the Department of Psychology at Queen's University, as he is shown in the accompanying photograph.

When he was called to Queen's, he had been asked by the Dean of Arts, Oscar D. Skelton, to build up the psychological side of the Philosophy Department (Blackburn, 1957) and this he began at once to do, with very great energy and effect.

In terms of undergraduate work, there was a sharp and dramatic change in course content just as soon as Humphrey took over. From a heavy concentration on the Greek and German philosophers, the Department changed to a broad offering of courses in psychology, as well as in philosophy.

By 1930, Humphrey and his new Associate Professor, Reginald Jackson, between them gave ten intramural courses in philosophy, of which five were actually courses in psychology. (*Philosophy 2*. Psychology: Texts – Pillsbury, *Essentials of Psychology*; Allport, *Social Psychology*; Kimball Young, *Source Book for Social Psychology*. *Philosophy 25*. Psychology of the Child: Texts – Woodrow, *Brightness and Dullness in Children*; Freeman, *Mental Tests*; Koffka, *Growth of the Mind*; Sandiford, *Educational Psychology*. *Philosophy 44*. Principles of Psychology: Texts – Ladd and Woodworth, *Physiological Psychology*; Lucas, *Conduction of the Nervous Impulse*; Adrian, *Basis of Sensation*. *Philosophy 48a*. Abnormal Psychology: Text – McDougall, *Outline of Abnormal Psychology*. *Philosophy 49*. History of Psychology: Texts – Brett, *History of Psychology*; Rand, *The Classical Psychologists*.).

This list shows very clearly how up-to-date and exhaustive the offerings of the Department of Philosophy had become in psychology. Nor were didactic lectures alone the final aim. By the year 1931–32, Jackson had left the Department, and Humphrey was running his courses with the aid of but one Lecturer, Dr. Gregory Vlastos. Nevertheless, a new course, *Philosophy 98*. Problems in Psychology, was that year introduced, with the following intent. "A specific problem of a minor character is taken up experimentally. A comprehensive report will be required, which will exhibit the results of the experimental work and give an account of the previous literature. The course is open for advanced students only, and by permission of the instructor." This certainly reads as if Professor Humphrey had begun in earnest to produce psychologists under cover of his Department of Philosophy!

In 1934–35, Gregory Vlastos was now Assistant Professor, and a new Lecturer had been appointed in 1933–34, H. Martyn Estall (now Emeritus Professor of Philosophy of Queen's University). On Estall's arrival he taught all of the courses that had been given by Humphrey (who was on leave that year), as well as yet another undergraduate course in psychology (*Philosophy 32*. Contemporary Trends in Psychology: Texts – Heidbreder, *Seven Psychologies*; Woodworth, *Contemporary Schools of Psychology*). In 1934–35 mention of graduate courses began to appear in the Calendar ("Graduate Courses: Lecture courses and directed special studies will be offered in the Department as needed").

In 1939, there was another addition to the Department when Donald Olding Hebb came from McGill to be appointed Lecturer in Experimental

Psychology. It is no surprise to find that a new course was added under his direction (*Philosophy 15. Experimental Psychology*: Texts – Boring, Langfeld and Weld, *Psychology*; Boring, Langfeld and Weld, *A Manual of Psychological Experiments*). The course description shows that the production of psychologists had now begun even earlier in the student's career. "The purpose of this course is to give an elementary knowledge of the experimental method as it is employed in psychology. During the first term the student performs selected standard experiments, and learns to evaluate the data obtained. During the second term, individual experimental projects are undertaken under the guidance of the instructor. Some consideration is given to methods of psychological testing and statistics."

By 1943, Hebb had departed for the Yerkes Laboratory, and an Instructor in Experimental Psychology, J.H. Houck (himself a Queen's MA, 1943) had been appointed. He was followed, in that same position, the next year by B.M. Springbett. In 1946–47 an undergraduate course in Clinical Psychology (*Philosophy 35*) was also being taught in the Department of Philosophy by the Professor of Psychiatry at Queen's, Dr. C. Homer McCuaig.

At the same time as George Humphrey was so radically changing the undergraduate curriculum of his Department he was, of course, also engaged in many other tasks of fundamental importance to the development of psychology in Canada.

In the early years of his appointment he had to beg or borrow laboratory space for his own investigative work wherever he could find it (how, at that time, would a Professor of Philosophy justify his need for a *laboratory?*).

Only the hospitality of the Department of Biology enabled him to carry out his classical work on conditioning effects using pure tones and arpeggios (Humphrey, 1927), and his studies of habituation in snails (Humphrey, 1930). It was, it will be recalled, Humphrey's so-called "Arpeggio Paradox" that Clarke L. Hull later sought to resolve in his discussion of the patterning of stimulus compounds as part of his influential *Principles of Behavior* (1943). Humphrey himself put his work on conditioning and learning together in his best book, *The Nature of Learning* (1933). The year before that he had, with his first wife, published a translation of Itard's *Wild Boy of Aveyron* (1932), to which he had also added a scholarly introduction.

In his time at Queen's, Humphrey also wrote the chapter on "Thought" for the first edition of Boring, Langfeld and Weld's *Psychology: a factual textbook* (1935). His book *Directed Thinking* (1948), although it was not published until he had left Canada, was written at Queen's and in it he acknowledges the help of, "My friends Gregory Vlastos, who critically read many of the chapters, Martyn Estall, and R.O. Earl, each of whom gave me expert advice."

As noted above, new mention of graduate course work in his Department began to be made in 1934, and by 1944 two regular courses had been established, *Philosophy 120* The Psychology of Thought Processes, and *Philosophy 125b* The Theory of Test Construction. During Humphrey's tenure about a dozen MA students were graduated whose thesis research could be said to be psychological in nature. His first graduate student was D.C.G. MacKay (Emeritus Associate Professor of Psychology of the University of British Columbia, and author, in this volume of the history of the Department of Psychology at UBC). MacKay was awarded the MA degree (in Philosophy and Biology) in 1930 for his study of learning in white mice. The first person to be awarded an MA in Psychology (instead of, as formerly, a master's degree in Philosophy, or in Philosophy and Biology) was F.L. Marcuse (now Professor of Psychology at the University of Manitoba).

Humphrey was also active in the application of psychology to military purposes, especially personnel selection, in the Second World War (Blair, 1966). He joined with other psychologists at that time as a founder-member of the Canadian Psychological Association (Myers, 1965). He was Secretary of the Association for the first three years of its existence, and then followed E.A. Bott as its second elected President. In his spare time he wrote two novels!

In 1947, St. John's College invited Humphrey over to Cambridge for a year as a Dominion Fellow. That same year, the University of Oxford, defying William McDougall's (1926) sarcastic prediction, managed to create a Chair of Psychology well *before* the end of the twentieth century; a Chair to which Humphrey was called, and thus lost to Queen's.

Over the years 1947–1949, a mitosis-like division can be seen to have taken place within Philosophy at Queen's. In 1947–48 it was still the "Department of Philosophy: Mental and Moral"; Brother Roger Philip was standing in for Humphrey, but the courses taught were still labelled as "Philosophy". In 1948–49 it had become the Department of Philosophy and Psychology, with the latter courses so labelled, and the faculty divided under these two headings. The psychologists at that time were Professor Roger Philip, Assistant Professor E.I. Signori and Instructors J.H. Houck and W.R. Thompson (later himself Head of the Department, 1966–72). In 1949–50 the division was at last completed, and the Department of Psychology now a separate entity, with J.M. Blackburn, E.I. Signori and J.A. Easterbrook as its faculty members.

The first Head of the Department of Psychology proper, Julian

Murray Blackburn was born in Hove, England, in 1903. An old Wykeham-ist, he was a graduate of both the London School of Economics (B.Sc. Econ., 1928) and of Cambridge University (Ph.D.,1933). While he was at Cambridge he had worked, under F.C. Bartlett, with the Industrial Health Research Board (1928–33). After holding a Rockefeller Fellowship at Yale University in 1933–34, he was then employed by the Medical Research Council (and also worked as a clinical psychologist at the Maudsley Hospital) over the years 1935–38. He became a Lecturer in Social Psychology at L.S.E. in 1939, where he remained until he emigrated to Canada in 1948. For one year he was an Associate Professor at McGill University, and was called to the Chair at Queen's in 1949. While he was still at L.S.E. he had published two brief texts, *Psychology and the Social Pattern* (1945) and *The Framework of Human Behaviour* (1947). He was a man who had, when he chose, great power to charm, together with a ready wit (which was, however, not always without its own barbed edge).

In the first years of his term at Queen's, much effort must have gone into building up the undergraduate curriculum in psychology. Just before Philosophy and Psychology were formally split apart there were seven lecture courses and three reading courses offered in psychology. A few years later there were fifteen lecture courses and three reading courses available. Perhaps because of Blackburn's own experience in applied and clinical psychology, closer links were also being forged, at this time, between the Departments of Psychology and Psychiatry. Dr. C. Homer McCuaig, who was Professor of Psychiatry and Superintendent of the Ontario Hospital, Kingston, was then listed in the University Calendar as a member of the Department of Psychology.

There was, between 1949 and 1959, for the academic ranks above Lecturer, a very rapid turnover of faculty in that Department. Thus, for example, E.I. Signori (now at the University of British Columbia) was an Assistant Professor for only two years (1948–50). H.E. Gruber (now at Rutgers University) was also Assistant Professor for two years (1950–52). L.R. Bowyer was Assistant Professor for one year (1950–51), L.J. Kamin (now at Princeton University) also held the same position for a single year (1956–57), as did G.L. Mangan (now at Oxford University) in 1957–58. In fact, the only constancy during this whole period seems to have been achieved by A.H. Smith (now retired from the Defence Research Establishment) who worked in the Department for four years (1952–56), and by Isabel M. Laird, who achieved the longest period of service, beginning her work in the Department in 1950, and remaining there until her retirement in 1970.

It was also during this period that W.R. Thompson (appointed Head of the Department in 1966) returned to Queen's in 1954 to spend two years as Lecturer in Psychology. He came at that time from McGill, where he had carried out some of the pioneering studies of the effects of early environmental restriction on later development in animals (see, for example, Thompson and Heron, 1954a; 1954b). He left in 1956 to take up a position at Wesleyan University in Connecticut.

During the ten-year period from 1949–59, thirteen graduate students emerged from the Department with the MA degree. Work toward the doctoral degree began to be offered in 1954–55, and the first Ph.D., J.W. Clark (now at Dalhousie University, and co-author, in this volume, of the history of the Department of Psychology at that University) graduated from Queen's in 1959.

It has already been noted that one or two graduate courses a year in psychology had been offered since 1944 onward. The total number of students, however, was very small (24 MAs and one Ph.D. between 1924 and 1959). This meant that such courses tended to take the form of "directed readings"; they were not taught in the same way as most of the graduate courses that we recognize today. It was, in fact, only toward the end of the first decade of Blackburn's tenure that major advances began to be made in the development of graduate studies within the Department. Those were boom times, so that such expansion was perhaps inevitable. Nevertheless, the start of these changes can be said, at the very least, to have coincided with the appointment of four new faculty members within three years, all of whom had previous teaching experience at the University of London. First, in 1957, came P.H.R. James as Associate Professor, a Cambridge Ph.D. who had worked at London's University College. Next, P.C. Dodwell, an Oxford D. Phil. (later Acting Head, 1964–66 and Head of the Department 1972–81) came from Birkbeck College in 1958 as Assistant Professor. Then, in 1959, came R.W. Payne and J. Inglis, as Associate and Assistant Professor respectively; both were London Ph.Ds who had formerly worked at the Maudsley Hospital and the Institute of Psychiatry of the University of London.

Each of these four men brought with him a well-developed interest in a particular research programme. James at once founded an animal laboratory in which to carry out his ethological studies on the phenomena of imprinting (see, for example, James, 1959). Dodwell had already begun his now well-known work on studies of visual perception (see, for example, Dodwell, 1961). Payne continued with his work in the exploration of thought disorder in psychiatric patients (see, for example, Payne, 1961) that eventually won him recognition in the form of the Stratton Research Award of the American Psychopathological Association in 1964. Inglis further developed his investigations of learning and memory disorder in the normal and the senile aged (see, for example, Inglis, 1959).

Payne and Inglis were appointed with a mandate to set up and develop a graduate training programme in clinical psychology at Queen's. The original impetus for this ambitious scheme came largely from the newly-appointed, dynamic – not to say aggressive – full-time Head of the Department of Psychiatry, Dr. R. Bruce Sloane, another Maudsley man, who is now Chairman of the Department of Psychiatry at the University of Southern California. He was, on his appointment to Queen's, also recorded (as Dr. C.H. McCuaig had formerly been) as a member of the Department of Psychology. He immediately began to press for the further development of clinical psychology (as well as psychiatry) within the University and in the local teaching hospitals. Those were also days of optimism and improvisation, so that funds were somehow scraped together, mainly from sources outside the University, to fund these two new appointments in psychology.

On their arrival, Payne and Inglis began, on the basis of their past experience in graduate teaching at the Maudsley, to set up, *ab initio*, courses for an MA programme in clinical psychology. The basic philosophy of this new programme was a clear reflection of their own adherence to a rigorous experimental approach to clinical problems, an approach that is still explicit in the current clinical training programme at Queen's.

The first descriptive course brochure was printed early in the summer of 1959. It outlined the programme as falling into three main sections, each with its own sub-sections. Section I comprised "Formal lectures and seminars" and its subsections included "Course 1. Abnormal Psychology (87 lectures, 24 seminars)". This was further subdivided into Experimental Method in Clinical Psychology, General Abnormal Psychology, and Psychiatry and Mental Deficiency. Course 2 included "Psychometrics, Theoretical and Applied (114 lectures)". Section II took care of "Practical Clinical Work and Research", being further subdivided into a Test Training Programme, supervised Clinical Work and Thesis Research. Section III specified the examinations to be taken in all of these areas.

Some 40 of the lectures in Psychiatry and Mental Deficiency were presented by Dr. Sloane and Dr. S.G. Laverty (another new appointment in the Department of Psychiatry in 1959), and 30 lectures were given by Dr. Dodwell on Psychometric Theory. With these exceptions, all of the other lectures and supervision were arranged and carried out by Payne and Inglis (for only four students in the first year of the programme!)

By the second year, 1960–61, five graduate courses had evolved from these beginnings, (*Psychology 124*. Theories of Personality; *Psychology 126*. Psychometrics; *Psychology 135*. Abnormal Psychology; *Psychology 136*. Psychiatry; *Psychology 137*. Method in Clinical Psychology); research work for the MA thesis was, of course, also required. In that same year, Ph.D. students began to be registered in the clinical programme.

By 1961–62 there had developed what is politely known as some degree of polarization between the experimental and clinical staff of the Department. The clinicians began loudly to complain of the weight of their self-inflicted work load: their battle cry was "More clinicians!". The experimentalists began to feel that this particular camel was now quite far enough into the tent; their battle-cry became "Preserve the balance!". One view of the efforts of the clinical programme at that time was later recorded in a piece of doggerel verse, part of which ran,

> Some viewed their scheme
> with jealous abhorrence,
> Called it just another Maudsley
> (on-the-St. Lawrence)!

A great paper barrage of memoranda and minutes certainly began to roll over the Department at about this time, and new appointments and apportionments were warmly disputed. Julian Blackburn, who had many other things to think about that did not necessarily concern his more junior staff (he had been President of the Canadian Psychological Association in 1956–57, was Editor of the *Canadian Journal of Psychology* from 1959–1965, and served on many national and provincial committees) obviously came to feel that his departmental Chair was turning into something of a hot seat. From time to time, *his* battle-cry might have been "A plague on both your houses!".

The fact of the matter, however, is that even the so-called "clinicians" in the Department had always insisted that their first allegiance was to the objective and experimental study of behaviour, so that the division between the two factions, even at this juncture, was perhaps more apparent than real. Between 1960 and 1963 there were four more Assistant Professors enlisted in the Department (D. Campbell, now at McMaster University, R. Ginsberg, now at San Jose State University, the late R.G. Rabedeau, formerly Chairman of Psychology at San Jose State, and A.G. Worthington, now at Trent University). Of these four, only Rabedeau, a physiological psychologist, had research interests that fell completely outside of any applied field. Thus, even at a time of some strife, new appointments were being made of a kind that eventually served to knit the Department into the more coherent and cohesive form that it has since attained.

In the meantime P.H.R. James had resigned in order to take up the position of Chairman of the Department of Psychology at Dalhousie University, a department that he developed with brilliant success. Later, for a brief spell, he was also Dean. A rather amusingly maudlin account of this phase of his career is to be found in the May, 1975 issue of the magazine *Impetus*; this article was written by Donald Cameron, who there found occasion to refer to Dr. James as "Prince Henry the Navigator", one name that he had never been called in all of his time at Queen's!

By 1962–63, graduate training in psychology had settled down fairly amicably into two streams, labelled general-experimental and experimental-clinical. There was still some disparity in the amount of course work and practical training that candidates in these two programmes had to undertake. In the general MA/Ph.D. programme, in addition to thesis work, students had at that time to register in a minimum of three out of four courses (*Psychology 114*. Advanced Statistics and Experimental Design; *Psychology 115*. Advanced Statistics and Multivariate Analysis; *Psychology 116*. Advanced Physiological and Comparative Psychology; *Psychology 117*. Advanced Experimental Psychology). In the clinical MA/Ph.D. programme, on the other hand, in addition to their thesis work, students now had to undertake six courses (*Psychology 124*. Experimental Investigations and Personality Theories; *Psychology 126*. Psychometrics; *Psychology 127*. Applied Clinical Psychology; *Psychology 135*. Abnormal Psychology; *Psychology 136*. Psychometrics; *Psychology 137*. Method in Clinical Psychology). Because of this discrepancy in the number of courses and amount of practical work required, a Diploma in Clinical Psychology was first awarded in 1962–63 to those students who had completed their initial year in the clinical Ph.D. programme. It was intended to show that the diplomate had undertaken the required theoretical and practical training in clinical psychology, without having completed a Ph.D. research project.

From 1924 up to the end of the academic year 1979–80, 268 students had received a total of 381 graduate degrees and diplomas in psychology from Queen's University. The 35 years between 1924 and 1959 account for only 25 graduates, so that in the 21 years since 1959, a total of 243 graduate students have come from the Department.

By 1964–65 changes were in the air. Julian Blackburn had withdrawn as Head of the Department, and Peter Dodwell was Acting Head. Seven new, full-time members had joined or were shortly to join the faculty (A.Z. Arthur, L.L. Cuddy, N.L. Freedman, J.B. Knowles, D.J. Murray, F.R. Staples, M.D. Suboski, R.G. Weisman, and G.J.S. Wilde) while several of the old guard had gone, or were just about to depart.

In 1960, Julian Blackburn had already been appointed, on behalf of Queen's University, as one of a group of advisers to the Board of Governors of the nascent Trent College in Peterborough; a group informally known as the 'Midwives' of Trent. In 1965, Blackburn resigned from Queen's to become the first Chairman of the Department of Psychology at that new University. He was Associate Dean of the Faculty of Arts there from 1969 to 1970, becoming Emeritus Professor of Psychology in 1973. He died in September 1974, and the next year there was established in his name the Julian Blackburn College of Part-Time Studies at Trent University.

Alan Worthington also went off to Trent in 1965, and R.G. Rabedeau and Rose Ginsberg left for San Jose State University in California. R.W. Payne and J. Inglis moved that same year to Temple University in Philadelphia, to set up a new Department of Behavioral Science at Temple Medical School.

In 1966, William Robert Thompson returned once again to Queen's, this time as Head of the Department of Psychology. Born in 1924 of Canadian parents in Toulon, France, and a graduate of the Universities of Toronto (BA, 1945; MA, 1947) and Chicago (Ph.D., 1951), he had worked in many university departments of psychology in Canada, the United States, and in Australia. An authority in the fields of developmental psychology and behaviour genetics (see, for example, Fuller and Thompson, 1960; 1978), he had held a Guggenheim Memorial Fellowship (1959–60) and had also been a Fellow of the Center for Advanced Studies in the Behavioral Sciences at Palo Alto in 1963–64. He came to Queen's, on this occasion, just as George Humphrey had done, from Wesleyan University in Connecticut.

So this academic circle closed again, and a new cycle was begun.

References

Bartlett, F.C. George Humphrey: 1889–1966. *American Journal of Psychology*, 1966, *79*, 657–658.

Blackburn, J.M. *Psychology and the social pattern*. London: Routledge and Kegan Paul, 1945.

Blackburn, J.M. *The framework of human behaviour*. London: Routledge and Kegan Paul, 1947.

Blackburn, J.M. George Humphrey. *Canadian Journal of Psychology*, 1957, *11*, 141–150.

Blair, W.R.N. In support. *Canadian Psychologist*, 1966, *3*, 185–196.

Boring, E.G., Langfeld, H.S., & Weld, H.P. *Psychology: a factual textbook*. New York: Wiley, 1935.

Calvin, D.D. *Queen's University at Kingston: the first century of a Scottish-Canadian foundation, 1841–1941*. Kingston, Ont.: Queen's University Press, 1941.

Dodwell, P.C. Coding and learning in shape discrimination. *Psychological Review*, 1961, *68*, 373–383.

Fuller, J.L., & Thompson, W.R. *Behavior genetics*. New York: Wiley, 1960.

Fuller, J.L., & Thompson, W.R. *Foundations of behavior genetics*. St. Louis: C.V. Mosby, 1978.

Gundy, H.P. Growing pains: the early history of the Queen's Medical Faculty. *Historic Kingston*, 1955, *4*, 14–25.

Gundy, H.P. Thomas Liddell: Queen's first Principal. *Historic Kingston*, 1971, *19*, 17–27.

Hearnshaw, L.S. *A short history of British psychology: 1840–1940*. London: Methuen, 1964.

Hull, C.L. *Principles of behavior: an introduction to behavior theory.* New York: Appleton-Century-Crofts, 1943.

Humphrey, G. *The story of man's mind.* Boston: Small, Maynard, 1923.

Humphrey, G. The effect of sequences of indifferent stimuli on a reaction of the conditioned response type. *Journal of Abnormal and Social Psychology,* 1927, *22,* 194–212.

Humphrey, G. Le Chatelier's rule, and the problem of habituation and dehabituation in *helix albolabris. Psychologische Forschung,* 1930, *13,* 113–127.

Humphrey, G. *The nature of learning: in its relation to the living system.* London: Kegan Paul, Trench, Trubner, 1933.

Humphrey, G. *Directed thinking.* New York: Dodd Mead, 1948.

Inglis, J. Learning, retention and conceptual usage in elderly patients with memory disorder. *Journal of Abnormal and Social Psychology,* 1959, *59,* 210–215.

Itard, J-M-G. *The wild boy of Aveyron.* (Translated by G. Humphrey and M. Humphrey, with an Introduction by G. Humphrey). New York: Appleton-Century-Crofts, 1932.

James, P.H.R. Flicker: an unconditioned stimulus for imprinting. *Canadian Journal of Psychology,* 1959, *13,* 59–67.

McDougall, W. *An outline of abnormal psychology.* London: Methuen, 1926.

Myers, C.R. Notes on the history of psychology in Canada. *Canadian Psychologist,* 1965, *6,* 4–19.

Neatby, H. *And not to yield. Queen's University. Volume I, 1841–1917.* Montreal: McGill-Queen's University Press, 1978.

Payne, R.W. Thought disorder and retardation in schizophrenia. *Canadian Psychiatric Association Journal,* 1961, *6,* 75–78.

Report of the Court of Error and Appeal of Upper Canada. *Weir vs. Mathieson: case on appeal from a decree of the Court of Chancery.* Toronto: Globe Steam Job Press, 1865.

Thompson, W.R., & Heron, W. Exploratory behavior in normal and restricted dogs. *Journal of Comparative and Physiological Psychology,* 1954a, *47,* 104–107.

Thompson, W.R., & Heron, W. The effects of restricting early experience on the problem-solving capacity of dogs. *Canadian Journal of Psychology,* 1954b, *8,* 17–31.

Further Reading

Anonymous – Citation: Julian M. Blackburn. *The Canadian Psychologist,* 1960, *1a,* 87.

See also notes in *The Canadian Psychologist,* 1956, *5,* 40; 1960, *1,* 141–143; 1961, *2,* 103; 1968, *9,* 82–84.

Note

The preparation of this chapter was begun with the assistance of a Leave Fellowship (Award No. W750081) from the Canada Council, and this aid is most gratefully acknowledged.

Several friends and colleagues have made many very helpful criticisms and suggestions. I would like to thank P.C. Dodwell and H.M. Estall for reading and commenting on the manuscript. I am particularly indebted to R.W. Payne who also very kindly provided me with a great deal of annotated documentation that dealt with the early development of the graduate clinical programme at Queen's.

The manuscript was also kindly read and constructively criticized by the late W.R. Thompson (1924–1979), Head of the Department of Psychology from 1966 to 1972, to whose memory this chapter is respectfully dedicated.

Chapter 5

Psychology at Western

by

Leola E. Neal* and Mary J. Wright**

The University of Western Ontario, popularly referred to in Canada simply as "Western", was established in 1878 but the history of psychology there begins 20 years later, in 1898. The years 1898 to the present can be divided into three fairly distinct periods: 1898–1929, 1929–1954, and 1954 to the present. These periods, each roughly 25 years, parallel the growth and prosperity of the University and reflect the social and scientific changes taking place in psychology.

The information about the earliest period, 1898–1929, is sketchy. The Board of Governors' minutes were written in longhand and there appear to be some inconsistencies and ambiguities in the records. Departmental records are non-existent, but it is known from university calendars that, in this period, the courses in psychology were taught by part-time lecturers in the Department of Philosophy. George B. Sage, an Anglican priest and lecturer in philosophy, was the first lecturer in psychology. Sage was born near Brantford, Ontario, and educated at Trinity College, Toronto. It is of interest to note that he was ordained in 1881 by Bishop Hellmuth, founder of The University of Western Ontario.

The course which Sage taught, an option for students in the second year of the general course, was described in the 1898–1899 calendar as "Sensation, Thought, Emotion, Volition". The first texts listed were:

* Professor Neal began her career at The University of Western Ontario (U.W.O.) in the Department of Philosophy and Psychology as a teaching assistant in 1935. Except for two years, when she was studying for her doctorate, she was associated with the department (part-time after her appointment in 1946 as Dean of Women) until her retirement in 1977. She was the author of the first part of this chapter, including the section on the Liddy Years.

** Professor Wright joined the Faculty at U.W.O. in 1946. She was Chairman of the Department of Psychology at Middlesex College from 1960 to 1963 and Head of the re-united Department of Psychology at U.W.O. from 1963 to 1970.

Angell's *Psychology* or Stout's *Groundwork of Psychology*. By 1927 the course content seems to have been expanded and included the nervous system, sensory and motor equipment, instinct, emotions, intelligence, habit, memory, perception, reasoning, imagination, will, and personality.

The second period began in 1929 when the University established a psychological laboratory and appointed a psychologist, Desmond Humphreys Smyth, as its "Director". Smyth had a Master's degree from McGill and held the rank of Assistant Professor of Philosophy and Psychology. A note on his appointment in the President's Report (1930–31) states: "For years the administration had been keenly aware of the great need for some such provision, only the inadequacy of the University's resources has made necessary the postponement of the required staffing and laboratory equipment". The report goes on to mention that "a new laboratory was built and equipped and has been serving a steadily increasing number of students".

This laboratory on the top floor of University College doubled as a classroom or office as required. By today's standards it was poorly equipped and woefully inadequate for both instruction and research. There is no record of the number of students enrolled in the psychology courses, but it should be remembered that in 1930–31 the total number of students registered in the University's three Faculties, Arts, Medicine, and Public Health, was 1302.

Smyth's appointment was terminated in 1931. In the same year Roy Balmer Liddy was appointed Professor and Head of a new department of Philosophy and Psychology. From that day until his retirement in 1954 the fortunes of Psychology revolved around Liddy.

The Liddy Years (1931–1954)

Liddy came to the University of Western Ontario from Mount Allison University in Sackville, New Brunswick. He was the Head of the Department of Philosophy and Psychology there and was highly respected as a scholar, teacher and administrator. He was hard-working and conscientious to a fault. His standards for himself, his colleagues and his students were high and set the tone for the department at Western.

Liddy was born December 6, 1886, at Bradford, Ontario, and grew up in a parsonage. He received his higher education at Victoria College and the University of Toronto where he received his Ph.D. His undergraduate training had been in Philosophy, Psychology and Theology and he was equally at ease in any one of these disciplines. As a philosopher he was influenced by R.W. Sellars[1] and A.N. Whitehead.[2] While on a sabbatical

Roy Balmer Liddy: 1886–1961

at the University of Chicago he studied with H.N. Wieman[3] who had earlier profoundly influenced his thinking in theology. As a psychologist his position was similar, in many respects, to the dynamic psychology of R.S. Woodworth. Woodworth's *Psychology* was the basic text for the introductory course for many years.

Liddy was the architect of the 4-year Honors program and in 1932 he introduced a graduate program at the M.A. level requiring a Thesis. The first M.A. was conferred in 1933. In 1935, only three M.A.'s were conferred in the entire University and one of these was in psychology. At this time the focus of the department, and indeed of the university as a whole, was on undergraduate work and on providing a liberal arts education.

Liddy like many of his generation believed that the introductory course was of paramount importance and that it should be the responsibility of the Head of the department (Liddy, 1946). He determined what would be taught and how it would be taught. Each student in the course, whether taught by Liddy or some other instructor, was given a hand-out which stated "the" definition of psychology and described the methods of psychology according to Liddy. A copy of this supplement is appended. During his regime, when there were numerous junior faculty members on sessional appointments, this was a wise policy which provided consistency, and a base from which to evaluate critically other schools of thought.

For Liddy, psychology could not be defined adequately as the science of the mind or as the science of behavior. It studied both mental processes (including conscious and unconscious) and behavioral processes. He believed that in the investigation of their data, psychologists are interested primarily in the general principles which apply to any aspect of human or animal activity. He contended that psychology studied its subject matter scientifically and this involved four steps: careful observation, formulation of hypotheses, the elaboration of these hypotheses and their testing. Observation might be subjective, objective, or both, and included experimentation where possible.

The 1930's were difficult years because of the serious economic depression. The University was heavily dependent upon private funding and money was always scarce. Even as late as 1945 the whole university budget was only slightly more than half a million dollars; $545,000 to be exact. Faculty salaries were low and departments were understaffed and overworked. It was not unusual to teach 15–20 hours per week, not including extension courses taught in London and in outside centres. Students in psychology were numerous when compared to those in other departments.

During this period, Liddy, Douglas J. Wilson an experimental psychologist with degrees from Toronto, Allison H. Johnson, a philosopher who taught introductory psychology and systems of psychology, and Leola E. Neal, a graduate assistant and teaching fellow with an interest in clinical psychology, were responsible for instruction in psychology.

The early 1940's were war years, an interlude when everyone, in addition to regular duties, was involved in the war effort. Some of the war-effort projects were individual, others were team efforts under the auspices of the newly formed Canadian Psychological Association (CPA). Liddy was a founding member of the CPA and its first treasurer. He served as chairman of a test research committee and persuaded two Insurance Companies (Wright, 1974, p. 115) to make grants which totalled $1000 to initiate a test construction research program. This program ultimately produced General Examination M, the classification test which was used in the Canadian Army.

Lionel S. Penrose, an internationally famous British scientist and researcher, was on the staff of the Ontario Hospital in London at this time.

Because of his expertise in test design and research methods he made an outstanding contribution to the psychological scene and to the test development program in particular. During this period Wilson joined the Royal Canadian Air Force, and Neal spent two years as a graduate student at the University of Toronto, returning to the University of Western Ontario in 1942. Throughout the War years Neal was associated with Penrose in various test-construction research projects.

In 1945 Gordon H. Turner, and in 1946 Mary J. Wright joined the faculty as Assistant Professors. Both had served overseas, Turner in Personnel Selection, Army, and Wright with the Canadian Children's Service and both had received their graduate training at the University of Toronto. Turner was interested in industrial and applied psychology and Wright in child development. Wright came to Western when Neal became a part-time member of the department on her appointment as Dean of Women.

In the hectic immediate post-war period, there was pressure from the provincial government on universities to expand to accommodate returning veterans. Student enrolment increased sharply and dramatically with demobilization. Liddy and a number of heads of departments, notably R.W. Torrens (Romance Languages) and M.K. Inman (Economics) were deeply concerned about the quality of teaching. In 1945 and 1946 many of the important introductory courses were being taught, of necessity, by junior faculty, often graduate students at the Master's level with no training or experience in teaching. A number of seminars or workshops on teaching methods were organized. On one occasion, S.R. Laycock a prominent educational psychologist from the University of Saskatchewan was the key note speaker.

During World War II, psychology was found to be useful and, after the war there was pressure from both the public and students on psychology to move towards the practical and applied. The demand for undergraduate courses in psychology and for graduate training was tremendous. At the undergraduate level psychology continued to be taught as a science and liberal arts subject, but at the graduate level the emphasis shifted to professional training, primarily in clinical methods.

In this period of rapid expansion, psychology flourished and, in 1948, psychology and philosophy separated (with some pain). Liddy became Head of the psychology department, Johnson Head of the philosophy department. In six years, 1948–1954, according to Wright (1963, p. 6) the Department of Psychology produced 47 Honor B.A.'s, 34 M.A.'s, and two Ph.D.'s. Numbers, while significant, tell only part of the story. Resources had not increased commensurate with enrolment and the story of that period is a saga of a small group of dedicated faculty and a group of mature students superior in intelligence and motivation. Many of these students held sessional appointments in the department and then did graduate work at McGill, Toronto, Western, or at American Universities such as Michigan, Minnesota, Pennsylvania State and Princeton. From 1950–53, Roger Philip (Bernhardt, 1958), a teaching Brother with wide teaching experience in a number of Canadian and American Universities, joined the Faculty as a Visiting Professor. His special interests were in experimental psychology and statistics and he acted as advisor to the first two PhD students. His breadth of knowledge and his skills were also of great benefit to all graduate students.

Because of a lack of adequate laboratory facilities and in part because of the applied interests of the majority of both the graduate students and the faculty of the department, field work largely replaced laboratory research and the department relied heavily upon community facilities and the cooperation of agency staffs for training and research opportunities. Several faculty members held appointments as consultants and many of the students were employed as psychological interns and research assistants in a variety of community settings. Chief among these settings were the Ontario Hospitals in London and St. Thomas, the Department of Veterans Affairs Psychiatric Hospital, the juvenile court and the schools. These working relationships began as early as 1930–31 when, according to the president's report, "… one phase of the growth of this Department (Psychology) may be seen in the cooperation of the Mental Health Clinic which operates in Western Ontario under the auspices of Dr. B.T. McGhie, Director of Ontario Government Hospitals. At no cost to the University, the services of Miss Lewis, the psychologist of the clinic, have been generously placed at the disposal of the Department. In the course of the academic year she conducts a course of lectures which, because of her special knowledge of abnormal psychology, are of distinct value to students".

It is difficult, and probably impossible, to assess the influence and significance of this field work on the Department and its students. Even a cursory glance at the titles of the theses produced at this time gives an indication of the importance of these resources. The Department recognized the contribution of many who were associated happily with it as teachers, clinicians, professionals and administrators and was especially grateful to three prominent local psychiatrists, E.S. Goddard, E.V. Metcalfe and George H. Stevenson, especially the latter. Dr. Stevenson[4] was "the" Professor of Psychiatry at the University, a former President of the American Psychiatric Association and Superintendent of the Ontario Hospital in London. For many years he taught a course in abnormal psychology in the Department of Psychology.

In the 1940's the University did not have funds to support research or to bring specialists and distinguished professors to the Department as guest lecturers and it had to rely upon financial support from outside agencies. In one year, 1949, three members of the faculty obtained grants: Liddy from the Ontario Department of Health for post-graduate training in clinical psychology, Neal from the same source to conduct a workshop in clinical psychology, and Turner from the National Research Council and Defence Research Board for special studies. The visiting lecturers were, for the most part, prominent psychologists from the United States such as N.H. Kelley, T.M. Newcombe, C.R. Rogers, R.R. Sears, and F.C. Thorne. They were a source of great inspiration to faculty and students. Their influence was also reflected in some of the thesis work. The emphasis, at Western on clinical rather than experimental psychology, sparked lively discussions about science vs. profession, and some criticism from other universities.

During these years, psychology was accepted in the University and the community. As a profession it was sometimes embarrassingly popular, but the object of derision if it failed to be a panacea. Occasionally, one got "the feeling" psychology was not always popular with other scientists or some psychiatrists, but it was popular with students.

The Faculty were active in university and community affairs. They served on important committees and boards inside and outside the university and were in great demand as public speakers. They helped establish the Canadian and Ontario Psychological Associations and served as officers in them. Academic psychology profited enormously from the efforts of these Associations.

Western at this time was not famous for its publications. Although some reputable articles were published, the Department was noted primarily for its teaching and its desire to produce well-rounded or "well-educated" students. Perhaps the most illustrious chapter in Western's history will be written by its graduates, many of whom are highly visible in American and Canadian psychology.

The third period in the history of the Department began after Liddy's retirement.

The Turner Years (1954–1963)

In 1954 Liddy's successor as Head was Gordon Haslam Turner. Turner obtained his Ph.D. at Toronto in 1939, just at the beginning of World War II. His first post-doctorate job was with the Young Men's Christian Association (YMCA) in Toronto, but from this he shortly went into war service. In 1941, when the Canadian Army established its Directorate of Personnel Selection, Turner was one of its first recruits. He served in this Directorate, both in Canada and in the United Kingdom, until 1945 when he obtained his discharge to take up an appointment at Western.

Turner was a humanist, and was deeply concerned about values and the condition of man in modern society. He was inspired most by the writings of persons such as Abraham Maslow, Carl Rogers, and Michael Polanyi (Turner, 1972, p. 64). In the early 1950's he became a convert to Group Dynamics on the "Bethel, Maine," style, and this seemed to have a profound influence on both his interests and attitudes in the years that followed. He became highly skeptical of the value of all types of psychological research, but especially of experimental research, (Turner, 1972, pp. 59, 61, 64). He also became distrustful of "authorities", especially the paternalistic type, and this lead him, eventually, into a lively career as an "activist" in campus politics.

When Turner became Head, he felt handicapped by strong anti-psychology feelings, which he sensed in the University community. He believed that these feelings had been induced by the President, G. Edward Hall, and then augmented by Liddy who had fought against them, perhaps too aggressively. Hall was appointed President in 1947, the year before psychology and philosophy were separated and an independent Department of Psychology was established. He had facilitated this separation, not to emancipate psychology, but to liberate and strengthen the Department of Philosophy. Hall was a medical scientist and his attitudes reflected the rather dubious view of psychology which was held by many Canadian medical people of his time. Hall was, however, ambitious for the University and strove, with great energy, to improve its quality. He valued scholarship, as well as scientific research, and he persistently "pursued a policy of bringing to the University men who were distinguished in their field ..." (Gwynne-Timothy, 1978, p. 287). He had noted the scholarship of a young philosopher, Allison Johnson, who had been at Western for approximately a decade. He therefore established a new Philosophy Department, made Johnson its Head, provided generous support for the expansion of its faculty and did all of this with, apparently, no communication with Liddy. Liddy always claimed that he had learned of it at a Faculty meeting when Johnson was called upon to speak about the philosophy course offerings for the academic year 1948–49. This first humiliation of psychology was quickly followed by a second, when introductory psychology, which had been for many years a compulsory course for freshmen, was downgraded to an optional course. Liddy was a proud and courageous man who, with much righteous indignation "stood up" for psychology and its worth during this difficult time, but his efforts seemed only to increase the strength of the tide against it.

Since Liddy's approach had failed, Turner decided to adopt a passive stance, especially with the administration, to make few demands and no trouble, and hope that this would facilitate a reduction in the anti-psychology climate. While waiting for more propitious times he concentrated on the Department and its internal affairs, and tried out his ideas about human relations and group dynamics in its administration. Looking back over the period of his Headship, Turner defended his non-aggressive stance by saying "there was no way anybody could have got anything going (for psychology) here ... given Hall's attitudes" (Turner 1972 pp. 52–53).

There is reason to believe that Hall had high hopes for psychology when Liddy, the elder stateman, stepped down and Turner, whose appointment Hall had promoted, became Head, but that he was soon disappointed by Turner's administrative style. There was, however, another factor which undoubtedly influenced Hall's attitudes. This was Turner's role in the new Faculty Association which was formed in 1955, the year following Turner's appointment as Head. Turner was the Association's first President. Although faculty resistance to Hall's administration had smouldered, almost from its beginnings, and had even, at times, flared into attempted coups to bring that administration down, the intrigues had been undercover. The founding of a Faculty Association was, however, a more open act of resistance, if not defiance, suspected of being the first step toward unionization.

The upshot of all of this for the Department was that it was treated very poorly. In fact, it was almost starved out. Its budget allocations became even more meagre than those meted out to Liddy. New and capable faculty in psychology were desperately needed, but authority to recruit at even the most junior levels was invariably delayed. Thus emergency appointments were frequently made and there was much staff changeover. Some degree of staff stability was, however, finally achieved after the appointment of Jaraslov Havelka, John Paul, and Frank W.R. Taylor in 1956 and of Morris Schnore in 1957.

From an academic point of view, the late 1950's were quiet years. The wave of war veterans had passed through. The undergraduates were a passive lot. The demand for graduate training had subsided. "Publish or perish" was an abhorred phrase to be applied in the United States, but not in Canada. Only a few statistics, which were easy to ignore in this climate, offered any portend of what the 1960's held in store. The Department was asked to project its needs for space and equipment, and it asked for, and obtained, a small laboratory for animal research in the biology building, but nothing more.

Thus, on the eve of the 1960's when the products of the post-war "baby-boom" were expected to flood the campus, the Department was totally unprepared to meet even its undergraduate, let alone its graduate responsibilities. It needed everything – laboratory space, up-to-date equipment, and above all high quality research staff who could sustain its graduate training program.

The Wright Years 1960–1970

The first major changes in the Department began to occur when the University implemented an unpopular scheme, a "brain-child" of the President's, which called for the establishment of at least two new Arts and Social Science Colleges, in addition to University College, in lieu of expanding the latter. The alleged reason for this was to keep undergraduate classes small when the expected expansion in enrolments occurred. The first of the new colleges (Middlesex College, its name derived from the County in which Western is located) was to be opened in 1960 and six new departments were to be established there. Psychology was one of these. Its faculty was to consist of half of the staff in psychology in University College, who would simply be transferred to their new quarters. In 1959 Mary Jean Wright[5] was appointed Chairman-designate of this new department.

Wright had been uncomfortable about the Department, feeling that it was not keeping up with developments in psychology elsewhere, and, in 1959, wasted no time in submitting a formal brief to the Dean-designate of the new College, outlining what the University would need to do if it hoped to develop a respectable modern department of psychology. This was an aggressive approach, which she took with some misgivings, not only because of the alleged unpopularity of psychology with the President, but because she thought it might be considered "unbecoming" in a woman. She was the first woman who had ever been appointed to the Chair of an academic department at Western. The brief was, however, favourably received by the Dean-designate and in 1960 the Department at Middlesex began to receive the support it needed. Funds were provided for new equipment, but what was more important, a decision was made to develop some specialized laboratory facilities for psychological research and to expand those facilities in a new wing of the College, still in the planning stage, which was scheduled to open in 1963. Furthermore, authorization for making new appointments was given early enough in the academic year to make it possible to conduct a responsible search for the kind of staff that was required.

The early progress made at Middlesex may have been due more to the influence of the Dean (Brandon Conron) than to any change in the President's attitude toward psychology. However, in the spring of 1962, an event occurred which clearly impressed the President and gave the Department some "kudos" in his eyes. This happened, because one of the promising young scientists appointed in 1961 (Robert Teghtsoonian) suddenly resigned at the end of his first year at Western, very late in the spring, when to replace him with someone of equal quality seemed likely to be impossible. Teghtsoonian left because he was not provided with adequate space for his animal research, thus underlining the need for proper laboratory facilities, but, of greater importance, was the fact that he was replaced by an even more promising scientist (A.U. Paivio) and this was brought to the attention of the President, not by internal, but by external means. Shortly after Paivio's appointment was confirmed, Hall received a scathing letter from his counterpart at the University of New Brunswick (President Colin B. Mackay) from which Paivio had been seduced, accusing him of "raiding" a smaller university and of stealing one of its best and most valued faculty members. Nothing could have delighted Hall more. It was the sort of initiative Hall had frequently taken himself and the kind he admired. He made a personal call to Wright, chuckling with glee, to insist that she compose an appropriate reply to President Mackay.[6]

The existence of two Departments of Psychology presented many problems, because they were jointly responsible for all instruction, and their Heads had to collaborate on all aspects of administration, including staff recruiting. Inevitably tensions developed between them over the latter, both the approach to recruiting and the type of new faculty that should be sought. Wright was promoting the development of a strong research-oriented department which was, if not repulsive to Turner, at least very unsettling and in 1962 he submitted his resignation from the Chair. This, plus the anticipated expense of equipping two laboratory-based modern departments of psychology, persuaded the University to re-unite the departments under one roof, in Middlesex College, and under one Head (Wright), and this was accomplished in 1963.

Wright's zeal to develop a "hard" science department surprised some, because she, like Turner, had done her graduate work in Toronto and had applied interests in child development and in early childhood education. She had consolidated those interests during World War II, which had interrupted her graduate training, while she served overseas with a group headed by W.E. Blatz. This group established a Teacher Training Centre and Demonstration Day Nursery in Birmingham, England to prepare personnel for service in Wartime Day Nurseries, and Wright taught there for over two years. Also, on her return to Canada, she did clinical work for a year on the Mental Health Clinic in Hamilton before resuming her doctoral studies at Toronto. She joined the faculty in psychology at Western (where she had done her undergraduate work) in 1946.

Wright's brief experience in the clinical field had led her to agree with Robert MacLeod (1955) who had concluded that psychology in Canada was indulging in "premature professionalism". Also, her experience in early childhood education had demonstrated to her the great benefits to be derived from a sounder data base. Therefore, she concurred with the post-war movement in psychology toward a return from the field into the laboratory, or at least into the research enterprise, until a more adequate base for the profession had been established. The discussions at the Opinicon Conference (Bernhardt, 1961) in 1960, which she attended as a "junior" recorder, confirmed her in this view. There was, however, an opportunistic aspect to what she attempted to do. When appointed Head she had sought the advice of Donald O. Hebb on how to go about developing a strong Department. He told her that if the Department was to thrive it must first earn the respect of the "hard" scientists in the University and that this could be done only by demonstrating that psychology did "hard" science, basic research. He pointed out that once this was accomplished, support for all aspects of psychology would be forthcoming. To act on Hebb's advice was Wright's greatest challenge, because it required obtaining the kind of expensive laboratory facilities which, until the mid-1960's, the University was unable or unwilling to provide. A beginning in physiological psychology was, however, finally made by forming a liaison with the Physiology Department, which loaned the department space. This made possible the appointment of Gordon Mogenson who joined the staff in 1965. Mogenson was highly regarded by the Head of Physiology, James Stevenson, and Stevenson was an influential person on campus. His admiration for Mogenson and his work did much to gain for psychology the kind of respect that Hebb said it required. It is noteworthy that at the time of writing, Mogenson is Chairman of the Physiology Department, although still associated with the Department of Psychology.

By the mid-1960's a number of very able new faculty had been acquired. Among them, besides Paivio and Mogenson, were D.N. Jackson, R.C. Gardner, J.P. Denny, H.O. Lobb, W.J. McClelland, T.J. Ryan, R.K. Knights and D.A. Chambers. All were active scientists and the amount of research funds obtained by them from non-university sources had been tripling annually. The number of publications produced by them was also growing rapidly and the number and quality of the graduate students being attracted was also increasing by leaps and bounds. Hall's administration was impressed. It provided generous financial support for the Department, made every effort to find space and convert it for specialized research, and agreed to build a new psychology building as soon as possible – and then came the "big" Faculty Revolt. This revolt completely tied the hands of the administration. All decision making was delayed until agreement had been reached on a revision of the University's Government. Finally, in 1967, President Hall resigned and the University slowly began to resume its normal administrative functions under a new Act,[7] which greatly increased the power of the Faculty, and a new President. Gordon Turner played a major role in the "Revolt" which was led by the Faculty Association, of which he was again the President in 1965–66.

After 1967 swift action was taken to provide psychology with the laboratory space it needed and within two years it was well equipped with such facilities in three adjacent buildings, one of them new. Also by the end of the decade, plans were completed for its future facilities in a new Social Science complex to be opened in 1972. The decision of the Senate to locate psychology in the Social Science Centre was not a popular one with a number of the faculty members in the Department. These favoured an alliance with the biological rather than the social sciences. A compromise was, however, reached when it was agreed that in the Faculty of Graduate Studies psychology would be classified as a Life Science.

During the second half of the 1960s the Department was successful in recruiting several additional outstanding faculty. These included Doreen Kimura, Milton Rokeach, Zenon Pylyshyn, Harry Murray, Neil Vidmar, Case Vanderwolf, Gary Rollman, Stephen Kendall, Richard Sorrentino, Will Reitz, Roger Stretch, David Pederson, Marvin Simner, Morton Rieber and several others, all of whom contributed importantly to the increasing prestige of the Department.

By 1970 Wright had achieved her goals for the Department. A strong research base had been established in a number of areas, including physiological, perception, learning and cognition, as well as social, personality, and developmental psychology. The faculty were highly productive and were attracting high quality graduate students for whom they were excellent models. The battle for space had been won and, after ten years, she decided it was time to resign from the Chair.

The McClelland Years 1970–

William J. McClelland succeeded Wright as Chairman. He had joined the faculty in 1960, had shown ability as an administrator and for some time was Assistant Dean in the Faculty of Graduate Studies.

McClelland did his undergraduate and MA work at the University of Toronto. He then went on to Bedford College, at the University of London where, in 1958 he obtained the PhD. His interests were primarily in the Clinical field. During his stay in the United Kingdom he spent two years as a Medical Research Council Fellow at Runwell Hospital in Wickford, Essex. On his return to Canada he took up a position at the St. Thomas Psychiatric Hospital and soon became Chief Psychologist there. From this post he came to the University.

In 1972 the Department moved into its new quarters which provided excellent facilities for all types of psychological research, under one roof, and it continued to prosper (Endler, Rushton & Roediger III, 1978). Although the mid-70's saw the end of the effects of the post-war "baby-boom" and were a time of declining enrolments and budget cuts, the Department not only maintained but increased its staff strength. It continued to attract established scholars, such as Charles Brainerd, as well as a number of promising younger scientists, among them James Neufeld, Mel Goodale, Tory Higgins, and Philip Rushton.

McClelland saw his primary task to be the strengthening of the applied side of the Department and this he has done with some success. In the 60's the Department offered only a Clinical program and this was primarily a program in experimental psychopathology. In the 70's it established a broadly-based Applied program which offered specialties in Medical, Community, Educational and Organizational psychology as well as Clinical psychology. However, anchored as it was in a Department committed to the advancement of knowledge, it was also strongly research-oriented. Another innovation of the 70's, which permitted the Department to offer still another applied specialty, was the establishment of a Laboratory Preschool which was located in the "heart" of the Department, on the fifth floor of its nine-story laboratory tower. The establishment of the Preschool had been promoted by Wright and she was its Director until her retirement. The availability of this facility permitted the Department to offer a specialty in Early Childhood Education as part of either the Masters or PhD program in developmental psychology.

Addendum

Finally, a description of "Pychology at Western" would be incomplete without reference to the academic psychology taught in the University's three affiliated colleges and the applied psychology taught in its Faculty of Education. Two of the affiliated colleges, Huron (Anglican) and King's (Roman Catholic) have separate Departments of Psychology and Brescia (Roman Catholic) has a Department of Social Sciences which offers psychology courses. However, all instruction in psychology, at these colleges, is at the undergraduate level. Huron College, which was the founding College of the University, and Brescia College have long histories and have taught psychology for many years.

A separate Department of Educational Psychology was established at Althouse College (Ontario's second training school for secondary school teachers) in the mid-1960's. It now has a teaching staff of thirteen and is part of the University's Faculty of Education.

In addition to the above a separate Department of Psychology was established in the new University Hospital which was opened in the early 1970's. Most of the members of this Department hold adjunct faculty appointments in the Department of Psychology and teach courses in applied psychology, sometimes at the graduate as well as at the undergraduate level.

Notes

[1] Liddy was impressed by and, in general, accepted Sellars' theory of reality, which was evolutionary naturalism, and his theory of knowledge, which was critical realism.

[2] Liddy was influenced by the views expressed by Whitehead, especially those put forward in his book "Religion in the Making".

[3] Liddy's thinking in theology was influenced especially by the views expressed by Wieman in his book "The Wrestle of Religion with Truth".

[4] For more information about Dr. Stevenson see "A Century of Medicine at Western" by Murray L. Barr. London, Canada. The University of Western Ontario, 1977, Pps. 354–355.

[5] An autobiographical sketch of Mary J. Wright is to appear in Agnes N. O'Connell and Nancy Felipe Russo (Eds.), *Models of Achievement: Reflections of Eminent Women in Psychology*. New York: Columbia University Press.

[6] A copy of Wright's letter to President Mackay dated June 20, 1962 and a copy of his reply dated June 29, 1962 are in the Department of Psychology's file (at U.W.O.) on A.U. Paivio.

[7] Bill Pr 31. 5th session, 27th Legislature, Ontario 15–16 Elizabeth II, 1967. An Act respecting the University of Western Ontario.

References

Bernhardt, K.S. Five New Fellows of the CPA (Brother Roger Philip). *The Canadian Psychologist*, 1958, 7, 96–98.

Bernhardt, K.S. (Ed.). *Training for Research in Psychology. The Canadian Opinicon Conference.* Toronto: University of Toronto Press, 1961.

Endler, N.S., Rushton, J.P., & Roediger III, H.L. Productivity and scholarly impact (citations) of British, Canadian, and U.S. Departments of Psychology (1975). *American Psychologist*, 1978, 33, 1064–1082.

Gwynne-Timothy, J.R.W. *Western's First Century*. London, Ontario. The University of Western Ontario, 1978. ISBN #0-7714-0014-4.

Liddy, R.B. Why students fail in psychology. *Bulletin of the Canadian Psychological Association*, 1946, *4*, 68–78.

MacLeod, R.B. *Psychology in Canadian Universities and Colleges*. Canadian Social Science Research Council, Ottawa, 1955.

Neal, Leola E. R.B. Liddy, Ph.D., L.L.D., H.L.F. *The Canadian Psychologist*, 1962, *3a*, 11.

Turner, G.H. Oral History Transcript. Public Archives of Canada, Ottawa, February 15, 1972.

Wright, Mary J. Psychology at Western. *The Canadian Psychologist*, 1963, *4a*, 1–4.

Wright, Mary J. CPA: The first ten years. *The Canadian Psychologist*, 1974, *15*, 112–131.

Further Reading

Anonymous – Psychologists in Profile: Mary Jean Wright, *The Ontario Psychologist*, 1976, *8*, 62–64.

See also notes in the *Canadian Psychologist*, 1961, *2*, 32–33; 1962, *3*, 11; 1963, *4*, 15–18; 1963, *4*, 123; 1967, *8a*, 371–374; 1967, *8a*, 134–135 and also in the *O.P.A. Quarterly*, 1959, *12*, 41; 1963, *16*, 23.

APPENDIX

Psychology 20

A Memorandum to Supplement Chapter I of Woodworth

1. *The Subject Matter of Psychology*

Psychology is defined as the scientific study of the activities of living beings. These activities are of three general sorts: conscious activities, unconscious mental activities and behavioral activities.

What are conscious activities? Seeing, hearing, tasting and other similar processes involving the use of sense organs are conscious activities. Recalling, imagining, reasoning and other responses akin to these are also conscious activities. Our emotional experiences – being afraid, being angry, being happy, etc., – are likewise included under the heading of conscious activities. Conscious activities, it is evident, are those of which we are aware. In other words to be conscious is to be aware. When we are unconscious, as in dreamless sleep or when deeply anesthetized, none of these processes is present.

Unconscious activities may be purely physical, such as the changes or processes which characterize any inanimate object at any given time. The sun, a stone, a drop of water, each is a complicated pattern of molecular activity. But there is unconscious activity which is intimately related to our conscious life and to our behavior. The information we have acquired but of which at the moment we are not aware, the abilities, the habits, the attitudes which are ours but which are not put into practice, or which we are not manifesting at any given time are a part of our psychological equipment. These activities – for they are activities – and all other such data, learned or unlearned, influencing intimately our conscious life and our behavior make up the second broad subdivision of the subject matter of psychology. These processes are sometimes denoted by the term the unconscious or the subconscious mind. It should always be remembered, however, that the phrase, the unconscious mind, is properly only a name standing for the activities just mentioned. It leads to confusion and error to suppose that the unconscious mind is either a container for the unconscious mental activities or a force that produces them.

If one asks in what sense these activities of which we are not conscious are a part of us, the appropriate answer is that they are physiological patterns within the organism. Information we acquired long ago which we still have and of which we are not now conscious is ours because it is a part of our nervous system. Connections among nerve cells in the cortex of the cerebrum of the brain have been established in the learning process and these brain patterns we retain. Sometimes muscles and glands are involved in these patterns. That would obviously be true in the case of many habits and emotional attitudes. Those patterns, then, within the organism which are intimately related to our conscious activities and to our behavior are the unconscious mental activities that the psychologist studies.

The conscious and the unconscious mental activities together constitute what is properly called the mind. It should not be forgotten, however, that the mind, for the psychologist, is not the name of a thing or force or substance. It is nothing other than a class term to denote these actually occurring processes, the ones called conscious and the ones called unconscious mental.

Besides these mental activities the psychologist studies, in the third place, the various movements that living beings manifest – their behavior. The rat trying to thread a maze, the child learning to walk, the human adult gesticulating, operating a machine, playing golf – all this is part of the subject matter of psychology. These activities are commonly called behavioral activities.

The psychologist, then, studies the activities of living beings and these are of the three general sorts just mentioned. Ordinarily of course, these activities take place not at different times but simultaneously. When we analyse the complex response of a living being to a stimulating situation we may discover that some of the constituents of his response are conscious, some unconscious mental, and some behavioral.

Psychology cannot adequately be defined as the science of the mind or as the science of behavior. It studies both mental processes and behavioral processes. Certainly it must not be thought of as the study of the soul or even of the mind if these be regarded as mysterious, occult entities differing from but in some way producing mental activities. The psychologist studies actually occurring processes. These, as has been said, may be classified as mental (including conscious activities and unconscious mental activities) and behavioral.

2. *The Method of Psychology*

Psychology studies its subject matter scientifically. This implies careful observation, including experimentation where possible, the formation of hypotheses (possible explanations for the observed data), the elaboration of these hypotheses (working out their consequences), and their testing by further observation. It is the use of this general method that makes any study scientific.

Observation in psychology may be regarded from various points of view. It may be subjective (introspection) or objective. Subjective observation is the observation of one's own conscious activities. When one attends to his memory of the events of yesterday he is using subjective observation. Objective observation is observation of behavior whether of lower animals, one's self, or others.

Observation may be experimental or non-expeimental. In experimental observation the conditions are under control. In observing we may attend to either the qualitative or the quantitative phases of objects. Mathematical techniques tend to make quantitative observation precise and exact.

The genetic (or developmental) method of observation and the case history method are other important types of observation. Psychologists, as later chapters in Woodworth indicate, make much use, too, of the interview and the rating-scale. The latter is one method of recording graphically the results of observation. The questionnaire and standardized tests are also psychological methods of observation. These all have their limitations but they are important types of observing, and they provide data for investigation and possible explanation. Without both observation and the use of hypotheses progress in the science of psychology would be impossible.

Chapter 6

Psychology at McMaster

by

P. Lynn Newbigging*

The Department of Psychology at McMaster came into formal existence on July 1, 1958.[1] At that time the departments of the University were grouped into two colleges, University College which included the humanities and social sciences, and Hamilton College which included the physical and biological sciences and engineering. On its formation, the Department of Psychology was located in University College. This was a matter of some disappointment to those of us here at the time (D.W. Carment, L.J. Kamin, P.L. Newbigging) since it was our intention to emphasize experimental psychology in the development of the Department and it seemed to us that the accomplishment of this would be facilitated were we viewed as one of the natural sciences and administratively grouped with them. This administrative arrangement was in fact achieved in 1962[2] and thereby hangs a tale whose telling I will delay for the moment until some background has been provided.

The early history of psychology at McMaster probably exhibits many points of similarity to that at other universities. The subject has been taught here since 1888, the year following the granting of the University's charter by the Ontario Legislature. Through the early decades the courses in psychology were offered by the Department of Philosophy until, in 1947, that department was renamed the Department of Philosophy and Psychology. The reasons for this re-naming seem not to be a matter of record but presumably reflect the intention of the chancellor and other academic administrators to strengthen the work in psychology beyond the two undergraduate courses then offered. It is recorded in the

* Professor Newbigging joined the Faculty of McMaster University in 1955 and was the Chairman of the Department of Psychology there from 1958 to 1964, from 1968 to 1972 and again from 1981–

University Senate minutes of the meeting of February, 1946,[3] as part of a discussion of faculty needs, that a full-time teacher of psychology should be appointed. The background of both members of the Department of Philosophy who were then teaching the psychology courses (Introductory and Social) was in theology and philosophy.

In the event, it wasn't until 1953 that R.H. Nicholson was appointed to the full-time faculty, the first person trained as a psychologist ever to be so appointed. Nicholson was tempted away from the University by the Ontario Hydro in 1955, but during his two years here he increased the number of the under-graduate courses from two to four[4] as the beginning towards the introduction of an undergraduate degree in psychology, and in other ways laid the groundwork for further development. I was appointed in 1955 to replace Nicholson. Significant dates and events of the immediately subsequent years are: 1957, the establishment of an Honours B.A. programme; 1958, authorization to offer the M.A. degree; 1959, authorization to offer the Ph.D. degree.[5] In 1963 the first two Ph.D. degrees in psychology were conferred by the University while in the period 1959 to 1963 inclusive, twenty M.A. degrees were conferred.[6]

In these changed days when proposed Ph.D. programmes in Ontario universities must survive planning and quality assessments before being considered by the government for funding, it is amusing to note that in 1959 when our Ph.D. programme was authorized by the University the Department had been in existence for only one year and had four faculty members (A.H. Black, D.W. Carment, L.J. Kamin and P.L. Newbigging), two of whom were new assistant professors (Black had been appointed in 1958 and Carment had completed his Ph.D. and had just been promoted from Instructor), and two newly promoted to Associate Professor. It is doubtful that a proposal from such a group to offer Ph.D. studies would receive serious consideration today.

Since 1959 the Department has grown at a rate of slightly more than one additional faculty member each year to reach its present size of twenty-four. Graduate student numbers have also grown and in recent years have stabilized at approximately fifty. The teaching and research interests of the faculty, now and in the past, are fairly reflected in the following tabulation by field of the M.A. and Ph.D. theses written by students in the Department over the years 1959 to the spring of 1976. It will be noted from the table that there are no theses on applied topics and this represents the outcome of a deliberate decision taken early in the department's life that we would develop an exclusively experimental department and thus concentrate our resources rather than spread them over a wide range of subject matter. It has long been my view that experimental and applied psychology are almost distinct disciplines,

TABLE I   M.A. and Ph.D. theses by field, 1959–1976

Type of Subject	Field of Psychology	M.A.	Ph.D.	
Human	Cognitive	9	3	
	Developmental	4	3	
	Learning	6	—	
	Perception & Psychophysics	12	12	
	Physiological	3	1	
	Social	5	3	
		39	22	61
Animal	Animal Behaviour	4	2	
	Learning	18	14	
	Perception	2	3	
	Physiological	18	13	
		42	32	74
	Totals	81	54	135

based on different values and with different objectives, and that each would prosper better if these differences were acknowledged by administrative separation.

This decision to concentrate faculty resources in experimental psychology was perhaps particularly important because it was coupled with another one; that was to keep the Department as small as possible given our responsibility to provide a broad education in psychology to undergraduate students whose numbers here as elsewhere burgeoned during the 1960's. The Department is still relatively small compared to those in other universities of comparable size but large enough, in our view, to provide viable groups with overlapping interests in the various fields of experimental psychology.

Let me go back now and describe chronologically those people and events that gave early direction to the development of the work in psychology here, a direction that I believe is preserved in the Department today.

The first influence of significance was undoubtedly that exerted by R.B. MacLeod whose wisdom and advice many of us have had occasion to value over the years. I had met MacLeod while I was at the University of

New Brunswick (1953–55). He visited there as he did other Canadian departments in the course of his survey of Canadian psychology for the Social Science Research Council.[7] One of the first things I did on my arrival at McMaster was to write to him to ask for his advice, particularly on setting up an undergraduate curriculum, but also more generally on the development of a department. The upshot was that he invited me to visit him at Cornell and he arranged introductions for me to the departments at Bryn Mawr, Bucknell, and the University of Pennsylvania. It was his thought that we could more effectively discuss matters of curriculum and department development face to face. The visits to the Bryn Mawr and Bucknell departments were particularly instructive since they each had ten to twelve faculty members, a size to which it seemed, at that time, McMaster might aspire.

These visits took place in November 1956. What specifically came of them is now lost to my memory except that, with MacLeod's encouragement, we set up here an undergraduate curriculum modeled on the Wolfle Report.[8] Over the next few years MacLeod remained a source of considerable help, particularly in the recruitment of faculty.

Of course, the most significant influences in the development of any department are those exerted by the members of its faculty. On those grounds there is no question that the nature of McMaster's Department owes a very great deal to D.W. Carment and L.J. Kamin who were both appointed in 1957 as Lecturer and Assistant Professor, respectively. The three of us formed a close working relationship from the beginning and were able always to represent psychology's needs to the administration with one voice.

At the time of his appointment, Carmet had just completed the residence requirements for his Ph.D. at the University of Toronto where he worked with Ketchum and Joyner. He completed his dissertation at McMaster and established a laboratory for work in experimental social psychology.

Kamin had completed his Ph.D. at Harvard in 1954 with R.L. Solomon and that same year came to Canada as a research associate with Bindra at McGill where he remained for one year. In 1955, on Julian Blackburn's invitation, he went to Queen's as a research associate and remained through 1956–57 as an Assistant Professor.

I met Kamin in Kingston in the fall of 1955 and again at the C.P.A. meeting in Ottawa in 1956. We had corresponded in the interim with a view to his moving to McMaster in the fall of 1956. McMaster was slow in taking the administrative action necessary to bring this about. At that time McMaster was a Baptist university with an eminent theologian, G.P. Gilmour, as its Chancellor and President. As was generally the case in denominational universities, the president had the ultimate authority in all matters, holding only those consultations which he deemed necessary and desirable. This was the situation in those years at McMaster and while Gilmour exercised his authority with wisdom and charity, exercise it he did.

In particular, he reserved final decision in all cases of faculty appointment. During 1955–56 he was heavily preoccupied by negotiations with the Baptist Convention of Ontario and Quebec which culminated in McMaster becoming a secular institution in 1957. The consequence was that we were not in a position to make Kamin an offer until the late spring of 1956 and his feelings of responsibility to Queen's, and I think also his affection for Blackburn, led him to decline. Continued negotiations resulted in his acceptance of an offer from us and his arrival here in the fall of 1957. He remained here eleven years, including a term as chairman, until enticed away in 1968 to chair the Department at Princeton.

Kamin brought with him an active programme of research which he vigorously pursued over the years. He was already gaining recognition as an accomplished experimental psychologist and without doubt that fact added credibility to our claim within the University that psychology was a science and, for administrative purposes, would be most appropriately grouped with other science departments. As I have already noted, that arrangement did ultimately come about and I now turn to a description of the events that were responsible for it.

Through the 1950's and into the early 1960's the undergraduate curriculum at McMaster, particularly in science, was rigidly prescribed leaving students few options even in their freshman year. We were anxious to attract some students with an interest in science into honours psychology but the curriculum made it impossible for the students in Year I Science to take our introductory course and so develop an interest in the subject. This situation we set about to try to change.

As alluded to above, the departments of the University at that time were organized administratively into two colleges: University College which included the humanities and social sciences, and Hamilton College which included the sciences and engineering. Each college had its own principal who reported directly to the president. The faculty, however, cut across this division and met as a single Faculty of Arts and Science which was administered by a senior dean. It was into a meeting of this faculty in the winter of 1958 that we introduced a motion that an opportunity be made available to science students to take first year psychology. The proposal sparked a lively debate, finding considerable support among the humanists and social scientists but none at all among the scientists. The attitude of the scientists was simple; it was that psychology was not a science and therefore courses in psychology did not belong in a science curriculum. The arguments they brought forward in support of their view were undoubtedly shaped by their own backgrounds in psychology which were dated by two decades and consisted of one or two courses taught for the most part by philosophers and theologians. The general tone was represented by a senior member of the chemistry department who prefaced his remarks in opposition by defining psychology for us as "the study of individual souls" (I think a definition of sociology was implied), surely not the stuff of science. Our motion was not voted on at that meeting but at a later, poorly attended one, when it carried twenty-three in favour and nineteen opposed.[9] The amusing thing was that the twenty-three in favour, apart from ourselves, were all humanists or social scientists; those opposed were scientists to a man. Thus, by being rejected by both sides, we got what we wanted. At a meeting of the Senate in October, 1959 this faculty decision was approved and science students were from then on able to complete their Year I which required physics, chemistry and mathematics with a choice of two from among biology, geology, a second mathematics and psychology.

Although initially relatively few science students availed themselves of the opportunity we had won for them the victory was by no means a hollow one, as at the present time some 20% of our honour students come from Year I Science. Further, the appearance of Introductory psychology as an acceptable Year I Science course facilitated the later acceptance of a B.Sc. Honour[10] stream to accompany the B.A. stream, and as well paved the way for our administrative move from University to Hamilton College in 1962 and thus full acceptance as a science department.

This was an important event in shaping the subsequent development of the Department. The problem was, given our exclusive emphasis on experimental psychology, the costs in terms of space and equipment were high and it was difficult to convince administrators with a background in the humanities that these facilities were essential if the discipline was to prosper. Our move to Hamilton College meant that we were responsible to a principal with a training in science and our requirements were readily understandable to him. When in 1967 the Faculty of Arts and Science was divided into separate faculties, our membership in the Faculty of Science, where we are today, makes retrospectively our earlier petitioning all the more wise.

Over the years the Department has been favoured by strong administrative support which enabled us to appoint in the early years some faculty who had already established reputations in research—W.H. Heron (1960), H.M. Jenkins (1963), A.B. Kristofferson and R.M. Pritchard (1965)—and this aided immeasurably in establishing a productive teaching and research atmosphere which enabled us to attract and hold the new Ph.D.'s to whom our major recruiting effort was addressed. Over the now eighteen years since the Department was founded, only eleven of those appointed to the faculty have left of their own accord for other places.

This relative stability of the Department can be accounted for in part by our slow growth which enabled new members to be integrated with those of us already here, in part by an equitable policy by the University in salaries and promotions, and perhaps most importantly, by the provision by the University of adequate space and equipment for the conduct of our work.

As with other departments our original space was in a temporary Army H-hut originally moved onto the campus to accommodate the influx of veterans in the immediate post-war years. As the Department grew, other temporary space was acquired and modified to our use. Such modified space can rarely provide the optimum in sound and temperature control needed for experimental psychology and in the mid-sixties we began to formulate plans for a permanent building. These plans were approved in 1967, the ground was broken in 1968 and we occupied the building in August, 1970. It provides some 57,000 sq. ft. of temperature- and sound-controlled usable space for research, offices and some classrooms, and has proved to be a splendidly workable building.

Last year we recruited our 24th member which fills the building according to the plan of its original construction. There seems here to be a fortunate conspiracy of circumstance since given the economic climate of the universities today, little if any expansion of faculty seems needed or, if needed, is economically possible. To maintain an intellectually viable department during what appears to be an extended no-growth period provides as much of a challenge as did the development of the Department in the expansionist 60's and early 70's. We will need all of our ingenuity to meet it.

References and Notes

[1] This was accomplished by a vote of the University Senate at a meeting held on January 28, 1958 and is recorded in the minutes of that meeting.

[2] The transfer was made on the decision of the then President and Vice-Chancellor, H.G. Thode, and made known to all faculty and administrative officers in a memorandum dated May 11, 1962. The significant paragraphs in that memorandum read as follows:

"During the past two years the transfer of this department has again been actively discussed and recently, for the purpose of curriculum, it has been agreed to include this department in the natural sciences division. As many activities of this department are closely allied to the life sciences, and because the research people of this department secure their support from the same national agencies as do the members of our present science departments, it seems logical to follow the academic pattern and include psychology with the natural sciences for administrative purposes.

Accordingly, effective July 1, 1962, this department will be transferred from University College to Hamilton College."

[3] University Senate Minutes, February 14, 1946.

[4] See McMaster University Calendars 1953–54 and 1954–58.

[5] The details of these programmes are to be found in the undergraduate and graduate calendars of these years.

[6] The names of these students are recorded in the records of the School of Graduate Studies.

[7] MacLeod, Robert B. *Psychology in Canadian Universities and Colleges*. Ottawa: Canadian Social Science Research Council, 1955,

[8] Wolfle, Dael (Ed.), *Improving Undergraduate Education in Psychology*. New York: Macmillan, 1952.

[9] These motions are to be found in the Minutes of the Faculty of Arts and Science dated December 17, 1958 and May 28, 1959.

[10] First described in the 1962–63 McMaster University Calendar.

Further Readings

Newbigging, P.L. "A Note on Psychology at McMaster". *The Canadian Psychologist*, 1956, 5, 76–77.

Newbigging, P.L. "Psychology at McMaster". *The Canadian Psychologist*, 1960, 1, 106–110.

PART II

The French Universities
of Central Canada

Introduction: An Overview*

The first two French universities to offer training in modern psychology, as distinct from philosophy, were the University of Ottawa and the University of Montreal. During the 19th century, like their English counterparts, both taught psychology as a relatively undifferentiated aspect of philosophy. The outstanding difference in this era was, however, that they held to a Thomistic philosophy rather than to Scottish Realism or British Idealism. The 1880 Calendar of the University of Ottawa indicates that students learned about the subject of mental philosophy through the works of Thomas Aquinus, Aristotle, and the French philosophers of Europe. Nevertheless, probably because it was surrounded, at that time, by a larger and more dominant English-speaking community, the University of Ottawa also acquainted its students with at least some of the trends in English mental philosophy.

Until well into the 20th century, the French Canadian philosophers maintained the Thomistic approach (Shevenell, 1948). Unlike the English Canadian philosophers, with their protestant heritage, they perpetuated a Roman Catholic outlook in the study of man. They intentionally resisted the forces of secularization and were reluctant to grant the burgeoning area of psychology a status independent of philosophy or religion. Although independent "Institutes" of psychology were established at Ottawa in 1941, and at Montreal in 1942, before separate departments of psychology were established in most of the English universities other than McGill and Toronto, both continued to foster a Roman Catholic orientation. Leery of positivistic experimentation the French Canadian universities were largely uninfluenced by the American behaviorism of the 1930's and 40's. However, in the 1940's some experimental research was begun in a small laboratory setting at the University of Ottawa and in the 1950's such work was also begun at the University of Montreal.

In general, the emphasis on clinical and applied psychology has been greater in the French than in the English Canadian universities. Through

* The assistance of Tory Hoff in the preparation of this overview is gratefully acknowledged.

the influence of R.H. Shevenell's Christian Personalism, most psychology students at Ottawa, for many years, trained to become psychological practitioners. Through the influence of Father Noël Mailloux and Adrien Pinard the same was later true at Montreal. Research remained secondary, and the heavy teaching loads that the professors were frequently required to carry made research virtually impossible. Much of the psychological research done in the French Canadian universities has been and is, increasingly in recent years, focused on specific needs in French Canada. This has been particularly evident in the area of psychometrics. Indigenous tests have been developed and other tests have been translated and standardized for use in the French Canadian setting. The research effort in this area has been substantial.

During the 1960's the number of psychologists interested in basic, rather than applied, experimental research, was increased at both Ottawa and Montreal. As a result, conflicts soon developed between these new scientists and the entrenched applied, professional psychologists and these proved difficult to resolve. By the end of the 1960's however, experimental psychology in the French Canadian universities, especially at the University of Montreal, appeared to have established a firm base. The work of David Bélanger in physiological psychology played an important role in this development. However, the emphasis in the department continued to be in applied research and professional training.

Reference

Shevenell, R.H. The teaching of psychology in Roman Catholic institutions in Canada. *Canadian Journal of Psychology*, 1948, 2, 112–113.

Chapter 7

Psychology at Ottawa

by

Anthony Paskus and *Joseph De Koninck**

Even if we accept Edwin G. Boring's claim that history moves on with its accustomed gradualness, we can still detect certain "critical" events that turn the movement in one particular direction rather than any other. For Psychology at the University of Ottawa the date October 4, 1941, represents such a "crucial" point because, on that day, the Institute of Psychology was born (Shevenell, 1946). On that day as well, the University administration authorized the title *Institute of Psychology* for the publication of the *Otis-Ottawa* Test. However, a whole stream of other important events preceded this one.

Not surprisingly, Psychology as a formal subject was introduced at Ottawa through its program in philosophy and consisted essentially of the coverage of "rational" psychology. In 1932, in the Faculty of Philosophy, a course described as a brief epistemology and history of psychology was offered as a complement to the one in so-called rational psychology.

The development of scientific psychology within faculties of philosophy in Catholic universities was the result of the reform of Canonical Faculties by the Sacred Congregation of Seminaries and Universities in 1935. Students in faculties of philosophy were required to include in their programs the scientific subjects that parallelled the various divisions of philosophy. The University of Ottawa was the first non-Italian Canonical

---

* Professor Paskus was a member of the faculty in psychology at the University of Ottawa, from 1973 to 1977. During his time there he worked on the preparation of a book on the history of psychology at Ottawa, and prepared an early draft of this chapter. Joseph De Koninck, director of the School of Psychology at Ottawa since 1978, expanded and updated the manuscript. The authors wish to thank Mary Wright, Henry Edwards and Maurice Chagon for their suggestions on earlier drafts of the chapter.

University to comply with the new requirements and, as a result, "scientific psychology" was developed as a foundation for the study of "rational psychology". The Faculty of Arts also contributed to this process. In 1933–1934, its academic calendar identified professor Raoul Leblanc as a professor of "experimental"[1] psychology. Two years later, another professor, Gustave Sauvé, received the title and the program in psychology was expanded to include three courses. The first (100a) was an introductory course, which dealt with matters such as the history and methods in psychology, while the third course (300a) included subjects such as child psychology, typology, and the psychology of the "noncivilized" people. Professor Leblanc used De La Vaissière's *Eléments de Psychologie Expérimentale*. This text book was written for those who were engaged in the study of philosophy. It aimed, therefore, at systematic presentation of the principal results obtained by the experimenters. Father Sauvé, however, wrote his own text: *Eléments de Psychologie Expérimentale*, – 112 pages, no publication date given.

Things continued unchanged until Father Sauvé was succeeded by Father Raymond H. Shevenell in 1938. Then, events began moving swiftly forward. On September 8th of that year, a laboratory of psychology was authorized by Father Joseph Hébert, the Rector of the University. It consisted of a room (15 × 45) taken over from the Department of Physics in the University's oldest building on campus at 135 Wilbrod. Shevenell had to furnish and equip the room himself as no funds were allocated for this purpose. He "borrowed" the lumber from the community's wood-work shop and made tables, chairs, and the shelves for the library. Most of the instruments like mazes, rotating chair, colour wheel and even a signal generator were made by the founder's skillful hands. The necessary material for these instruments was found either in the junkyard or bought in separate parts and then put together by the laboratory's "mechanic" Father Shevenell. On January 1, 1939, it was opened for experimentation. The following year, each student in Shevenell's class of 26 had an opportunity to play the role of experimenter in psychological demonstrations (Shevenell, 1946, p. 234–235).

The importance of Shevenell's laboratory stems not only from its role in the development of psychology at Ottawa, but also because in that same room the Canadian Psychological Association was conceived, if not born. In December of 1938, the American Association for the Advancement of Science (AAAS) held its annual meeting in Ottawa. The Canadian psychologists, being in charge of one section of the programme, held their own meetings. During one of those meetings at 135 Wilbrod, the decision was made to form an Association of Canadian Psychologists.[2]

From "Institute" to "School" to "Faculty" to "School"

The efforts to establish psychology as a unit in the University were culminated by the official foundation of the *Institute of Psychology* in 1941. It functioned first within the Faculty of Arts. By 1941–1942, its offerings doubled to six courses under the heading Positive Psychology. The following year's calendar listed as many as 14 different courses under the heading of Scientific Psychology, including four courses in experimental psychology with laboratory, and three courses in methodology, including statistics. This indicated to the old guard (the philosophers) that Shevenell meant business in making his "new" psychology really new. In 1949, the School became the Department of Psychology and Education in the Graduate School of the University. It had eleven full time professors and 62 graduate students (52 M.A. and 10 Ph.D.). By 1950–1951, 23 Psychology-Education courses were offered covering more specialized fields in Psychology. In 1955, the Department was elevated to the School of Psychology and Education. Ten years later (1965), it was transformed into the Faculty of Psychology and Education of the "new" University of Ottawa.[3] In 1967, however, under pressure from the Ontario Department of Education, a separate Faculty of Education was formed, but from 1967 to 1977, Psychology at Ottawa kept the status of a Faculty which provided unique financial and academic autonomy. For a few years it even organized itself into departments, and in 1970 had four intimately linked departments: General-Experimental (director, L. Dayhaw), Physiological Psychology (director, W. Barry), Child (director A. Sidlauskas), and Clinical-Counselling (director, G. Chagnon).

Shevenell retired as dean in 1973. He was replaced by Henry Edwards and, because of fear that the departmental structure would generate unwanted divisions, a "programmes" structure was reestablished in 1974.

In 1977, following the Senate's reform of the Institution's academic structure, the Faculty of Psychology became a School of Psychology within the Faculty of Social Sciences. The Dean of Psychology became Associate Dean of Social Sciences and Director of the School of Psychology. While a school at Ottawa is now much like a department, it has added autonomy in the development of agreements with external agencies for the benefit of its programmes.

This almost record number of changes in academic structure for Psychology has been equalled by an almost equivalent number of changes in physical settings. The creation of the professional training units and the expansion of the School to the Faculty required additional space. Lack of space on the University's central campus led to the expatriation in 1969 of the Faculty's administration, its main laboratories and its own library, to the former Grand Seminary of the Diocese of Ottawa (three miles south of the main Campus). By that time, Psychology was spread into nine different locations on and off campus. The erection of Lamoureux Hall in 1978 allowed Psychology to be repatriated on campus, where it is however still spread over four locations. The psychology and education library collection has now been integrated into the main library on campus.

The Pioneers

In 1954 Robert MacLeod presented a report to the Canadian Psychological Association on his survey of Psychology in Canada, and in it, according to the *Chronique Universitaire*, concluded that "quatre universités au Canada peuvent prétendre entraîner des psychologues dans l'ordre suivant: l'Université de Toronto, l'Université d'Ottawa, l'Université McGill, l'Université de Montréal. Cette classification est fondée sur quatre facteurs: 1) le nombre et la valeur des professeurs; 2) l'organisation pratique d'une riche bibliothèque spécialisée; 3) l'outillage adéquat du laboratoire, 4) le fonctionnement des cliniques; le Centre d'Orientation et le Centre Psycho-Social."

Shevenell later noted in the minutes of a meeting: "Quand l'Institut fut officiellement classé deuxième au Canada, le personnel auquel l'Association donna du poids fut: R.H. Shevenell, A. Sidlauskas, V. Szyrynski et L.T. Dayhaw". Indeed, the remarkable achievements of the Institute and the School of Psychology were the result of the determination of several pioneers. Lawrence Dayhaw who obtained his Ph.D. from Louvain was the expert in experimental psychology and statistics. His "Manuel de statistiques" has been used extensively by francophone students in Psychology and Education throughout French Canada. He became professor Emeritus in 1974. Agatha Sidlauskas dominated the development of the Child Clinical area. She established the Child Guidance Centre (later Child Study Centre) in 1953 and persuaded the University and the government to erect the magnificent six-story building which has housed it since 1969. She headed the Centre until 1979 when she retired. Victor Szyrynsky, who retired in 1979, was for many years the professor of Psychotherapies. His approach was that of systematic eclecticism. To those names, one must add that of the late Paplauskas-Ramunas who held the chair of history. Finally, one of the first graduates from psychology at Ottawa, Maurice Chagnon, joined the pioneers and became Shevenell's right-hand man for a quarter of a century. He was very active in the Guidance Centre which Shevenell created in 1942. He introduced within the centre services that were to lead to the development of the Child Guidance Centre, the student Counselling Centre, and the University's student placement office. Having served as the University's Vice Rector Academic from 1965 to 1977, Chagnon has since returned to his duties in the School of Psychology.

The dedication of these pioneers went beyond their teaching. At the beginning, faculty salaries were very low. Shevenell, being a member of the Oblate Order received no salary at all. He lived on an allowance. In 1942 his assistant, Maurice Chagnon, agreed to work for $50.00 a month. Dr. Dayhaw, Dr. A. Sidlauskas and all the teaching staff (as well as the secretary, Juliette Morisset) made financial sacrifices for the good of the Institute.

The programmes and their aims

It is interesting to note that from the very beginning, undergraduate courses in Psychology were offered by the Faculty of Arts and not by Psychology even though the courses were offered by psychology professors. In 1963, when Arts started to offer a B.A. with concentration in psychology, it asked a professor from psychology, Raymond Vaillancourt, to coordinate the courses. It was only in 1973 that the Faculty of Psychology introduced its own B.A. with concentration in psychology and in 1976 a four-year honours programme. In the previous years, the efforts had clearly focused on graduate training. Besides graduate degrees in Education, the Master of Psychology (M.Ps.), the Master of Arts in Psychology (M.A.) and the Doctorate (Ph.D.) with specialisation in experimental, clinical, and child clinical psychology were awarded.

Enrolments in these graduate programmes increased very rapidly. From 62 students in 1950, the school increased its graduate enrollments to 410 (152 doctoral and 258 masters) in 1961. Unfortunately, the number of staff did not increase accordingly and this resulted in heavy teaching loads for the 13 full-time professors. Indeed, in some cases, a professor directed 20 theses, taught three or four full courses during the school year and two additional courses in the summer. In this context, it is not surprising that the School's research undertakings assumed lower priority than teaching or the supervision of graduate students. When in 1965 the University became a publicly funded institution the additional funding allowed an increase in full-time teaching staff to 44. Greater emphasis on undergraduate training and staff research has lead in recent years to a voluntary decrease in graduate enrollment.

Throughout its history, although the School has offered graduate training in the whole spectrum of psychology, the bulk of its students and staff have been in the professional areas and its major contribution has been in the production of Canadian psychologists in applied areas. For three consecutive years (1962–1965), of the total number of Ph.D.s in psychology produced in Canada, 30% to 36% were from the Ottawa School of Psychology.[4] For the period 1961–1970 its share of Canadian doctorates in psychology was over 18%.

The principal aim of the School was to prepare scientists-professionals. It followed, though not always with complete success, the general outline of the Boulder model. A unique feature of Ottawa has been the absence of the traditional split between experimental and clinical psychology. This is probably due to the important influence of the founder who himself developed both the experimental and the clinical components of the school, and initially hired as professors a number of his graduates who followed his orientation. This phenomenon is clearly demonstrated by the contribution of William Barry, who was director of the Department of General-experimental Psychology (1976–1974) and subsequently director of the clinical programme (1975–1978) and for years taught both Physiological and Abnormal Psychology. For his teaching, he received the University of Ottawa Teaching Award in 1976.

Another unique feature of Psychology at Ottawa has been the use of internal training units for clinical/counselling internships. Here again, Shevenell was the pioneer. He founded the Guidance Centre in 1942. The Child Guidance Centre followed in 1953 (director, A. Sidlauskas), the Psychological Services in 1965 (director R. Shevenell) and the University Counselling Services in 1965 (director S. Piccinin). While providing services to both the University and the community, these centres also provided practical training for graduate students. Today the value of such units is generally acclaimed, and this model is used by an increasing number of psychology departments.

The Founder: the man and his philosophy

In his 1968 report to the Rector of the University, Shevenell wrote: "From the start, this Faculty chose to formulate a Christian personalism that would respect the human person in all its attributes". Christian personalism, in its theoretical form, meant to Shevenell the Thomistic philosophical anthropology. He was thoroughly at home with it, and appreciated its emphasis on the whole man with his biological, psychological and spiritual dimensions. He always insisted that the study of man should utilize the insights of a variety of disciplines, including psychology, philosophy and theology. In the 1930's and 1940's, this message sounded like heresy to the "old guard" (the philosophers) and an anachronism to those in psychology who believed only in "the assignment of numerals to objects or events according to the rules". He was a humanist at heart. He became personally and deeply involved in the Guidance Centre, where he could put into practice whatever he or others had discovered in theory.

His philosophy also predominated in his teaching and reflected itself in his attitudes toward his students and staff. According to a former student: "In class, he was lively and imaginative. Outside the classroom, he was part of the group. The first among equals." Reports from former students almost unanimously portray the staff of the Institute as being extremely approachable. The word "appointment" was unknown in the student-teacher relationship. Openness, accessibility and warmth pervaded the whole school.

With the arrival of a number of staff members from other universities, the School has lost its religious orientation and has come to resemble most other departments of Psychology. However, Shevenell's[5] holistic approach and the closeness of professors and students in the training units prevails. In the later years, efforts have been made to strengthen the experimental components of the graduate programmes, while retaining an essential integration of the experimental and the professional. To date, this has succeeded. It will be a continuing challenge for Ottawa to keep it that way.

A Bilingual Psychology

Consistent with the commitment of the University of Ottawa, the Institute of Psychology has been bilingual from the beginning. It has contributed to bilingualism mainly in the area of psychometrics. In the early forties, diagnostic tests for French-speaking Canadians were badly needed. Immediately, the Institute moved into this virgin field bringing with it all its resources. In 1942–1943, of the class of 24 students, all except two were working on test construction, or the translation and adaptation of tests to the French-speaking population in Canada. Tests translated and adapted by Shevenell and his students included personality inventories such as the Allport-Vernon-Shevenell, Bell-Ottawa, Bernreuter-Ottawa, Brown-Ottawa, Examen pour le Personnel, Mes Goûts et mes Aspirations, as well as the Otis-Ottawa and the Ottawa-Wechsler intelligence tests, and other instruments. The Ottawa-Wechsler project was initiated and carried through by Maurice Chagnon with the help of L.T. Dayhaw, V. Szyrynski and Eva Labrosse. This project was financed by a grant from the Federal Department of National Health and Welfare. This grant was the first large research grant given to one of the University's units. The Fowler-Parmenter-Ottawa Self-scoring Interest Record was translated and adapted under the direction of L. Isabelle. These tests were and still are being used. As of March 31, 1976, 6,040,529 copies had been sold, including manuals and study samples.

While Ottawa was inactive in this area during the fifties, a psychometric lab has recently been revived and is developing bilingual Canadian versions of tests such as the Otis-Lennon School Ability Test.

Research on bilingualism and cross-cultural comparisons is also actively conducted, and Ottawa has proved to be an idealy suited location for such research.

Bilingualism in course offerings has presented a real challenge. The undergraduate student population is approximately 60% French and 40% English. At the graduate level, it has generally been the opposite. At the undergraduate level, separate French and English sections of each course have been offered, while at the graduate level the approach has been to offer bilingual courses, meaning that both languages are used in class. In practice, this approach was less successful. Because certain professors could not teach bilingually, and because many unilingual English students were admitted to the graduate programmes, the tendency was to use English, on the grounds that most francophones "understood English"! Recently, major efforts have been made to recruit more bilingual staff and to offer more courses in French at the graduate level. A recent revision of the graduate programme calls for the availability of compulsory courses in both languages. With its intent to seek OPA and APA accreditations, Ottawa may very well be the first university to offer such accredited programmes in French.

Concluding Remarks

In the process of sketching the history of Psychology at Ottawa, certain conclusions have been reached.

1. From the beginning Psychology at Ottawa developed a strong professional character. It made a considerable contribution to psychology in Canada by preparing a great number of clinicians. In spite of its recently increased emphasis on experimental research, its strength is still in the clinical area and is likely to remain there.

2. Albert Wellek, one of the renowned West German psychologists, recently stated that "without philosophy, every psychology is just a collection of empty facts". If the next revolution in psychology attempts to connect these 'empty facts' with the aid of philosophy, then Ottawa was in the vanguard of this movement. From its inception, it persistently attempted to integrate the philosophical and psychological views of man. Shevenell, the founder, strongly believed that candidates for the graduate school should have a broad and deep humanistic training. His influence prevails.

3. Some Canadian psychologists are beginning to search for a distinctive identity for Canadian psychology. Berry (1974) has suggested that such an identity might be found through the study of problems which are unique in Canada such as French-English biculturalism and bilingualism. The day to day experience of bilingualism and the location of Ottawa place the faculty there in an optimum position to study these problems.

Notes

[1] The term experimental psychology really meant an empirical psychology as opposed to a rational psychology. There was no laboratory experimentation except for a few class demonstrations.

[2] If there is some doubt about CPA's place of birth, there seems to be little doubt about its conception. As K.S. Bernhardt put it, certainly the first signs of pregnancy were visible "here in Ottawa" (K. S. Bernhardt, 1947, p. 52). See also Wright, 1974, p. 114.

[3] In that year, the University of Ottawa became a "public" institution funded by the Government of the Province of Ontario.

[4] This information was taken from *Canadian Graduate Theses*, edited by R. Thompson. National Library of Canada, 1973. It contains, however, some errors of omission.

[5] Shevenell is now Professor Emeritus and is at 71 still actively involved in Graduate Teaching and internship supervision.

References

Bernhardt, K.S. Canadian Psychology – Past, Present and Future. *The Canadian Journal of Psychology*, 1947, *1*, 49–60.

Berry, H.W. Canadian psychology: Some social and applied emphases. *The Canadian Psychologist*, 1974, *15*, 132–139.

MacLeod, R.B. Psychology in Canadian Universities and Colleges. A report to the Canadian Social Science Research Council, 1955.

Shevenell, R.H. L'Institut de Psychologie et le Centre d'Orientation. *Revue de l'Université d'Ottawa*, 1946, *16*, 234.

Wright, M.J. CPA: The first ten years. *The Canadian Psychologist*, 1974, *15*, 112–131.

Further Reading

Anonymous – R.H. Shevenell, *The Canadian Psychologist*, 1959, *8*, 68–69.

Isabelle, Laurent, "La Psychologie A L'Université D'Ottawa". *Canadian Psychologist*, 1968, *9*, 6–12.

Shevenell, R.H. "The School of Psychology and Education of the University of Ottawa". *The Canadian Psychologist*, 1962, *3*, 7–10.

See also notes in *The Canadian Psychologist*, 1965, *6*, 376; 1967, *8a*, 374–380; 1969, *10*, 485 and also in the *Bulletin of the Canadian Psychological Association*, 1943, *3*, 58–60; 1944, *4*, 80–81.

Chapter 8

Psychology at Montreal

by

*Luc Granger**

The development of the "Département de Psychologie" of the "*Université de Montréal*" parallels closely the history and problems of psychology in the province of Quebec. The problems that this department has experienced during its brief history have their origins in two basic facts: linguistic isolation (which has led to problems in recruiting qualified North American staff and in acquiring some renown) and the emphasis which has been placed on regarding psychology as a profession. Yoshi (1970) emphasized the latter problem when he wrote: "In Quebec, a majority of French Canadian psychologists are interested in applied psychology. The experimental research sector is still undeveloped and our universities keep on training practitioners". (p. 377). Appley and Rickwood (1967) had earlier observed: "As it is, the present situation leads to a medium or long term weakening of academic psychology in Quebec. Being ignored in his province and having almost no facilities to do good work, the young graduate, especially the English-speaking one, will tend to emigrate to the U.S. or elsewhere in Canada, where he will find better working conditions". (p. 11). In the following pages, an attempt will be made to give an overview of the development of psychology at the Université de Montréal. This Department has passed through three main developmental phases since its foundation. The ideas, and the men and women responsible for them, will be briefly examined, and an attempt will be made to highlight the department's successes and failures.

---

* Professor Granger joined the Faculty in psychology of the University of Montreal in 1968 and became Director of the Department of Psychology there in 1980.

Birth (1942–1945)

The "Institut de Psychologie" was founded in 1942 by the "*Faculté de Philosophie*" of the "*Université de Montréal*". Its creation was due to the initiative and efforts of Reverend Father Noël Mailloux. He gave it the mission of training "psychologists who will not be simply what is currently called psychotechnicians, but true specialists, able to criticize theories, and facts and to organize them in an harmonious and powerful synthesis in continuity with philosophical knowledge". There is little to tell about this era, except to underline the tremendous work of Noël Mailloux who, during the first three years, was the only full-time professor in the department. He had to build a three-year curriculum with the assistance of ten lecturers. During this period, the *Institut* granted the degrees of *baccalauréat* in psychology after the first year, of *licence* after the second year, and of doctorate after the third year. It is evident that the emphasis was more on curriculum development than on research. The creation of the *Institut de Psychologie*, however, opened the way for scientific psychology and its first permanent appearance among the French-speaking population of the province of Quebec.

Infancy (1946–1963)

During the 17 years between 1946 and 1963 the "Institute" gradually developed its modern image. It was during this phase that research started and that the department won some outside recognition. It began with a slow but gradual increase in the number of staff members, particularly full-time ones, as shown in Table I. From a single member in 1945, the staff increased to five in 1950, and to 19 in 1963. Conversely, the number of lecturers diminished progressively, falling from 21 in 1943 to 7 in 1963. Among the new faculty appointed were Pinard, Bélanger, Lavoie, Clerk, Lussier, Décarie, Laurendeau, Cormier and Cardu who were the principal architects of the department and who contributed most to its reputation.

The curriculum underwent major transformations and began to reflect a preoccupation with the training of professional psychologists. At the program level, research was regarded as one specialization and there were many others of an applied nature. The training model was the well known "scientist-professional" one, which assumes that the applied psychologist must first receive a solid theoretical and scientific training. In the 1945 calendar, it was stated that the main goal of the *Institut* "is to conduct graduate teaching in order to give the students a precise

Table 1

Number of staff members by three year periods

	FP	AS	A	SL	L
1942	1				10
1945	1				21
1948	1	2			20
1951	1	3			20
1954	2	9	3		6
1957	2	8	4		10
1960	3	10	3		8
1963	3	11	3	2	7
1966	6	11	4	8	6
1969	9	6	13	14	25
1972	9	14	27	13	13
1975	13	17	34	7	13
1978	20	26	20	1	15

FP: Full professors
AS: Associate professors
A: Assistant professors
SL: Senior lecturers
L: Lecturers

knowledge of the different areas of psychology and of their application. It is also to encourage the student to do research and practice in these areas". Every student in psychology, whether interested in an academic or a professional career, was required to go through the same basic program of studies.

As early as 1946 the length of the program was extended to 4 years. After the first year, the student was granted a *baccalauréat*, after the second a *licence*, and after the fourth a doctorate. Specialization began gradually, at the doctoral level. For example, from 1953 to 1963, the doctorate was granted only after the student had had one year of professional practice. The 1953 calendar stated: "the fourth year completes the additional program for the doctorate. However, the degree will not be given before the student has completed at least a year of professional practice". In 1954, the length of the *licence* program was extended to two years and that of the doctorate reduced to one year. This was probably due to the fact that many graduates started their professional career immediately after being granted the licence. In 1957, the Department offered ten possible specializations at the doctoral level: experimental psychology, psychometrics and projective techniques, human relations, social psychology and anthropology, clinical psychology, industrial psychology and vocational guidance, delinquency and criminality, religion and ethics, psycho-pedagogy, and finally, military psychology. One may be slightly skeptical as to the degree of specialization which could be offered by a department claiming ten fields of specialization with only 14 full-time staff members and 10 part-time lecturers. This is one of the factors which may have impaired the development of the Department. This situation is attributable to the fact that, at that time, the *Institut de Psychologie* was the only French-speaking department of psychology in Quebec. Consequently, it had to cater to the needs of all professional psychology in the province. Fortunately, this anomaly did not last long, and by 1958, only five areas of specialization were offered, and these were the precursors of the options still provided at the graduate level at the time of writing.

At that time, the *Institut* was also offering certificates of study, the best known of which was the one in psychopedagogy. This certificate, which required three years of study, was created through the joint efforts of the *Université de Montréal* and the *Fondation Richelieu* whose main goal was to promote studies in juvenile delinquency. The program leading to the certificate became autonomous in 1971 with the creation of the *Ecole de Psychoéducation*.

Research at the *Institut* first developed along two main axes: studies in intellectual development and psychophysiology. The studies of intellectual development started in the early fifties out of a preoccupation with psychometrics. A research group led by Barbeau and Pinard was interested in the measurement of intellectual capacities and worked at the construction of an I.Q. test for French Canadians. The result was the development of the "Barbeau-Pinard" general intelligence test which is one of the few intelligence tests specifically designed for the French-speaking population of Canada. A growing desire to understand intellectual functioning led this group to study the various aspects of intelligence. This resulted in the development of the *Test Différentiel d'Intelligence* through the collaboration of Laurendeau, Parent and Guy Lavoie. During the same period Laurendeau and Lavoie designed a general intelligence test for the primary school population. It quickly became apparent, however, to these scientists, that the problem of intellectual measurement had to be studied from the standpoint of a definition of intelligence. Consequently, Pinard and Laurendeau oriented their research toward the study of the development of cognitive functions from the standpoint of the theory of the Swiss psychologist, Jean Piaget. This work led to several publications and, particularly, to a book (Laurendeau and Pinard, 1970) which gave the *Laboratoire d'études des fonctions cognitives*, an international reputation as one of the main research centers working on Piaget's developmental theory.

During the same period, at the instigation of professor Bélanger, and with the collaboration of Dr. Robert B. Malmo from McGill University, the *Institut de Psychologie* began a series of studies on physiological psychology from the standpoint of activation theory. This theory exerted, during the sixties, a considerable influence on the psychophysiological studies of motivation and emotion. The research group of Bélanger (to which Ducharme made a major contribution) began a series of inquiries using mainly animal subjects. This research program reached its peak at the end of the sixties and made an important contribution to the clarification of the concept of physiological activation.

At the end of this period, when professor Adrien Pinard was appointed chairman of the *Institut* to replace Father Noël Mailloux (who had occupied the post for more than 16 years), a series of events occurred which were to lead the Department to an accelerated growth and diversification. Two "political decisions" involving the direction of the Department were to have a major influence on its future development and on the conception of the training of psychologists in Quebec and, to a certain extent, across all Canada.

The first of these was made public in Professor Pinard's presidential address to the Canadian Psychological Association. In his speech, he questioned the universally accepted "scientist-professional" model for psychology. According to Pinard, "the fact is, that the scientific production of the average professional is poor, and I think, along with many others, that this is mainly due to a motivational problem. In fact, it is foolish to expect the average professional to be a scientist at the same time". (Pinard 1964, p. 192). This led Pinard to propose the creation of two types of complementary, but different, training programs for psychologists: one for those interested in professional psychology and one for those interested in academic psychology.

The second political decision was for the *Institut* to play an instrumental role in the creation and in the organization of the Corporation Professionnelle des Psychologues du Québec, whereby psychology, as a profession, would acquire legal status.

Adolescence (1964–1978)

If adolescence is characterized by rapid growth, and a reevaluation of the accepted value system, accompanied by painful anxieties, this is indeed a description applicable to the development of the *Institut* from 1964 to 1976. During this period, there was a rapid increase in the number of staff members and as well important curriculum modifications which reflected a new conception of how psychologists should be trained.

The increase in the number of full-time staff members was mainly a consequence of the growth of the student population. During the sixties, psychology became one of the most popular subjects among the students at the college level. This led to an increase in the number of students applying for admission to the *Institut*. The staff grew from 22 in 1964 to 51 in 1970 and to 66 in 1978. This represents a 300% increase in a little more than 10 years.

In 1963 Professor David Bélanger was appointed chairman of the *Institut*. He immediately introduced a series of modifications in the curriculum intended to represent the two main goals of the Department: the training of professional psychologists and of academics. In 1963, the *baccalauréat* program was extended to two years. The program for the *licence* was reduced to one year, and that for the *doctorate* extended to two years. In 1968, the first diplomates of the new colleges in Quebec, i.e. Collèges d'Enseignement Général et Professionnel (C.E.G.E.P.s), reached the University level and, it became necessary to increase the length of the *baccalauréat* program to three years. Simultaneously, two types of programs were adopted at the graduate level. M.A. and Ph.D. programs were designed for those whose main interest lay in research, and the Maîtrise en Psychologie et Doctorat en Psychologie programs were designed for those preparing for a professional career. The author believes that the *Institut* was, at the time, the only department in the world offering such a division. It goes without saying that the application of this policy was not affected without ruffling some feathers! The conflict reached its peak during the summer of 1969, when the staff voted for the division of the department into two separate entities, corresponding more or less to the two types of graduate programs offered.

However, this division was never to take place. In June 1969, the term of Bélanger as chairman ended. There was no candidate for the chairmanship. Finally, Father Mailloux was persuaded to accept the post and he believed in the necessity of maintaining the unity of the department. He received the indirect help of the University administration, whose intention it was to centralize academic management and to make major modifications in the power structure. A great number of Faculties were abolished, and almost all the Departments were reunited into one super-structure: the *Faculté des Arts et des Sciences*. During this interval, the *Institut de Psychologie* officially became the *Département de Psychologie*. For a few years, the Department continued to live in the illusion of unity.

In 1973, Bélanger accepted a new term as chairman of the Department. He tried, with the help of Roger Lapointe and the members of the program committee, to modify the program in order to put an end to the existing conflicts and to reunite the department. Unfortunately, this proved less than successful, mainly because of rigid differences of opinion. This led a group of professors in January 1975, to send a petition to the Dean of the Faculty asking for the creation of an autonomous department of academic psychology. After a vote by the members of the staff on this issue, the authorities decided on the nomination of a committee to study this problem. This committee suggested a division of the department into two sections: Applied Psychology and Fundamental Psychology. Now after three years a new committee is evaluating the results of this experiment. The members of the Department nourish the hope that this problem will be solved once and for all, so that the energy of everyone concerned can be directed to the acquisition of knowledge instead of being wasted on internal conflicts.

With all their apparent intensity these conflicts are not exclusive to the *Département de Psychologie* of the *Université de Montréal*. They are but the reflection of tensions which have affected psychology everywhere since World War II. Psychology, like all of the human sciences, is concerned, at the same time, both with knowledge and with technology. This is a fact that must be recognized by all, eventually. The simple fact that a learned society like the Canadian Psychological Association has become aware of such a reality (as evidenced by establishing applied and experimental divisions) is an encouragement for the future.

During recent years the Department has taken responsibility for the vocational guidance program. Until 1968, two schools at the *Université de Montréal* were training professional guidance counselors, the *Faculté des Sciences de l'Education* and the *Institut de Psychologie*. In 1968, the University granted the Institut an exclusive jurisdiction over the teaching of Psychology. By 1974, the guidance program as such disappeared and became what it should always have been: a special training program in psychology. In 1974 also, as a consequence of a strong public interest in the communication media, the Department opened a Communication Section. This Section became an independent Department in June 1980.

It becomes very difficult to study in detail the development of research during this period. As in the case of the training program there was a rapid growth and diversification in research activities. During an earlier period the number of research workers in the Department increased rather slowly. Today the Department has several research laboratories for work in all of the major fields of fundamental and applied psychology. This evolution took some time. As a matter of fact this period was characterized more by the construction of a modern research infra-structure (hiring of technicians, acquiring new equipment, etc.) than by an outstanding scientific productivity. An effort was also made to involve the Department in the scientific power structure (Science Council, Medical Research Council, National Research Council, etc ...). Even if, at the beginning of this period, scientific productivity did not immediately follow staff increase, a careful examination of the situation prevailing over the last two years shows a positive increase in productivity. In the coming years, the Department should attain a productivity level proportional to its actual resources and potentialities.

To conclude this analysis of the 1963–1978 period, it could be said that a good part of the energies of the faculty were spent on a necessary but costly process of reconstruction. It seems, however, that the Department is now coming of age and that it is in a position to fulfill the hopes for it of its founders.

In the preceding pages an attempt has been made to present a brief review of the ideas of the men who were istrumental in the creation and the growth of the *Département de Psychologie* of the *Université de Montréal*. It is hoped that it has been shown that for an organization as well as for a human being, the present is perfectly understandable only in the light of the past.

References

Appley, M.A., Richwood, J. *La psychologie au Canada*. Etude spéciale 3, Secrétariat des Sciences, Ottawa: Conseil privé. 1967

Laurendeau, M., Pinard, A. *The development of the concept of space in the child*. International University Press, New York. 1970

Pinard, A. Le modèle scientiste-professionnel: synthèse ou prothèse. *Psychologie Canadienne*, 1964, *5*, 187–208.

Yoshi, P. Psychologie au Québec: présent et avenir. *Psychologie Canadienne*, 1970, *11*, 377–385.

Further Readings

Anonymous – Citation: Professor David Bélanger. *The Canadian Psychologist*, 1965, *6a*, 294.
    – Award of Centennial Medals, 1967 (Reverand Pere Noël Mailloux). *The Canadian Psychologist*, 1968, *9*, 229–231.

See also a note in *The Canadian Psychologist*, 1970, *11*, 75 and also a note in the *Bulletin of the Canadian Psychological Association*, 1943, *3*, 29–30.

PART III

The English Universities of Western Canada

Introduction: An Overview

The first universities in Western Canada were Manitoba, Saskatchewan, Alberta, and British Columbia. Each was, from the start, a provincial or public, as opposed to a private institution, and each was established shortly after its founding province joined confederation (Manitoba and British Columbia) or was newly constituted by Canada as a province (Saskatchewan, Alberta). All were essentially products of the 20th century and none, except Manitoba, the oldest of the four, had any roots of a sectarian type in its past.

In 1870 when Manitoba became a province of Canada it had three denominational colleges. These were St. Boniface (Roman Catholic), St. John's (Anglican) and Manitoba (Presbyterian). In 1877 when the university of Manitoba was founded it began as an examining body to set standards for and coordinate the efforts of these three colleges. It was not until 1900 that the university itself became a teaching institution. At that time it assumed responsibility for instruction in subjects which, because of their cost, were not taught by the colleges, such as science and later the professions.

The provinces of Alberta and Saskatchewan founded their universities in 1906 and 1907 respectively, and two years later were offering instruction, but in British Columbia, although an Act to establish a university was passed as early as 1890, no classes were offered until 1915. From 1899 some post-secondary education could, however, be obtained in British Columbia. In that year the Vancouver High School, functioning as an affiliate of McGill University, began offering first year courses in arts. By 1902 second year courses were also offered and in 1906 a McGill University College of British Columbia was established. This college functioned until the University of British Columbia finally opened its doors (Harris, 1976, p. 226).

Although, when teaching began in the universities of the West, psychology was no longer considered to be simply a special branch of philosophy, in all of them psychology was first offered (as it had been in the eastern universities) by departments of philosophy or by professors who occupied Chairs of Philosophy. The first philosopher to be appointed at Alberta did, however, have some serious training in psychology. This was J.M. MacEachran who joined Alberta's faculty in 1909. MacEachran had studied philosophy at Queen's under John Watson, where he earned his first Ph.D., but he had then gone to Germany, where he studied with both Wundt at Leipzig and Stumpf at Berlin. He obtained a Leipzig Ph.D. and, although this was also in philosophy, his thesis being on American Pragmatism, he gained, in Germany, not only a considerable knowledge about the new psychology, but a keen interest in it. During his first year at Alberta he offered an introductory course in experimental psychology using as a text William James' *Psychology: Briefer Course*. It is not surprising therefore, that in the west, the first university to establish a department which formally recognized psychology as a discipline other than philosophy was Alberta. A Department of Philosophy, Psychology, and Education was established there as early as 1933, and in 1935, it became the Department of Philosophy and Psychology. MacEachran was the department's Head and he continued to hold that post until his retirement in 1945.

Relationships between philosophy and psychology appeared to be so congenial at Alberta that the administrative ties between them were not broken until 1960, making Alberta the last of the four western universities to establish a separate Department of Psychology. However, psychology thrived there in both the late forties and the 1950's. MacEachran's immediate successor was another philosopher, John Macdonald. However, Macdonald had received some training in psychology at Edinburgh and was prepared to support its development. The first real psychologist was appointed at Alberta in 1937. He was Douglas E. Smith, a Canadian who had taken his first degrees at Queen's, but had then gone to Chicago and later Harvard for his Ph.D. where he studied physiological psychology, along with Donald Hebb, under Lashley. In 1952 Smith became Head of the Department and served in this capacity for five years until he was made a Dean. It was not, however, until 1960 when a separate Department of Psychology was established that psychology at Alberta began to develop its contemporary image. The first chairman of this new department was Joseph R. Royce, an American with a Chicago Ph.D. who had studied under Thurstone. Royce was an effective administrator and, during the expansionist period of the 1960's was able to create a strong research-oriented, theoretical-experimental department which could mount and sustain a strong doctoral training program. Among those who helped him develop the department was Thomas Nelson, who succeeded him as Chairman in 1967.

Modern psychology came to Manitoba in 1920 when H.W. Wright joined its faculty. Although basically a philosopher Wright had studied psychology with Titchener at Cornell and in the 20's and 30's he exerted steady pressure on the university to recognize psychology as a discipline separate from philosophy. For a time at Manitoba, the chairmanship rotated on an annual basis between the philosopher and the psychologist in what was then a two-man department. When Wright took his turn as Chairman of what was officially the Department of Philosophy, he took every opportunity to refer to it as the Department of Philosophy and Psychology. Thus, for historians, he created considerable confusion about just when such a combined department was actually established. The official date appears to have been 1946, but this new Department had but a short history. In 1947 Philosophy and Psychology were divided administratively and a separate Department of Psychology was established.

Although in the early post-war period conditions at Manitoba were favourable for the development of a modern Department of Psychology and some promising young psychologists were recruited for the faculty, among them D. Carleton Williams who joined the staff in 1946 and succeeded Wright as Chairman of the Department in 1948, the stay of such people was short-lived. Williams left to accept a post at Toronto in 1949 and there followed a period of instability during which the department was administered by an Acting Chairman, B.M. Springbett. However, in 1953 John Zubek was appointed Head and he provided strong leadership. Zubek, who had been trained at Johns Hopkins, brought an experimental, research orientation to the department and began to develop a competent faculty which could offer sound graduate training.

Saskatchewan, as well as Manitoba, established a separate Department of Psychology in 1947 and appointed a psychologist, Tom Cook, to be its Head. Although Cook remained at Saskatchewan for only two years he succeeded in finding a capable successor, Gordon A. McMurray, who brought stability to the department and shaped its image for 21 years (from 1949 to 1970). McMurray had been trained in physiological psychology at McGill and he determined to establish at Saskatchewan a strong academic, experimental and research-oriented department. However, until the beginning of the expansionist period in the late 1950's and early 1960's, it remained a small two- or three-man department. Even so, graduate training began in the late 1940's and although in the early years this was only at the Masters level, by the end of the 50's it included doctoral training. During the late 50's and early 60's the department had a strong faculty which included such people as Gordon Mogenson and Neil Agnew.

At British Columbia the first psychologist to be appointed to the Department of Philosophy was Jennie Benson Wyman (later Pilcher). She came to the university in 1926 and taught, in addition to an Introductory Course, a course in social psychology. Pilcher had been a student of Terman's at Stanford and appears to have been interested primarily in testing and its applications in education. In 1935 another psychologist joined the staff. This was Joseph Morsh, whose Ph.D. was from Johns Hopkins where he studied with Knight Dunlap. In 1936 psychology was formally recognized as an important discipline in its own right and the Department of Philosophy became the Department of Philosophy and Psychology. This new department was, however, headed by a series of philosophers until 1945 when S.N.F. Chant was appointed to the Chair. Chant, who, before World War II, had taught at Toronto, set out to strengthen the psychology side of the department and by 1951 had increased the number of psychologists on the staff to six and had obtained authority to offer graduate training to the doctoral level. The doctoral program was, however, slow to develop. This was because, three years after his appointment as Head, Chant was made a Dean and for several years thereafter, psychology lacked strong leadership. When Chant became Dean he gave up direct control of the department, but a philosopher became its Chairman and Chant continued to be the spokesman for psychology. Also, in 1958 when a separate Department of Psychology was finally established, Chant became its head, even though he continued as Dean. An Acting Chairman, Edro Signori, was appointed to carry out everyday administrative duties and this unsatisfactory arrangement continued for as many as seven years with Signori as Acting Chairman (1958–1962) and then Acting Head (1962–1965). Signori's position must have been a most difficult one. He had little opportunity to take the initiative and during his years as "Acting" Chairman or Head the university continued to make a series of what appeared to be half-hearted, abortive attempts to recruit a new Head. Finally in 1965 an internal appointment was made. Douglas T. Kenny who had joined the faculty in 1950 was made Chairman. For five years Kenny gave the department the leadership it required, but then he was appointed President of the University. Another period of uncertainty for psychology followed, during which Signori again functioned as Acting Head. Thus, it was not until 1972 when a new Chairman, Peter Suedfeld, was found that the work, started by Kenny, of building a strong research-oriented department worthy of a university such as the University of British Columbia, was completed.

Chapter 9

Psychology at Manitoba

by

*Morgan W. Wright**

The University of Manitoba came into existence in 1877. It represented the confluence of three educational streams: Catholic, Anglican and
Presbyterian. Its initial function was administrative, only taking over a
teaching role in 1900 when three professors from the colleges were
persuaded to teach for half time, paid by the University.

The history of academic psychology in Manitoba can be said to start in
1920, with the appointment of Henry W. Wright to the Department of
Philosophy. Henry Wright was a student of Titchener, at Cornell,
graduating at the turn of the century. He came to Manitoba in 1920 from
Lake Forest College, Illinois, where he was acting President. Just what
induced him to leave the lush environment of Lake Forest for the arctic
remoteness of Manitoba was a continuing mystery to his wife, though she
became very actively involved in the community, perhaps just to keep
warm.

The University of Manitoba, at that time, was a collection of
denominational colleges with an organizational and directional hub, the
University proper. The University's department of Philosophy, to which
Wright was appointed, was chaired by a bright acerbic philosopher,
Rupert Lodge, a graduate of Oxford. The two men were appointed at
almost the same time and retired within a year of each other. They were a
study in contrasts. Rupert was quick, lively, sarcastic and forceful –
Henry quiet, thoughtful, scholarly, and a political innocent. The chair-
manship rotated each year. When Henry was Chairman, it was the
Department of Philosophy and Psychology, when Rupert was writing the

* Professor Wright joined the Faculty of the University of Manitoba in 1956. He is
currently the Director of the Psychological Service Centre there. He is the son of Professor
Henry W. Wright who was the first professor of psychology to be appointed at the
University of Manitoba. He is *not* related to Mary J. Wright, the co-editor of this book.

annual report, it was just Philosophy. An inkling of an underlying drama – the emancipation of psychology from philosophy, can be read into Henry's annual report to the president in 1923 when he wrote – "pending the establishment of a separate Department of Psychology" – which then pended for a quarter of a century, being finally realized in 1947, on his retirement. In the same report he offered thanks to the Board of Governors and Council of the University of Manitoba for a modest grant to establish an experimental laboratory in psychology.[1]

The "emancipation" was slow in coming but it is clearly discernible as one reads between the lines of the university calendars. In 1921 one course was taught in Psychology, the text books by William James and Pillsbury. In 1923 Experimental Psychology came into being, Woodworth's *Psychology* being used. Also, at that date, a social psychology course was introduced – McDougall's *Social Psychology* and a text by Henry Wright – *The Moral Principles of Democracy*. In 1927 a course in applied psychology was offered to extra-mural students. By 1935[2] five psychology courses were being taught by Henry Wright, totalling some sixteen hours of lecturing per week. The first graduate course came in 1938 – with readings listed by such authors as Spearman, Koffka, Lewin, Sherif, and Tolman. A course in Abnormal Psychology (Boring, Langfeld, and Weld) and in 1942, Personality (Allport) rounded out a substantial program.

The calendar also provides other clues to the development of an increasingly independent infant. As indicated, psychology crept into the calendar initially, only when Henry Wright was Chairman. However, in 1932[3] psychology courses were listed separately from philosophy courses and in 1936[4] psychology was listed separately as a discipline in the calendar. Finally, in 1947, on his retirement, a separate and distinct department of psychology became a fact, which, I know pleased Henry Wright far more than being made Professor Emeritus and receiving an honourary doctorate of Laws from the University of Manitoba.

Although Henry's early writings were clearly in the area of ethics, a significant shift occurred in the mid-thirties. By 1933, at 55 years of age, he had written four books and thirty articles, all of which could be broadly classed as philosophical. Following 1933 he published another twenty-five articles, eighteen of which appeared in psychological journals. In 1934 he published an article[5] of 25 pages in the University of Toronto Quarterly. It was a scholarly review of current motivational theories, stressing the fact that what had been the province of ethics was now that of psychology. It was called "Understanding Human Nature and Social Relations" and painted an optimistic picture of the contribution psychology was to make, applying objectively obtained data to the understanding of human conduct. One quotation, in particular, caught this reader's attention, attributed to a Professor Hocking.[6] "What the social desire seeks, is the social desire itself – in another person". Although a bit enigmatic, it catches the flavor of a concern that was increasingly to catch Henry's interest – that of the hows and whys of social communication, with its foundation being based on shared meaning. A development that played a major role in Henry's conversion from the philosophical to the psychological, was the emergence of the Canadian Psychological Association. Ten of his last twelve papers appeared in the Journal of the Canadian Psychological Association and the Association's annual meeting was the high point of his academic year.

During the latter period he was ably assisted by several staff members, including P. Hampton, J. Burns, K. Sayons, S. Hogg, D. McLeod, and D.C. Williams. He was delighted when Carl Williams was appointed his successor, and disappointed when Carl was lured away to the east where he became, eventually, President of the University of Western Ontario. Bruce Springbett followed Carl, as acting chairman, until the arrival of John Zubek in 1953.

The second era of Manitoba psychology was introduced by John P. Zubek. The contrast between Wright and Zubek was marked. Whereas Henry Wright was broadly concerned and scholarly, and interested primarily in establishing psychology at the University of Manitoba as a distinct academic discipline, John Zubek was first and foremost a scientist. He worked at the cutting edge of knowledge as he vigorously pursued new areas of psychological investigation. He was highly productive, wrote (or edited) six books, contributed fifteen chapters to books edited by others and published more than 80 articles in scientific journals. What surprised the writer was the fact that in 30 of these articles, a graduate student was named as first author, although the impetus for the work and its direction were clearly John's. How tragic it is that he died at such a relatively young age.

John Zubek was not an easy man to work for or with. He demanded much of himself and others and was not a natural administrator, a fact which was recognized by making him a research professor in 1962. However, he was the driving spirit of the department, not only when he was Head, but also afterwards. The new psychology building, which presently houses close to sixty psychologists, was largely a product of his efforts. He promoted it, planned it, and obtained funds for it from various research grants. Whereas Henry Wright established psychology within Manitoba, John made psychology at Manitoba known internationally. In 1973, in a report by Lisa Martel on achievements in Canadian Science and Technology, prepared for the Ministry of State in Ottawa, his research laboratory was described as the "world's leading centre on sensory deprivation".

This is not the place to do full justice to John Zubek or to assess his impact upon Psychology, Manitoban or otherwise. This has, however, been done elsewhere (Harper & Bross, 1978). The writer often disagreed with John and this led to some lively altercations, but what was appreciated, I hope on both sides, was that differences were openly expressed and there was nothing covert. One always knew where and why John stood on an issue. Despite this, he was personally very sensitive to criticism and emotionally vulnerable. His most valuable contribution, at a local level, was his impetus to research. He was a dedicated and enthusiastic investigator who was always ready to share his findings and his excitements. His later research centered mainly on sensory deprivation, an area in which he became an international authority. Unfortunately, this also drew the ire of an aroused student body who saw in his work the inspiration of the devil. He was challenged to defend his investigations against charges of "brain washing" and scientifically directed "mental torture". Although most of us dismissed these charges as nonsensical (easier to say now than then), I believe John was deeply hurt and confused by the charges.

John graduated from the Universities of British Columbia (B.A.), Toronto (M.A.), and Johns Hopkins (Ph.D.). However, I think he was influenced most by Donald Hebb with whom he worked at McGill before coming to Manitoba. John's scientific credentials were clearly established; however there was another side to him that was not so apparent. He dabbled successfully in the stock market and supported philanthropies of his own choosing. As an example, after a very respected and beloved psychologist, Clifford Robson, from United College (now the University of Winnipeg) died under tragic circumstances, John Zubek established a teaching award in Professor Robson's name.

After two hard "acts" to follow Alfred Shephard initiated a third epoch in 1961. As time passed and the department grew, it became less easy to identify the department with an individual. With Henry Wright there was no problem, *he* was the department. With John Zubek the department was still largely manageable by one person. With the coming of Alf Shephard the scene changed. When John Zubek was elevated to Research Professor there were five full-time faculty members, when Alf stepped down in 1973 there were upwards of fifty. A similar phenomenon (a sudden increase in psychology professors) must have occurred at other universities. At Manitoba it went from eighteen in 1969 to thirty in 1970, and thereby hangs a tale. The tale has to do with an energetic and somewhat devious professional group, led by a daughter-in-law of Henry Wright's, Marion Wright, who with the help of Alfred Shephard convinced the administration that a clinical program should be made available at the University of Manitoba. This led to the appointment of some dozen clinically-oriented professors and the establishment of a psychological clinic which was associated with the department.

Shephard did his undergraduate work at the University of British Columbia and his graduate work at the University of Iowa. Before coming to Manitoba, he taught for more than a decade at the University of Toronto. In many ways his orientation to psychology fell somewhere between that of Henry Wright and that of John Zubek. Like Zubek he did relatively "hard-nosed" experimental research. This was on motor functioning. Like Wright, he had an abiding interest in broad, systematic questions in psychology. This latter may have grown out of some preliminary interest and training which he had in theology. Earlier it was suggested that Titchener inspired Wright and that Donald Hebb inspired Zubek. The writer thinks that E.A. Bott of the University of Toronto was the person who most inspired Shephard, for at times, when he listened to Alfred lecture to honours students on methodology, his "deja-vu" experience was compelling. He was once again listening to E.A. Bott, a truly unforgettable experience.

Alf's approach to administration was conciliatory and therapeutic rather than decisive. He would listen patiently to all sides of a question and then wait hopefully for a solution to emerge, which, oddly enough, often did. The department burgeoned under his stewardship in all areas, its total complement increasing tenfold. This placed new and not-as-yet-experienced burdens on the Head, effectively making him a captive of the system and demanding all of his time and energies. Perhaps with a sigh of relief, he passed the mantle on to John Adair in 1973.

However, before turning to John Adair, some comments should be made about the development of the clinical training program. As early as 1958, John Zubek had recommended to the President, the establishment of a clinical training program for psychology students. In 1958 Jim Nickels was appointed as director of such a program and, with the author, began scouring the countryside for clinical psychology professors, eventually attracting a well-qualified group, all of whom were Americans. This was not a deliberate policy. The sad fact was that there were few comparably trained Canadian clinical psychologists, and those who were, preferred the Ivy'd East to the Western boondocks. This caused, however, a minor whirlwind, better known locally as the second war of 1812, with which Adair was required to cope. Several of the Canadian professors resisted the onslaught of their neighbors from the south. Fortunately, there were no serious casualties, and John Adair survived relatively unscathed although, as an American himself, he must have felt uncomfortable at times, administering a Department in which a group of Canadian enthusiasts seemed bent upon some form of nationalistic purge.

These academic fireworks shouldn't blind one to the very significant contribution John Adair made to the Department and to the profession. Prior to his stewardship the academic model of the Head was that of "the distinguished senior professor at the helm". Increasingly this had become an inappropriate solution to the running of a highly diversified and complex organization. In recognition of this, John proceeded to reorganize the Department with tireless energy and devotion. Additionally, he played an active part in provincial psychological affairs and received the Manitoba Distinguished Psychologist award in 1980. Not content with contributing locally, he served as President of the Canadian Psychological Association in 1979–80, a remarkable record, which is far from finished.

Another John, John McIntyre, followed Adair as head. McIntyre, a graduate of Calgary and Illinois, inherited most of Adair's problems, plus some others. Both Johns hailed from areas in which men are a little "larger than life" – Texas and Alberta – which may explain their willingness to take on a job that any sensible person would avoid.

The fact is that the Department of Psychology at Manitoba is a very vigorous and productive enterprise as measured by research, scholarship and teaching and, as well, it provides an atmosphere with a healthy degree of controversy and dissention. Currently there is concern related to the maintenance of academic standards in the face of applied training pressures. Certainly at one time, professional psychologists sat outside departmental doors, waiting for whatever crumbs of recognition and support came their way. Now there is almost a role-reversal at the University of Manitoba, with the majority of graduate students opting for applied programs and careers. Recently a strong Behaviour Modification group within the Department has developed a doctoral program, under the leadership of Gary Martin, which may well merge with the even larger clinical program. This could escalate anxiety about what is already seen (by some) as a top-heavy applied emphasis.

These problems are not unique to Manitoba. They involve balancing the values of research and practice, in considering whether a separate doctoral degree (a Doctor of Psychology) is appropriate for students working towards professional careers. This issue, among others, will undoubtedly keep John McIntyre from becoming bored during his headship. Fortunately, John McIntyre is a staunch Canadian, a good hockey player, *and* from Alberta. That's a combination hard to beat.

Notes

[1] University of Manitoba Annual Report, 1922–23, pp. 40–41.
[2] University of Manitoba Annual Report, 1935–36, p. 35.
[3] University of Manitoba Arts and Science Calendar, 1936–37, p. 4.
[4] University of Manitoba Arts and Science Calendar, 1936–37, p. 5.
[5] Understanding Human Nature and Social Relations. *University of Toronto Quarterly*, Vol. 3, 1933–34, pp. 321–348.
[6] IBID – p. 330.

References

Harper, D.W., & Bross, M. The effect of unimodal sensory deprivation on sensory processes: A decade of research from the University of Manitoba. *Canadian Psychological Review*, 1978, *19*, 128–144.

Further Readings

Anonymous – D.C. Williams. *The Canadian Psychologist*, 1959, *8*, 71.
Hebb, D.O. John Peter Zubek. *The Canadian Psychologist*, 1974, *15*, 398–399.
Janisse, M.P. John Adair. *Canadian Psychological Review*, 1979, *20*, 145–147.
McCormack, P.D. "Psychology at Manitoba". *The Canadian Psychologist*, 1962, *3*, 38–42.

See also notes in *The Canadian Psychologist*, 1962, *3a*, 122; 1965, *6*, 69; 1968, *9*, 81–82.

Chapter 10

Psychology at Saskatchewan

by

Gordon A. McMurray*

The pattern of change over three decades of a recognizable institutional entity such as a university department has many facets. There is, *first* of all, the pattern shown by the individual department in such growth indices as number of staff, students, classes offered, and the size of the physical plant. This development has been extremely rapid in all Canadian universities and forms a very salient characteristic if one wishes to describe the changing patterns of university growth in Canada. It is of interest to examine the degree to which local changes have followed this general trend. The *second* aspect of development is that formed by the ever-changing individual contributions of the members of departments, reflecting the interactions between the individual and the social setting. These interactions are decisive in determining the product of growth: the teaching, the research, and all the professional activities. The history of a department told in these terms often shows the great influence of a single contribution. A *third* facet of the developmental pattern reflects the overall orientation of the department towards the discipline it represents. There may be shifts in emphasis which alter decisively the historical character of a department. No where else is this more important than in psychology, because of the wide variety of interests, goals, and activities that characterize psychologists.

It is from these three different aspects that I wish to consider the history of the Department of Psychology at the University of Saskatchewan. As I do this it appears that the whole pattern of change falls into three clearly discernible phases. Let us look at each.

---

* Professor McMurray joined the Faculty of the University of Saskatchewan in 1949 and was the Chairman of the Department of Psychology there from 1950 to 1970.

Phase 1–1947–1957

The University of Saskatchewan was small in its beginnings in everything except the concept of future development. The numbers involved may be realized when we read in the first calendar that:

> In September, 1909, students will be admitted into either the first or second years of the B.A. or B. Sc. Course. If four or more apply before September 1st, 1909, for admission into the third year of the B.A. Course, provision will be made for the necessary classes.

When classes did open in 1909, the faculty consisted of President W.C. Murray and four professors. There were 70 students who paid an annual tuition fee of $30.00, with partial students paying $6.00 for each course. Yet this small group had the administrative framework of a Chancellor, Senate, Board of Governors, and President. It was to occupy a site set aside on the east side of the South branch of the Saskatchewan river eventually comprising 2550 acres about 350 of which, with a frontage of over half a mile on the river, had been designated for campus building to replace the downtown building where classes had begun.

The University at this early point had also set its goal of close integration with the needs of the province. The 1910 calendar, referring to the university, states:

> Its watchword should be service – service of the state in things that make for happiness and virtue as well as in the things that make for wealth. No form of that service is too mean or too exalted. It is as fitting for the University, through correspondence classes, extension courses, supervision of farmers' clubs, travelling libraries, women's institutes or musical tests to place within the reach of the solitary student, the distant townsmen, the farmer in his hours of leisure or the mothers and daughters in the home, the opportunities for adding to their stores of knowledge and enjoyment; as it is that the University should foster researches into the properties of radium or the causes and cure of swamp fever; provided, of course, that it is better fitted than any other existing agency for that particular work.

This concern with the practical needs of a province in the early stages of development has remained a characteristic of the University and one which was to have much influence in the later development of psychology. Psychology, taught as part of philosophy, was part of these earliest beginnings. Dr. W.C. Murray, the first university president was himself a philosopher-psychologist and was listed in the Calendar as a lecturer in the Department of Philosophy. The head of this first department was Professor Ira McKay who, at this time, combined Philosophy with Political Science.

One of the basic courses offerd by this department was Philosophy 1: Logic and Psychology. The text for the Psychological part of the course was Titchener's *Primer of Psychology*. Also, part of the elective examinations for Honours in Philosophy was based on the reading of James' *Principles of Psychology* and Wundt's *Lectures on Human and Animal Psychology*. It appears that, from the first, students in Saskatchewan received a traditional introduction both to the established school of structuralism and to the functionalism that was developing in America.

This particular course in psychology continued for several years. The 1911–12 programme again used James and Titchener, but introduced a minor, although interesting, change when Philosophy 1 was renamed Psychology and Logic (from Logic and Psychology). This probably recognized a change in emphasis, because the new title persisted with few changes in the course except the introduction of new texts such as Stout's *Manual of Psychology*.

In 1919–20 Professor J.A. Sharrard was Profesor of Philosophy. Philosophy 1 remained as before, but Philosophy 10: Social Psychology was introduced and offered in alternate years with Philosophy 14: Aesthetics, Psychology and Philosophy. Over a period of years the offerings in psychology assumed a definite pattern. The general introduction was no longer part of Philosophy, but became a separate course (Philosophy 5) using Woodworth's *Psychology: A Study of Mental Life*. This was followed by Philosophy 51: Advanced and Experimental Psychology with Woodworth's *Experimental Psychology* as text and two half-courses Philosophy 52a: Social Psychology and 53b: Psychology of Aesthetics. The Experimental Psychology was regularly alternated with the Social Psychology and Psychology of Aesthetics sequence. Professor Sharrard taught all these classes and, before he retired, was here to meet the onslaught of students, war veterans and others, which came after the war*.

The sequence of classes evolved by Professor Sharrard is also significant in that it gave the students a straight-forward presentation of traditional general and experimental psychology along with an early interest in Social Psychology.

* World War II

The formation of the Department of Psychology became possible when on October 8, 1946, the Faculty of Arts and Science passed a recommendation for the establishment of a separate department, followed by ratification by the University Council and Board of Governors. This move clearly followed the direction set generally by North American universities. It was made natural by the appearance within the Department of Philosophy of a clearcut sequence of courses that were heavily influenced by the early leaders in the emergence of psychology as an independent scientific discipline. Such men as Titchener, James, Woodworth, Dashiell, Kimball Young, Gardner Murphy wrote the texts that were determining the content of the courses. The other and decisive influence as far as the University of Saskatchewan was concerned was that Professor Sharrard who had developed this sequence of courses retired in June 1947. It was a natural break for the establishment of a new professorship.

The new department actually started classes in 1947–48 with T.W. Cook as first professor of psychology. Dr. Cook came from Toronto and was generally regarded as an experimental psychologist with particular interest in human learning. His first assistants were B. Quarrington from Toronto, as instructor, and B. Springbett from Alberta, as lecturer. That year the university calendar listed three full courses and four half-courses in Learning, General, Social, Abnormal, and Industrial Psychology. The following year B. Quarrington left to do further graduate work at Toronto. He was replaced by W.H. Bexton from Waterloo Lutheran as the young department contined to offer the equivalent of six full courses.

This department operated within the framework of the College of Arts and Science and the autonomous College of Graduate Studies. It represented academic psychology in Saskatchewan and remained its sole representative until 1965 when a second department of psychology for Saskatchewan was created at the University of Saskatchewan in Regina, later known as the University of Regina.

The other main centre for psychology in Saskatchewan was in the College of Education. The emphasis there on psychology started earlier than in the Arts and Science Faculty when S.R. Laycock joined the staff in 1927. Professor Laycock, later Dean of Education, was particularly concerned with Child and Adolescent Psychology, the Psychology of Adjustment, and Mental Testing. As early as 1940 he was offering four full courses in these areas. Professor Laycock, an expert communicator both by radio and by writing, used his expertise to promote mental health movements in the field of education, penal corrections, and medicine. He was for a long time "Mr. Psychology" in Saskatchewan. His particular orientation, however, was very different from that which had been set for psychology earlier by the Department of Philosophy and carried into the new programme introduced by Professor Cook. It was possible that his presence had much to do with the traditional academic stance assumed by the new department of psychology.

The next academic year, 1949–50, saw a nearly complete changeover in the small department when Cook left for a position with the Defence Research Board and Springbett left to complete doctoral work at McGill University. The Department was also reduced in size, as the only replacement was G.A. McMurray who that spring had completed his Ph.D. at McGill. He was appointed as assistant professor and acting head of the department while Bexton continued as instructor. The following year McMurray became head of the department and held this position until 1970. Bexton continued for another year until he left in 1951 to do graduate work at McGill.

From this time until 1957 psychology continued as a two-person department with the department head and one assistant, usually an instructor. In 1953, however, the second member was R.A. Rennie with the rank of associate professor and already considerable experience in university teaching. Professor Rennie remained with the department until his death in 1973, although in 1958 he assumed the responsibility of Director of Student Counselling and, later, Dean of Students. This meant that his participation in departmental affairs was very much reduced.

At this point we might pause to look at the contribution of an individual to the pattern of change in the Department because Professor Rennie was a significant agent of change. This came largely from his ability as a teacher. He was a clear, well-organized, popular lecturer who attracted many students to psychology. The increase in student interest in psychology was, of course, a general phenomenon in Canadian universities at that time, but at Saskatchewan, Professor Rennie provided the kind of situation in which such interest could grow.

In the general growth of the department, the first phase stands out as a long developmental plateau. The staff remained at two and the space allotments minimal. From 1950 the Department's temporary home was in the new Medical Building. This came after the earliest years when the only space was shared offices for the faculty. The space in the Medical Building provided one office for the two staff members, an adjoining office that was used as a senior laboratory, and the opportunity to use the large physiology laboratory for the course in experimental psychology. Classroom space was always adequate either in the Medical Building or, as happened more often, on some other part of the campus. This was because at this time the Faculty of Arts and Science, with the exception of the Departments of Physics and Chemistry, had no home of its own. The faculty was acquiring strength and diversity, but a separate identifiable Arts and Science building did not come until 1968. So the Department of Psychology was not unique among the Arts and Science departments in the way that it started with gradual growth. It was probably unique, however, in the rapid rate of change that occurred in later stages of development.

The typical teaching assignment at this time was for Rennie to give a section of Introductory Psychology and courses in Social Psychology and Personality; while McMurray gave a section of Introductory Psychology, a course in Experimental Psychology, and a seminar dealing with different topics selected from year to year. This load of three courses was standard in the College of Arts and Science at the time. The Department of Psychology, however, did generally have large classes. The typical section of Introductory Psychology with over 100 students was very much as it has remained until today. There was also a pattern of enrolment emerging which remained for many years. This pattern was that of large classes in Social Psychology and Personality with small classes in experimental areas.

Teaching was the main funtion of the small department, although at an early stage McMurray introduced research on perceptual studies of closure, the effect of repeated measurement on visual illusions and, in particular, on the effects of analgesic drugs on thresholds for pain and the pain response to the cold pressor test. The appearance of Osgood's work on the semantic differential method for the measurement of meaning also led to his interest in applying the technique to such phenomena as the fittingness of signs to words and phonetic symbolism.

The department's close association with physiology began when the cooperative use of their laboratory space made its possible to carry on the laboratory work in Experimental Psychology. This led to research with Professor L.B. Jaques of the Department of Physiology on the effects of psychological stress on physiological indices such as growth, blood coagulation, and capillary resistance. G.J. Mogenson, a 1955 M.A. graduate from the department, worked with Dr. Jaques at this time. Later he returned to the faculty to institute a tradition of research in physiological psychology which has continued unbroken through H. Weinberg, G. Winocur, R. Stretch, and T. Wishart until the present.

This departmental work did not cost the university much financially. A typical salary would be approximately $4000 with very little cost for expansion of staff or space. It is revealing to examine the differential growth between Psychology and departments such as Chemistry, Biology and Physics. Each one started with one man in 1910 (although Psychology was then in Philosophy), but in 1933–34 Philosophy still had two with

Chemistry eight, Biology five, and Physics five. As late as 1956, Psychology was still a two-person department while Chemistry, Biology, and Physics had reached nine, eight, and seven respectively. Psychology was not the only department with such a long, restricted growth phase, although it was certainly one of them and the one that stood out in the size of its student-staff ratio.

At this time the department, small as it was, had probably assumed the overall orientation to the field of psychology which it was to maintain until the 1960s. This may be described as academic, experimental, research-oriented, with a strong interest in developing senior undergraduate courses and the opportunities for research, thesis-centred, graduate work. In retrospect it seems to me that this was a rather undeliberated orientation growing out of the background of McMurray's graduate training at McGill, coupled with a fairly strong tendency at the time for this to be the predominant attitude of psychology as a discipline. It also was influenced by the general atmosphere of the University of Saskatchewan which, I think, placed its highest values on research. It is of interest to note that this orientation at the undergraduate level has changed little over thirty years. The undergraduate programme has expanded greatly in the number of courses, and a much better distribution of enrolment has been achieved, but the traditional, academic orientation described above has remained essentially unchanged.

This orientation was not popular among the students, but this conflict has occurred over and over again in most departments of psychology. Students select psychology for their major because of an interest in people, only to be disappointed by the emphasis on experimental research and statistics. This non-fulfillment of expectations occurred also in the professional schools that wanted a general course in psychology, which they thought would improve their students' ability to understand and work with people. The department tried to meet the demands of these schools by offering a general introductory course which was followed by others in such diverse areas as Social Psychology, Personality, Applied, Statistics, Experimental, and History and Systems. Most of the senior students who took Honours courses developed a fair background in both scientific and applied psychology, but many of the regular majors were somewhat one-sided in their acquaintance with the different fields, having elected only the more applied courses.

Looking back on the long, slow beginning of the department it seems that much of this was due to the general administrative atmosphere of the university. As noted above, the university favored academic, research interests, and, at this time, fostered especially sciences such as Biology, Chemistry, and Physics. The Social Sciences and Humanities did not receive much administrative support. Psychology, in particular, headed almost from its beginning by a new Ph.D., was not given high priority in the plans for growth.

The fact that growth did start to occur in the late 1950's seems directly attributable to an interesting change in student demands. At the beginning of the first phase in the department's history, Saskatchewan students had, for the most part, very practical objectives in mind when attending university. They preferred the natural sciences or the professions and took only as many courses in the humanities and social sciences as were required. This trend in student interest began to change when the interest of many was captured by disciplines that appeared to be more directly concerned with man. Psychology was one such discipline and it had the added advantage that a profession of psychology was also developing. This development was led in Saskatchewan by the Psychiatric Services Branch of the Saskatchewan Department of Public Health. The early work of this branch was inspired by the novel research ideas of Dr. A. Hoffer and Dr. H. Osmond who were pioneers in the search for a biochemical basis for schizophrenia. The excitement generated by their research was communicated to many young psychologists whose names have become well known such as N. Agnew, T. Ayllon, D. Blewett, L. Elkin and R. Sommer. Some combination of these influences started to produce steady pressure on the Department. Classes grew, and more and more students sought graduate training in psychology in order to achieve professional status. The problem was that a hard-pressed, two-person department, with little in the way of physical facilities, could not meet such demands.

Phase II – 1957–1967

This phase began when Neil Agnew and John Nash joined the departmental staff as part-time lecturers. They had come to Saskatoon to work primarily at the newly completed University Hospital, Dr. Agnew as research psychologist in the Psychological Research Centre, and Dr. Nash as chief clinical psychologist. Agnew, a native of Saskatchewan who did his graduate work at the University of Toronto, returned to the province as Executive Director of the Saskatchewan Division of the Canadian Mental Health Association. Later he became Research Psychologist in the Psychiatric Services Branch and when he moved to Saskatoon became Chief Research Psychologist. Nash completed his Honours B.Sc. and Ph.d. at the University of Edinburgh between 1946 and 1953. He came to Saskatchewan from a position as Chief Psychologist for the Department of Public Health in New Brunswick.

These men were interested in an identification with the university and partly because of this, as sessional lecturers, they contributed much more to the Department than the amount of salary they received directly from the University would justify. The content of the classes they offered was close to their respective interests and, since they were given at a senior level, enabled the Department to offer a little more breadth in its program. This contribution to the department from psychologists employed at the University Hospital has continued without interruption. It testifies to the value that applied psychologists place on a university contact. It resulted in invaluable aid during this period of growth, but it did not provide a permanent solution.

In 1959 the Department moved, for the first time, to space of it's own, in the New Arts Building. This consisted of departmental offices, a large-class laboratory, and a laboratory with small animal housing facilities intended for research in physiological psychology. As it turned out these quarters were inadequate within a few years, necessitating another move to space which in turn became insufficient in an even shorter time.

The growth in the full-time staff began in 1958 when G. Mogenson and D. Sydiaha arrived with their newly-acquired Ph.D.s. It is significant that both of these men, born and educated in Saskatchewan were, after their senior graduate work at McGill, happy to return to Saskatchewan to begin their careers. Their appointments were of great importance to the department because their solid contributions over several years had a decisive influence. In most respects they, along with Rennie and McMurray, created the cohesive forces that held the department together during the growth stresses of the early 1960's.

The growth stresses during this period centred around the difficulties of recruitment in Saskatchewan. At this time the student pressure was gradually moving the University's administration to relax it's restrictions on staff growth in psychology. More money was available for the new staff, but the problem was that expansion of staff in psychology was occurring at this time all over Canada. This was particularly noticeable in Ontario, but was paralleled in Alberta and British Columbia. The result was that every new Canadian Ph.D. graduate available for university teaching was offered numerous positions. In this kind of situation the department did not fare too well. For the graduate of the larger Eastern universities there were too many nearby opportunities to consider the more drastic move to the relative isolation of the prairies. If some venturesome persons decided they would like to "go west" it was usually all the way to the very attractive developments in British Columbia and Alberta. The standard solution for this shortage of Canadian candidates was to turn to young American graduates, but, even for these the smaller, more isolated, centre in Saskatchewan was not particularly attractive.

This led to a period during which the Department, in order to meet some of the demands created by the increasing student preference for behavioral sciences, was made up of a few full-time members and several part-time lecturers. The latter were recruited largely from psychologists working in professional settings close to the university. It was in this situation that the orientation of the Department was re-established.

The Department continued to be an academic, research-oriented one. But the focus of the academic and research activities remained broad, mostly because Mogenson and Sydiaha, the two younger staff members were active in very different fields. Mogenson was a physiological psychologist and very quickly developed research interests in the exploration of brain function by means of intracranial stimulation. The broad demands of undergraduate teaching meant that he could not be exclusively concerned with such research, but would be teaching in general experimental areas of learning and motivation with an emphasis on the physiological mediators. Sydiaha's return was prompted by an agreement between the University and the Psychiatric Services Branch as to the need for reinforcing applied training in the province. He had started as an applied, industrial psychologist, but developed his interests primarily in social psychology and personality. It is here that he made a decisive contribution through his devoted response to heavy demands for teaching and research. He ensured the continuing commitment of the department to these areas often when he was nearly alone to do so. Later, during this phase, another permanent staff member, C. Bernhardson, taught the undergraduate class in Personality and also the classes in Statistics. As the department grew Bernhardson's research and teaching interests turned more towards statistics, and he has continued to develop the department's competence in this area which psychologists have generally felt to be of great importance.

The close of this phase saw the department with a full-time staff of eight, but still hard pressed to keep up to the students' demands both at the undergraduate and graduate levels and part-time lecturers were still being used. Thus, while many Canadian Psychology departments grew dramatically in the early 1960's the growth here was much more modest.

Phase III – 1967–1976

The opening of this phase saw conditions ready for rapid change in the department when it moved again, to a new location in the Arts Wing.

This new space, although it became inadequate in a few years, provided a clearly indentifiable unit for psychology with good quality facilities for many activities. Departmental offices were provided close to an adjoining workshop and laboratories for physiological psychology, social psychology, perception, and learning. The unit contained an undergraduate laboratory with a central lecture room and adjoining small rooms for indvidual research projects. There were also specialized animal housing and surgical areas; electronic stimulation, recording, and timing facilities; and ready access to a good computer.

This move was accompanied by a pronounced change in the general recruitment situation. The rapid growth of most departments had slowed down and, at the same time, an increasing number of Ph.D.s had been produced and were looking for university posts. As a result enlargement of the permanent staff became more possible and a period of catching-up to student demands could begin. The growth that ensued was not rapid, but it had settled into a steady pattern. In 1967 the faculty consisted of nine full-time and three part-time members. By 1972 there were sixteen full-time and four part-time members and after the fairly intensive recruiting year of 1975 the faculty grew to eighteen full-time and six part-time members. During this same period the faculty of the affiliated St. Thomas More College which, as will be noted later, took a full part in departmental acitivities, had increased from two to four. This gave the department an effective full-time faculty equivalent of twenty-four.

This growth was made largely through the appointment of young Ph.D.s at the assistant professor level. Appointments were guided particularly by the need to meet the heavy student enrolments in the areas of Social Psychology and Personality. Aside from this general requirement the main determinant of appointments was individual qualifications. This continued until 1971 when priority was given to the clinical area.

The young and expanding faculty, together with an increasing number of graduate students, began to promote revisions in the departmental programme. Their interest was in applied training at the graduate level with a more structured programme and a more vigorous search for the best graduate students. The undergraduate programme was also carefully scrutinized and ultimately re-organized.

Much of the revision started in 1970 when McMurray resigned as head of the department and was succeeded by R. Stretch. Dr. Stretch came to the department from the University of Sheffield with research interests in the study of drugs using methods of operant behaviour analysis. He resigned in 1973 to concentrate on research, and was succeeded in 1974 by M. Brown. It has been mainly since that time that the forces set in motion for change began to take definite form. Dr. Brown came to Saskatchewan from the University of Waterloo with broad interests in research and applied areas that were well suited to the emerging programme.

The main changes which resulted at the undergraduate level were the introduction of a wider variety of courses and a system of prerequisites and class limits which did much to correct imbalances in enrolment. Although the programme was given more structure and depth, its character remained as a basic research-oriented presentation of the major areas of psychology. At the graduate level, many more classes were introduced; there was greater structure in degree requirements; and more opportunities for doing practicums in clinical and applied research settings were provided. The numbers of carefully selected students were set at a fairly fixed enrolment of ten in each year of the two-year MA programme and approximately five at the Ph.D. level. New methods of evaluating students were also tried.

The expanded programme retained the possibility for general experimental degrees organized mainly on an individual basis, but put the main emphasis on the area of clinical psychology. This was followed in 1976 by the introduction of a programme in applied social-personality which focused on the development of expertise as a research worker and consultant in applied settings.

This explicit formalization of the programmes, changed the direction of graduate work in the department, but fitted in well with the traditional orientation of the university which had, from its beginning, emphasized professional training and the importance of making teaching and research serve the needs of the province. The university's orientation made it easier to secure appointments in applied areas and facilitated the close integration of the department with the University Hospital and governmental and community agencies on a province-wide basis. The emphasis on applied psychology was also, of course, the product of the interests of the new faculty and students.

⌈ The expansion and formalization of graduate work grew out of a long period when graduate studies were organized on an individual basis. Such informal work started very early with the award of an MA degree to I. Mackintosh in 1949. It continued with a few Master's students over this early period. The focus was not on formal course work, but on a research project individually supervised by a staff member whose interests were close to the student's project. It was a research-apprentice model influenced no doubt by the English universities and by McGill which had a decisive effect on Saskatchewan through the early faculty appointments of McGill graduates.⌉

The number of graduate students increased gradually from the two or three of the early years to the 14 to 18 registered each year from 1967–1972.

There was little change, however, from the model of the research apprentice working with an individual faculty member. The students were almost entirely candidates for the MA degree, but some Ph.D.s were granted. The first one was to T. Weckowicz in 1962, followed by Z. Pylyshyn in 1964, D. Gold and H. Klem in 1966, S. Guraraja in 1970, and T. Dineen, L. Shepel and B. Corenblum in 1975.

No history of the department would be complete without reference to other groups in the province interested in psychological services and education with which it was closely associated. These include the Departments of Psychiatry and Psychology at the University Hospital, the Institute for Child Guidance, and the University Counselling Service. Dr. D. Sydiaha in 1974 took over as director of the latter service and it has become closely integrated with the Department. Invaluable help has also been received from members of St. Thomas More College which became a federated college within the University of Saskatchewan in 1936. When the Psychology Department first offered courses in 1947–48, a section of Introductory Psychology was taught by a member of the staff of St. Thomas More. After this college added faculty in pscyhology to a total of four and introduced courses in Social Psychology, Personality, and Developmental Psychology, all teaching there and in the University Department was integrated and a tradition of full participation of the college staff in all departmental activities was established. The result has been that the St. Thomas More faculty has played and continues to play an important role in meeting the extensive demands on the department.

The Department was also intimately involved in the formation of the Saskatchewan Psychological Association (SPA) which was established in 1954. The SPA was the first such association in the prairie provinces. It started very small. The author can remember an occasion at one of the earliest meetings, held at the University Hospital, when everyone left the meeting room together to go for coffee and all were able to occupy a single elevator, and Morgan Wright, the first president, remarked "I'll bet this is the only association in the world that could hold its meetings in an elevator".

The Association, nonetheless, has continued without a break since its formation. It has been active in securing legislation regulating professional psychological services in the province and in promoting educational activities among its members. Annual week-long seminars have been held and have brought to Saskatchewan many outstanding contributors to teaching and research in psychology. At one such seminar there was another memorable happening. Our guest had been Dr. Bruno Bettelheim who had been with us for a week to give a series of excellent presentations on his work. When he was leaving Neil Agnew was to see him off, pay the honorarium, and generally assure that all went well with the visitor. Neil told us later that his final act was to write the honorarium cheque for five hundred dollars. This time, inadvertently, he wrote the amount as five dollars and handed over the cheque with a flourish. Dr. Bettelheim looked at it and then said with mock sadness, "So that is what you thought of me?".

The Department of Psychology, now nearing the close of Phase III, a phase marked by reorganization, is ready to enter another phase which should be marked by stable growth and the development of quality in teaching and research. Many of the old problems still plague the Department, notably the difficulty in recruiting sufficient staff to meet the demands of large class enrolments, and in obtaining adequate office and research space. The classes are still large with 1678 students enrolled in Introductory Psychology and 1304 in 19 upper class courses. At the undergraduate level the programme remains very much a descendant of the one first offered thirty years ago by the Department and before that by philosophy. At the graduate level new emphases and new directions, have arisen, but these are popular with students and there is strong competition for the places open for MA and Ph.D. students each year.

Further Readings

Bernhardt, K. S. Five new Fellows of the C.P.A. (Dr. Thomas William Cook). *The Canadian Psychologist*, 1958, 7, 96–98.

McMurray, G.A. Psychology at Saskatchewan. *The Canadian Psychologist*, 1961, 2, 45–49.

See also a note in *The Canadian Psychologist*, 1960, 1, 64.

Chapter 11

Psychology at Alberta

by

Thomas M. Nelson*

Most if not all the histories collected here cite the academic events and settings from which their teaching and research in psychology emerged. It was different here. The antecedents were political, namely those sorrounding the creation of new provinces out of the Alberta, Assiniboia, Athabasca and Saskatchewan Districts of the old Northwest Territories (*Alberta and Saskatchewan;* 1981). Nothing was settled until the spring of 1905 and no serious thought could be given to the question of a university until afterwards. It is clear that John M. MacEachran, who was then considering whether or not to pursue study of Philosophy and Psychology in Germany, could not have yet planned to come here.

Once geo-political issues were resolved in Ottawa and a Premier elected, things moved ahead rapidly. At the first meeting of the Legislature it was decided to create a University. Premier Rutherford was especially concerned that the basis for high quality advanced education be firmly established during his term of office. He reserved the portfolio of education for himself and devoted enormous amounts of time to assure that a University was launched under circumstances most favourable to its development (Johns, 1981). Yet he acted quickly by announcing the appointment of Dr. Henry Tory on March 30, 1908.

The same night from the same platform Tory outlined the basis upon which he wished to develop the University. Tory stressed the need for appointing scholars. No one, he said, should teach who did not have the equivalent of the Ph.D. degree, and the University should be built around the Arts and Sciences, not applied disciplines as planned in Saskatchewan (Johns, 1981). He soon made four appointments to provide for

* Professor Nelson joined the Faculty of the University of Alberta in 1964. He was Acting Head of the Department of Psychology there in 1965–66, Associate Head in 1966–67 and Head from 1967 to the present.

teaching English, Classics, Modern Language and Mathematics. These four were joined by others in 1909, notably Dr. John M. MacEachran, Ph.D., Queen's University; Ph.D., University of Leipzig.

John MacEachran was born in or near Glencoe, Ontario, eventually inheriting a family farm there. He did not come from an academic family, but showed promise in public school and, on this account, was encouraged by a school master to matriculate at a university. He chose Queen's and once there admitted to having vacillated about choice of a major. At one point MacEachran considered some branch of engineering very seriously. Finally, however, he settled upon philosophy. It seems likely that it was during his time at Queen's, where he obtained an M.A. and Ph.D.[1] in philosophy that he also began to read psychology, although we have little information about how he developed this interest. Surely at some point MacEachran decided he must go to Germany and complete his education by studying psychology.

He left in 1906 and presented himself to Stumpf in Berlin, spending what he describes as an ineffectual period of about nine months there. He apparently got little encouragement from Stumpf although he did accrue his first laboratory experience in psychology. Sometime in 1907, he decided to visit Wundt in Leipzig. He found Wundt more receptive than Stumpf.

MacEachran had many conversations with Wundt before settling on a thesis topic. Education was very much an individual matter in Leipzig and Wundt apparently discussed a wide range of topics with each of his students before agreeing to supervision. Since Wundt wrote on philosophy as well as psychology and physiology, he eventually suggested that MacEachran write on pragmatism; something new to the continent. Since this was a topic which lay near the interface of philosophy and psychology, MacEachran assented. He began course and thesis work at once, being already very competent in German. At the same time, Wundt assigned his "American"[2] to one of his laboratory assistants to assure that he left Germany with a sound experimental education. I gathered from MacEachran that his committee required no specific course work. They simply gave him notice of the scope of his examination, which was to be philosophy as a major subject, cultural history as a first minor and psychology as a second minor.

The University of Alberta Archives cares for MacEachran's *Kollegien-Buch*[3] as part of its permanent collection. This shows that he had taken 19 courses at Leipzig during three semesters: Summer 1907, Winter 1908, Summer 1908. Seven of the courses were in psychology and twelve divided between philosophy and cultural history. The psychology courses were: PSYCHOLOGY OF FACIAL SENSES given by Wirth; PSYCHOLOGY

given by Wundt; INTRODUCTION TO PSYCHOLOGY by Klemm; PSYCHOLOG-
ICAL LABORATORY by Wundt; HUMOUR AND COMEDY by Volkelt; PSY-
CHOLOGY by Wirth; PSYCHOLOGICAL LABORATORY by Wirth and PEDAGOGY
IN THE SCHOOLS ACCORDING TO HERBART by Volkelt. Closely related to
psychology were HISTORY OF PHILOSOPHY given by Wundt and HISTORY OF
PEDAGOGY by Volkelt.

When his thesis was finished he, of course, gave it to his supervisor.
Wundt told him to come back in a year after he had had time to read what
he had written. This suited MacEachran very well. In 1908 he went to
Paris to study with the distinguished sociologist Durkeim and the brilliant
philosopher Henri Bergson. Also, he had heard of Binet's exploratory
work in intelligence and hoped to take lectures from him. In his later years
he seemed to regard the radical and novel exposition of Bergson with
some reservation, although I noticed that the first M.A. student he
supervised – this was in 1913 – wrote about Bergson's theory of memory.

After Paris, MacEachran travelled in Italy to satisfy a long standing
interest in the fine arts. There he purchased a number of good items.
One wall of his house displayed a Rembrandt sketch purchased while
travelling and oils from recognized Italian painters were prominent on
others. He shared this interest with Wundt. MacEachran liked to relate
how he and Wundt chanced to meet at a gallery one day and how pleased
he was to receive a lengthy and knowledgeable lecture on the collection
being exhibited as they strolled through together.

Upon returning to Berlin he found his thesis suitable for defense. The
committee was assembled and his examination begun. MacEachran
remembered many of the questions asked him. MacEachran, playing the
role of Wundt, asked the question in German, translated, gave his answer
in German and then translated this. He was fluent and apt to lapse into
German entirely when discussing his examination.

Best recalled was that part of the oral where Wundt asked the
question, "What is an idea, Dr. MacEachran?" He reports to have said
that an idea is "a copy of a copy of a sense impression". Apparently this
was very much to the Master's liking. Wundt is reported to have said,
"We need not examine this man further, gentlemen. It is a farce beyond
this." MacEachran's thesis was published with the title *Der Pragmatismus*.

Despite his education in the New Psychology, MacEachran was not
fully convinced of the value of introspective research. A curious
eclecticism characterized MacEachran's thinking about psychology
throughout. The laboratory outlook was Wundtian and his experimental
pride the "Hipp Chronoscope", but his favourite text book was *A Briefer
Course* by William James.

The solution to the enigma of MacEachran's psychology may reside in MacEachran's pragmatism and the immense impracticality manifested by the New Psychology. True to his pragmatic leanings, MacEachran admitted that he dared to ask Wundt what the possible usefulness of experimental psychology might be. Predictably, Wundt was disparaging, saying something like "Oh you Americans, always asking for something in the way of practical application. Grasp the fact that experimental psychology has just begun! Give it the required time to develop! The applications will come in proper time, don't worry about that. But first we need at least two to three centuries of very careful laboratory measurement." We shall see later that this advice was disregarded: Alberta moved toward applied psychology quickly.

If we have solved one MacEachran riddle, there are two more difficult. Why did a man who possessed such academic qualifications and a very refined taste accept an appointment at a frontier university housed in space rented from a public school – the whole being created by a legislature meeting in first session three years previously? MacEachran was always vague about this but I gathered that he had been recommended to Henry Marshall Tory who was constantly raking the country to locate top quality scholars he might entice to Alberta. Tory was a very convincing man by many accounts (Johns, 1981).

The other mystery is – why did he stay? His answer to this was Algerian – 'A man should stick to what he starts to do.' Others, not so charitable, suggest that he had found a comfortable niche – as one put it – 'he was a big frog with a loud croak in a damn small pond!'

Very possibly, Alberta can claim to have Canada's longest unbroken program of instruction in modern psychology serviced by qualified psychologists. There can be no doubt that MacEachran was more interested in philosophy than psychology, but there also can be no doubt that MacEachran was a psychologist as well. The important things about MacEachran and psychology in Alberta are the following: 1) he taught courses in modern psychology every year from 1909 onwards; 2) from the very first it was possible to have some concentration in psychology to the extent of one junior and two senior level courses (Smith, 1975); 3) it was possible to pass the first examination set in psychology without taking recourse to philosophy[4]. 4) once the psychology program started it continued to expand in scope. For example, beginning in 1911 it was possible to obtain an M.A. as well as a B.A. degree by studying psychology; 5) MacEachran remained active in professional psychological circles. He was one of the founders of the C.P.A. and he became its first Honorary President in 1939. 6) the Canadian Psychological Association constitution was written in Edmonton as an assignment to a then fresh Ph.D. from Harvard, Douglas E. Smith (Smith, 1975); 7) MacEachran was a prominent participant in the eugenics program launched in Alberta, somewhat to the embarrassment of the University at the present time. This appointment was probably linked in some fashion to his background in psychology. More will be said about this later.

MacEachran Years: Development of Psychology program (1909–1915)

It is sometimes said that the high tide of confidence in Western Civilization was reached in the decade just prior to World War I. Certainly confidence in the future of Alberta and Edmonton was never greater. Edmonton registered a population of 700 in 1892 and was given the status of a North West Territories town. By 1904 the population had risen to 8,350. In 1911 the population had escalated to approximately three times this, and then more than doubled during the year 1911–1912, reaching a number in exess of 50,000. By the year 1915 the population was about 75,000 persons.

The development of psychology which kept pace was not modeled along Wundtian lines.[5] The 1909–1910 Calendar saw one course titled PSYCHOLOGY AND LOGIC introduced. The text for the psychology portion was William James *Psychology: A Briefer Course*. This course was afterwards continued but renamed. In 1913–1914 there were 439 students registered in the University and a substantial increase in course offerings in psychology occurred. Several options were opened to students at senior levels which expanded the range of topics appreciably. In addition to the first course now called PHILOSOPHY II, which involved two hours of psychology and one hour of logic per week, PSYCHOLOGY III[6] and PSYCHOLOGY IV were introduced. The first was designed to provide advanced general psychology for two hours per week and social psychology for one hour. The second promised education in comparative psychology including animal evolution and child psychology for two hours per week and racial psychology, which involved lectures about the psychological basis of language, myth, art, custom and morality for one hour a week. MacEachran appears to have taught the junior course and one senior each year, alternating between the senior courses. In the same year MacEachran introduced honours/graduate courses in PHYSIOLOGI-CAL PSYCHOLOGY, ABNORMAL PSYCHOLOGY and PSYCHOLOGY OF RELIGION.

The last Calendar prepared in peacetime (1914–1915) reorganized the psychology sequence as PHILOSOPHY 1, PSYCHOLOGY 51, PSYCHOLOGY 52, PSYCHOLOGY 101, PSYCHOLOGY 102, PSYCHOLOGY 103. As before psychology courses were separated from philosophy courses, each having its own place in the Calendar.

The more monetary minded may be interested to know that MacEachran's salary as a professor reached $4,900 during this period. He appears to have earned it since he carried virtually the entire undergraduate philosophy program as well as the psychology program.[7] Moreover he was responsible for a substantial honours instruction in both philosophy and psychology, and supervised at least one M.A. student. In addition, he was carrying out the administrative duties associated with the office of Provost of the University, an appointment he had been carrying out since 1911 (Macdonald, 1958) and accepted officially a year or so later.

MacEachran told me that at one point he found himself beset with responsibility for eleven courses, some of them falling outside his specialty of psychology and philosophy. He said he had insufficient time to write out notes and was able to manage this incredible load only by memorizing each lecture as it was being delivered! MacEachran was a very busy professor by any standard and frugal too. Smith (1975) shows no expenditures on Supplies and Sundries during the Developing Era. The first entry is $25.00 spent during the year 1915–1916.

MacEachran: First War Emergency (1916–1920)

Nineteen hundred fourteen saw the speculative development bubble burst in Edmonton, causing a sudden large decline in the number of persons in the city. It also saw Canada deeply involved in war. A large number of University of Alberta students and staff served and many gave their lives in service (Johns, 1981). Growth in numbers stopped.

MacEachran himself joined the Western Universities Battalion, Canadian Infantry, and later served as a paymaster in France (but probably not with the 196th Battalion). He was replaced by a man by the name of W.S. Dyde, who was connected to Robertson College – a theological school – and later by J.M. Berry, who had received an M.A. degree from the University of Alberta.

New courses were nonetheless introduced in 1915–1916 and 1916–1917. Two of these were a move towards application. PSYCHOLOGY 53 was described as 'Psychology in Relation to the Practice of Medicine'.[8] It met only one hour per week. The second and third courses were at honours levels: PSYCHOLOGY 104 presented 'Educational Psychology' and PSYCHOLOGY 105 'Experimental Psychology.' Here again we witness the broad innovative drive of MacEachran.

MacEachran: Applied Years (1921–1936)

Development of Psychology resumed with the return to peace. Berry left in 1921 but during the same year two additions to staff were made. One was John Macdonald, appointed Assistant Professor, who held an Honours M.A. in Philosophy, the M.A. being the first degree at Edinburgh. Most of Macdonald's course work was taken in psychology even though the degree that was awarded specified 'Philosophy'. He received instruction from psychologist James Drever who occupied the Chair there at that time.

Macdonald had also previously held a post at the University of Bristol and, therefore, was experienced in teaching (Arvidson and Nelson, 1968). He was one of the most significant appointments MacEachran made. During his long service at the University of Alberta he maintained an excellent reputation as a teacher and helpful colleague.

Notwithstanding his excellence as a teacher, he and a number of others came under pressure from President Tory in 1926. This led him to take a leave of absence, which eventuated in award of the Ph.D. from Edinburgh, again in Philosophy.

Macdonald had a keen interest in educatuon as well as psychology and philosophy (Macdonald, 1938). This was later helpful in having education of public school teachers moved from normal schools to the university. Macdonald was to become Dean of Arts and Science in 1945. He stayed until the time of his retirement in 1952.

The second appointment was Earl D. MacPhee as instructor. He stayed until 1925 at which time he left to accept appointment at the University of Toronto. MacPhee later became an industrial psychologist in private practice and then even later Dean of Commerce at the University of British Columbia.

In the decade of the 'twenties', the program veered sharply in the direction of applied psychology. PHILOSOPHY 1 was removed and courses appear with the titles APPLIED PSYCHOLOGY, EDUCATIONAL PSYCHOLOGY, INDUSTRIAL PSYCHOLOGY, LEGAL PSYCHOLOGY and PSYCHOLOGY AND ECONOMIC PROBLEMS. However, courses of a more theoretical character were also added in the area of Macdonald's chief interest (social psychology) as well as three courses with clinical content – NORMAL and ABNORMAL PSYCHOLOGY, PSYCHOPATHOLOGY and PSYCHOPATHOLOGY (ADVANCED). The latter were designed to be of interest to students of medicine. The courses representing Social Psychology used William McDougall's classic textbook.

Years of Adversity

Alberta was prosperous in the 1920's and two persons definitely related to education were added. The first was Dr. M.E. Lazerte who later became the first Dean of the Faculty of Education. The other was H.E. Smith who later became the second Dean of Education. In addition to these there were three others; a Samuel R. Laycock who instructed in both Classics and Psychology, a William Line who instructed only during the 1924–1925 academic year and a Brother (Roger) Philip.

The latter was on staff at St. Joseph's College,[9] but was a specialist in experimental psychology with a good background in mathematics. Brother Philip eventually developed a fairly wide range of undergraduate-type experimental equipment and was given charge of the Hipp chronoscope. This precious piece of brass was the big capital acquisition of the department, costing a large sum in the earlier years. MacEachran believed that it was necessary to retain a person specially skilled in its use and this, he told me, was one reason for appointing Brother Philip originally.

The University had 1,560 students in 1929–1930. Wall Street 'crashed' at the end of October 1929 and the first eight years of the 1930's were the depression years.

Despite a grave shortage of funds (Johns, 1981) administrative reorganization was still feasible and some new courses could be put forward. In the 1933–1934 Calendar the Department became that of Philosophy, Psychology and Education. This arrangement lasted for only two years after which there was a Department of Education.

Academically the first course in clinical psychology appeared in 1930 at honours level. A course titled SOCIAL PSYCHOLOGY is also noted in the 1933–1934 year along with PSYCHOLOGY FOR STUDENTS IN NURSING which is, however, listed as PHILOSOPHY 3 for some reason. Another course, PHILOSOPHY 2, was renamed GENERAL AND SOCIAL PSYCHOLOGY AND LOGIC, later to revert to the familiar PSYCHOLOGY AND LOGIC title.

Several courses were removed from the 1934–1936 list and transferred to the new Department of Education. One new course was inserted called PSYCHOLOGY IN RELATION TO SOCIAL REFORM. New staff were not added during this portion of the Applied Years and salaries fell somewhat.

It is now the time to say something about MacEachran's controversial involvement with the Mental Health Movement in Alberta, if for no other reason than to clarify that these activities were *not* those of the Department itself. It should be said, firstly, that MacEachran's motives appear to have been those of the reformer of prisons and other such institutions. In a paper titled "Criminals are not Reformed by Brutality and Inhumanity" (MacEachran, 1932), he heatedly argued that then existing methods of treating lawbreakers were both ineffectual and unjust. Secondly, MacEachran was identified with the Mental Health Movement in Canada to the extent of developing a philosophical justification for the movement (MacEachran, 1932) and was probably on the Eugenics Board as much from philosophical convictions as because of his background in psychology.

The Mental Health Movement, which was widespread, led to the establishment of the Alberta Eugenics Board in 1928. The Board was assembled in accordance with an act designed "to prevent the mentally ill or the mentally deficient from passing on mental illness or metal deficiency to offspring". This act was amended several times (Frost, 1942).

A four-man Board established under the act was empowered to order sterilization without the consent of persons judged mentally deficient. The Board was empowered to authorize doctors to sterilize mental patients if they, or a husband, or wife, or guardian consented (Frost, 1942; *Edmonton Journal*, 1974). Sterilization rarely involved neutering, although this did occur when there was a history of violence. According to T. Kibblewhite[10] who served as secretary to the Board, all decisions to sterilize were arrived at by the Board upon the advice of a diagnostic group using as evidence case history materials, psychiatric interviews and intelligence test data. MacEachran was Chairman of the Alberta Eugenics Board from 1919 to about 1955.

The act was repealed 42 years later, in 1972. During this time approximately 4,500 persons were presented to the Board and about 2,500 actual sterilizations occurred. Criticism was later directed against the wisdom of the legislation and the possibility of ethnic bias was raised (*Edmonton Journal*, 1979; *Edmonton Journal*, 1974).

Departmental members other than MacEachran were not involved with the operation of the Alberta Eugenics Board.[11] Employees of the Provincial Government made measurements and evaluations.[12] A survey of the activities of the Alberta Eugenics Board was made the topic of a thesis by a mathematics student (Frost, 1942).

MacEachran: Introduction of Laboratory Psychology (1937–1940)

We are fortunate to have a record of the personal memories of Douglas Elstow Smith, who arrived on campus in September 1937 to take up teaching duties as a Sessional Lecturer in Psychology (Smith, 1975). Brother Philip had been called to another post and Smith was a replacement to improve the 'science side' of Psychology.

Smith added considerable strength and prestige to the Department.

A Canadian, he held a B.A. and M.A. degree from Queen's and had studied with Karl Lashley, the noted physiological psychologist, first at the University of Chicago and later at Harvard, where he obtained the Ph.D. He also had studied under E.G. Boring, Gordon Allport and Henry Murray, which qualified him to teach a variety of courses (Arvidson and Nelson, 1968).

His first impressions are stated in these words:

I had my first sight of the Arts building from the 105th Street Bridge, as I was being driven to the campus, because there were then many vacant lots in the Garneau area, especially along the river bank. I still remember how impressive and attractive the location and the stone-trimmed brick buildings were at this first contact.

In the first year I was conscious of an interesting mixture of traditional (even out-dated) and progressive approaches in the Department. For example, the official name of this Department had been Philosophy and Psychology since 1933, while most psychologists in Canada were still members of Departments of Philosophy. Although the contemporary pattern in the United States was separate departments of psychology (and I had carried on graduate studies in two of them), I was pleased that the University of Alberta recognized psychology as a separate discipline, though in this and other instances combining disciplines in a single department (as it continued to do for many years).

The organization of courses seemed somewhat unusual, and sometimes old-fashioned. One of the courses I taught that year was Philosophy 2, a junior introductory course in psychology and logic normally given by Dr. Macdonald. This arrangement followed a pattern found in philosophy offerings in many Commonwealth universities and originally established in England. My other courses were: Psychology 51, a senior introductory course in psychology; Psychology 61, a two-hour-per-week course in general psychology for second-year medical students; and Psychology 62, a one-hour-per-week course in abnormal psychology for third-year medical students. Dr. Macdonald's other courses (not given in 1937–38) were one in social psychology and social anthropology and one in sociology. Dr. H.E. Smith gave an undergraduate course which had recently been adapted from an honors course in clinical psychology. A course in legal psychology was in the Calendar but had not been offered for some time. There were honors courses in experimental psychology, physiological psychology, abnormal psychology and the psychology of religion.

The curriculum for the honors program seemed particularly anachronistic. The calendar provided that courses and "specific work" would be prescribed for each honors student in the Department, who also wrote a series of "final examinations" in the last year. The three programs were: Honors in Philosophy and Psychology; Honors in Psychology and Philosophy; and Honors in Philosophy and Greek. If the final examinations reflected their preparation, students interested in philosophy did six-sevenths of their work in philosophy, while any students interested in psychology could do no more than half their work in that subject. This was not just a matter of terminology; for example, my first degree (awarded in 1933) had been B.A. with Honors in Philosophy and Economics when my specialization had really been a strong major in psychology and a minor in political science. My first comments on the curriculum here seemed to produce no interest in change; there were then no candidates for honors psychology, and I decided not to try to change the curriculum until a more favorable opportunity occurred.

Text-books for the two introductory courses had been ordered well before my appointment, and I was far from satisfied with them. In Philosophy 2, Dr. Macdonald was using in the psychology part of the course *Elements of Human Psychology*, by Warren and Carmichael, published in 1930. This was a revision of a much earlier book, *Human Psychology*, by Warren; and Carmichael as joint author had not produced the modernization I would have expected from a distinguished and up-to-date experimental psychologist. In Psychology 51 I inherited from Brother Philip *Introduction to Psychology*, by Boring, Langfeld and Weld. These senior psychologists had been dedicated Titchenerians, and when their book was published in 1935 reviewers expressed surprise that the emphasis was about the same as that of a text by Titchener some decades earlier. In Psychology 61 there was no text, as I remember; in Psychology 62 there was a slim volume by a British psychiatrist, largely theoretical and with a Freudian emphasis.

I found Psychology 51 a very demanding course. One reason was the importance at that time of a distinction between junior and senior courses. First-year students in Arts and

Science were restricted to junior courses; to be promoted to second year they were required to pass five such courses in one year (a repeated first year, still restricted to junior courses, was very common). In the second and later years they took four senior courses per year; not only was each course more extensive but also students were more mature, and were the survivors of the selection process of promotion from first year. Psychology 51 was thus more comprehensive and detailed than the psychology portion of Philosophy 2. A second factor was the requirement in the Calendar for "laboratory work and projects", with no laboratory hours in the list of hours per week. In practice, therefore, I had to organize laboratory projects for some 60 students per year, with no laboratory assistants (Smith, 1975, pages 1–4).

Smith received a second appointment as Sessional Instructor in 1938, and shortly afterwards was appointed Lecturer on a permanent basis. One of his first assignments was to teach HISTORY OF PSYCHOLOGY, an honours course he had managed to get put into the Calendar while yet an Instructor. EXPERIMENTAL PSYCHOLOGY was also introduced as a separate junior course and required three hours of laboratory per week. The course in ABNORMAL PSYCHOLOGY was restructured to stress the biological and social factors related to maladjustment and diminish the 'dynamic' approach taken by psychiatrists and Freudian psychologists.
   Notwithstanding the good rapport Smith had with MacEachran, which led to easy changes in curriculum, laboratory research apparently still had a low priority. MacEachran neglected to support his requests for laboratory research space and his research was consequently restricted to an experiment conducted in cooperation with a friend in the Department of Biochemistry (Smith, 1975). His impression of the research facilities of the Department of Philosophy and Psychology as it became officially known in 1935 are not exciting.

   I found in the Department more equipment than had been available at Queen's when I was a student there (but of course far less than Chicago and Harvard had possessed). There were several performance tests of intelligence, some instruments for studying sensation (including a hand-held perimeter and a Galton whistle), a kymograph and an ergograph, a model of the human brain, and similar standard small equipment. the Hipp Chronoscope was there, and even then out of order; there was also a Dunlap Chronoscope (a more modern but elaborate and clumsy instrument which could be used for precise research when in working order). These were typical of large and expensive pieces of equipment doubtless obtained for some former member of the Department for research, but of very limited use for general laboratory experiments.

In retrospect the attempt to introduce laboratory psychology seems to have been largely abortive. Brother Philip was moved by his order in 1937 and Smith left campus for a post in the Canadian Army in 1941 before he could consolidate the concept of true research laboratories. Moreover the experience he gained in the Personnel Selection Unit of the Army during World War II reduced his enthusiasm for experimental psychology when he returned after the war. No further permanent staff appointments were to be made for eleven years, until 1948.

Enrolments had increased at a painfully slow rate. There were only 2,327 students registered in the whole University during the semester following the outbreak of World War II (i.e. on 1 September 1939).

MacEachran: Second War Emergency (1941–1945)

The war years must have been a somewhat depressing period to be in charge of a department. Now too old to seek active service, MacEachran could only bid goodbye to staff placed on leave of absence and see his personal domain reduced to provide spaces for temporary wartime programs (Johns, 1981). Replacements for departing staff were difficult to secure and if even a part of the calendar was to be covered, increasing use had to be made of graduate students and even senior undergraduates. Budget for salaries and equipment were being cut at times and enrolment in various courses had to be temporarily suspended. Two junior undergraduate courses were permanently removed from the Calendar and two were renamed. Nothing was added.

MacEachran is now at the end of his career. Before we bid him good-bye, let us briefly share some of his reflections.

His retirement started a month after the surrender of Germany and a few weeks after the capitulation of Japan. The culture which he both loved and respected best was that of Imperial Germany. He wrote with affection of how Germany had given the world the concept of academic freedom, and had provided a setting where students could totally commit themselves to study (MacEachran, 1945). He spoke often of the beauty of the poetry of Goethe and the music of Wagner (Nelson, 1972). He told me that he was long determined that he must have a German-trained psychologist appointed to staff and would have had his old teacher in

1915, the historian of psychology, Otto Klemm, except for the eruption of the war. He regretted that the appointment of Klemm was not politically feasible after the war. But this culture was no more. And if MacEachran was regretful of the distance World War I had put between Canada and Germany, he was more horrified at the Germany World War II exposed. In 1945 he shared these sombre thoughts with us.

"The German Universities received a severe set-back during the Great War. Their scientific activities were, of course, directed toward the needs of war. They were depleted of students and the professors were impoverished by the disastrous inflation which followed. The old ideals, however, remained till the rise of the Nazi regime, when everything in the form of freedom of thought, freedom in teaching, and freedom in research activities was ruthlessly destroyed. The libraries were invaded and very valuable collections of books were burned in public. What was left of these famous institutions was now deliberately and thoroughly turned into the service of the war-machine. If Germany is ever to regain her self-respect and the respect of the world, she will need a drastic cleansing of her national and spiritual life, and one of the first steps in that direction must be the restoration to the Universities of the free intellectual life and ethical idealism that made them during the four hundred years preceding the Great War, world-renowned as centres of learning." (page 7, MacEachran, 1945).

John Macdonald Years (1945–1952)

Following MacEachran's retirement in 1945, Macdonald, then Professor of Social Philosophy and Social Psychology and a native of Scotland, became the fourth Dean of Arts and Science and Head of the Department of Philosophy and Psychology. Macdonald continued to carry this area as a teaching Dean. Smith, newly returned, could be expected to carry courses in history, experimental and honours courses other than in the social area.

Due to the return of verterans, enrolment in psychology became very heavy, more than double what it was in the last peacetime year (Macdonald, 1958). Unfortunately, the University did not act at once to increase staff but Macdonald was able to promise Smith that the psychology side of the Department would be strengthened. Space was increased making it possible for Smith to begin to establish a psychological laboratory, and research equipment was purchased in enough quantity to justify a part-time summer assistant to help assemble it. Experimental Psychology was faring better under Macdonald.

In 1948 Macdonald made provisions for the appointment of Donald Spearman, a graduate of McGill University. Spearman's area of expertise was Clinical Psychology, which fit Macdonald's perception that a junior Ph.D. was necessary to teach ABNORMAL PSYCHOLOGY AND MENTAL HYGIENE.

The one additional appointment of a psychologist during the Macdonald years was Lolita Wilson (1951). This was split with Student Counselling and further strengthened the clinical area. A course THEORY OF PSYCHOMETRICS was added to the Calendar but this was in fact only the lecture portion of the then existing course THEORY AND PRACTICE OF PSYCHOMETRICS. Wilson much later left to teach at Simon Fraser University.

Before the Macdonald years ended, D.E. Smith was offered the Headship at Queen's University creating a conflictful situation. Accepting appointment at Queen's would return him to his Alma Mater and locate him close to his father and brother. He talked to Macdonald who wished him to stay. By this time the Smiths had established a family who were reluctant to relocate, so when Macdonald offered him the rank of Professor, he accepted. The offer was confirmed by the Executive Committee of the Board of Governors in 1949, as was the custom at that time.

D.E. Smith Years (1952–1957)

Upon Macdonald's retirement in 1952, Douglas Elstow Smith, the psychologist, became the third Head of the Department. In 1957 he was to become the sixth Dean of Arts and Science and in 1963, the first Dean of Arts.

Smith was born in a small town about 15 miles from Kingston, Ontario, the son of a 'railroad man'. The family moved frequently but he was able to attend university. His original intention was to major in Law and History, but this changed when he was exposed to the lectures at Queen's University given by George Humphrey, who later became the first Director of the Institute of Experimental Psychology at Oxford. Humphrey eventually supervised his M.A. thesis and advised him to go to the University of Chicago for a Ph.D. and to study Educational Psychology there so as to have 'two strings to his bow'. In Chicago he fell under the influence of Karl Lashley and a fellow graduate student, Donald Hebb. He quickly forgot Humphrey's advice and desired to become a Physiological Psychologist. He and Hebb then moved to Harvard with Lashley. Both Smith and Hebb completed their Ph.D. there, remaining fast friends to this day.

At Alberta Smith was a popular teacher known in the student body as 'Rat' Smith to separate his interests from those of 'Education' Smith. He was also known as 'Monkey' Smith. There were no caged primates at that time and the epithet 'Monkey' was based upon an amazing repetoire of contorted positions he would suddenly assume during lectures to 'stimulate interest in psychology'. He retired in 1975.

Smith was the first Head in 40 years to devote his whole efforts to the development of programs in the Department. His period of administration was brief, only five years, but active. He brought in Lawrence C. Walker in Social Psychology (who left in 1956); A.J.B. Hough who was attached for the most part to Student Counselling, but who taught PSYCHOLOGY OF RELIGION for many years; Joseph L. Lambert, an American who did a philosophical analysis of Tolman's Theory of Learning for his Ph.D. dissertaion; and Esther Milner (who left in 1960).

Smith was a bear for organization and much housekeeping was done to improve the Calendar. Importantly, the first course having specific developmental content was approved for teaching (Psychology 42, GENERAL AND DEVELOPMENTAL PSYCHOLOGY).

⌐A major development during his time was the forming of a Teaching and Counselling Service in the Department of Philosophy and Psychology. Legislation to control the practice of psychology was lacking as yet and there was a dearth of qualified individuals to do diagnostic testing and personal counselling. The plan he and Spearman reached was to provide supervised practical experience to students interested in obtaining clinical experience while at the same time extending service to clients at either a nominal charge or at no charge. This plan allowed Spearman to spread his available clinical time over more clients than he was able to see before. The service was first budgeted in 1956–1957 and still functions with Dr. Spearman as its Director.⌐

Anthony Mardiros Years (1957–1960)

Upon Smith's assumption of the position of Dean, the Department added Sociology to Philosophy and Psychology, and plans were laid to create several new departments. Mardiros, a philosopher specializing in the writings of Ludwig Wittgenstein, helped the University achieve these ends.

During his tenure as Head, five new psychologists were put on staff. Added were Charles Uhl and Raymond C. Miles, both Experimental Psychologists and Peter F. Remple, who was appointed one-third time in Psychology and two-thirds time in Student Counselling Services.

In 1959, Edgar Howarth, specializing in personality theory, was appointed by Smith, having been recruited by Miles from R.B. Cattell's laboratory at the University of Illinois. Howarth, who had obtained his Ph.D. from the University of Melbourne, was to greatly assist the Department in the next several years to start the process of course expansion and creation of a Ph.D. program. He taught courses in many and diverse areas while permanent staff were being sought.

The fifth was Joseph Russell Royce, who was appointed Professor of Psychology and named the first Head of Psychology.

J.R. Royce Years (1960–1967): Department of Psychology

Royce and MacEachran are possibly the most significant appointments yet to be made at Alberta: One formed the basis upon which psychology was to develop, the other a) started the actual Department, b) started the 'Center for Advanced Study in Theoretical Psychology', c) decided faculty affiliations and d) selected and appointed the staff who were to determine the ultimate form the Department would have. Under Royce's direction the Department began its bid for international stature.

Royce was an enthusiastic, friendly man whose distinguishing mark was a quick, short, soft laugh. Born in New York in 1921, Royce studied at the College of the City of New York, Denison University, Ohio State University, and the University of Chicago where he earned his Ph.D. in 1951 studying with Thurstone. He came to Alberta from the University of Redlands (California). His major interests included theoretical-experimental, comparative, and physiological psychology, as well as factor analysis.

Royce says he arrived believing that he was to be interviewed for a position as a Professor, not intending, or even wanting, to be considered as a candidate for Head which was also being advertised. When it became clear that he could have the Headship, he became interested enough to ask A.G. McCalla, then Dean of Graduate Studies, what obstacles would be placed in the way of assembling a first class department. McCalla said 'none'. Royce also found that Smith would give him his full cooperation as Dean of Arts and Science. His support continued even after 1963 when as Dean of Arts he could have questioned the large number of appointments being made in Science.

The separation of Arts from Science created a dilemma. Staff in the social, personality and clinical areas were considered Arts, while Royce and others he already recruited were biologists and considered Science faculty. The resolution was to keep the Department in both. This has been continued to the present day where roughly half of staff are in Arts and half in Science. It was proven to be a very workable arrangement given the cooperation we have had from the succession of Deans in both faculties.

At the time the faculty divided, plans were laid for two new buildings: a Henry Marshall Tory building for the Arts Faculty and a Biological Sciences building for Science. It so happened that psychology could move to either, but the Tory building would make space available several years earlier.

Since 1951 the Department had been located in renovated basement space in the Arts building previously occupied by Physics, and the space situation had become so critical with the numerousness of new appointments that it was tempting to move into Tory. In spite of the advantages of early relocation, it was decided to wait until the Biological Sciences building became ready because this promised better laboratory spaces. This required securing and renovating temporary space, much of it in Garneau, a residential area adjacent to campus on the east.

In 1961–1962 Robert Sommer, William Blanchard and Ludwig Von Bertalanffy came to Alberta; Sommer represented perception, Blanchard personality, and Von Bertalanffy theory. The latter is now widely considered to be the originator of General Systems Theory.

The next year Stanley J. Rule, W.N. Runquist and W.A.S. Smith were appointed. Rule was capable in auditory perception and scaling and had a sufficiently strong interest in methodology to make him desirable to teach statistics as a replacement for Uhl who had resigned. Runquist already had a good reputation in verbal learning and would give general strength to experimental psychology and replace Miles. Sam Smith was eclectic and came as much to assist in administation of the Department as to teach. All three were undergraduates at Redlands and Royce knew them as undergraduate students. Brendan G. Rule, a social psychologist, started that same year too, but as a sessional instructor. She was later appointed to regular staff, part-time, then full-time.

In 1962–1963 an extension branch of the Department was established in Calgary and A.E.D. Schonfield and M. Humphries were appointed to teach there. Schonfield later became first Head of Department at the University of Calgary.

The Ph.D. program was also instituted in 1962–1963 supplementing the M.A. and M.Sc. degrees offered up to that time. Required doctorial courses were experimental design and systematic-theoretical including history. A total of 22 graduate courses were catalogued. About half dealt with empirical research or experimental methodology. The remainder were in history, theory and clinical areas. The number of graduate students greatly increased and admissions were handled by a committee although the Head could, and did, admit separately when he chose to do so. Stipends were $2,100 to $2,700, plus a travel grant of up to $250.

In 1964 Sommer resigned, but the number of regular staff was nonetheless increased to 16 by the appointments of T. Nelson (visual perception), W. Rozeboom (learning and theory), R. Walley (physiological), and T. Weckowicz (experimental psychopathology). The latter held an M.D. as well as Ph.D. and was appointed jointly with Psychiatry. The same year the Department housed its first Post Doctoral Fellow, a physician, J.W. Urshel, and appointed A.B. Carran as a full-time Research Associate.

In 1964 Royce became convinced that it would soon be feasible to develop some kind of a theoretical centre, the first anywhere in the world devoted exclusively to psychology. He asked for and was granted sabbatical leave. He spent it lecturing in Europe and developing a proposal for the centre. W.A.S. Smith continued to help him here, although Smith had already accepted a position in central administration. W.A.S. Smith later became the First President of the University of Lethbridge, Dean of Arts at Simon Fraser University and First President of Athabasca University.

After a comical exchange with Royce and W.A.S. Smith in spring 1965, I agreed to act as Head while Royce was on sabbatical leave starting August 1965. Royce then signed a number of appointment forms, asked me to 'carry through' on a number of others during his absence and told me his wishes in regard to salaries and promotions of staff members. Following his brief, nine new staff were taken on in a single year, as many as the total appointed during the first 39 years and more than any other year since. In 1965–1966 appointments were still made without the benefit of interview visits, but this was the last year that the University routinely refused requests to fund such visits.

Staff acquired were the following: J.E. Drevdahl (creativity and factor analysis), who unfortunately died April 1966, N.M. Ginsburg (comparative), B.H. Schaeffer (animal learning), D.L. Schaeffer (personality and clinical), R.G.A. Stretch (operant learning), P. Swartz (personality systems and aesthetics), and K. Wilson (cognitive), joint with Computing Science. K. Dabrowski, the eminent developmental psychologist and psychiatrist, became visiting professor, appointed joint with Educational Psychology and Psychiatry. Dabrowski was soon to have considerable academic influence in the University. The second Visiting Professor was H. Steinmetz, appointed to provide instruction in the industrial area. L. Wilson resigned. A theoretical conference was held in 1965 at Banff with the title "Toward a Unification of Psychology". This was the first of a series continuing to the present.

In 1966 Royce returned and I stayed on as Associate Head. During the year the Center for Advanced Theoretical Study in Psychology came into existence officially and Royce resigned to become its first Director, a post he still holds. The Center was designed to provide for graduate and post-graduate level research in systems and theory in all areas of psychology[13].

In 1965 Gordon Hobon received his Ph.D. with W. Runquist as his supervisor. He was the first student at the University to do so in Psychology. Hobson later became Chairman at the University of Victoria.

For a number of years McCalla, Dean of Graduate Studies, attended many of the oral Ph.D. candidacy examinations and every thesis examination given in psychology to assure that the newly won privilege was being discharged up to standards. All graduate programs were still being administered by the Head with no delegation of responsibility allowed. This requirement has been gradually relaxed over the years so that at present a Chairman is required to be little more than the signing authority.

By the summer of 1967 the Department had a publishing staff of 23 professors, active laboratories, a Center devoted to the study of theory, an undergraduate course calendar of 24 courses made up of 13 courses in Arts and 11 in Science, a graduate calendar of 33 courses and a viable graduate program through the Ph.D. level. Large sums were now regularly spent upon equipment and ample space in a new biological sciences building was hoped for.

The Last Fourteen Years (1967–1981)

In the summer of 1966 Joe Royce returned to re-assume his duties as Head of Department. I briefed him about the events of the year, he thanked me and then said he would like me to stay on in administration part-time. I initially refused because I did not relish taking up the role Sam Smith had filled. A few days later Joe returned with an offer I should not refuse: he would arrange for my appointment as Associate Head and would divide the duties. Joe would like to keep responsibility for salary, promotion and appointment, but I should have most of the rest. He assured me that this appointment would be for the year only and that once the Center for Advanced Study in Theoretical Psychology was approved, he would again have the time to run the Department on a day-to-day basis. I accepted and the arrangement worked surprisingly well for a short time. However, not long afterwards Royce informed me that the Center would require a Director and that he intended to be this, which meant that he would resign as Head. He further told me that there would be an open competition for a replacement and that I should give consideration to running. I did so and was selected.

In 1967, as before, the position of Head was a very important one. It entailed appointment 'without definite term' and could be continued indefinitely 'at the pleasure of the Board'. Many appointed at that time expected to hold the post until retirement. Notwithstanding this, a decision was shortly made to dispose of this position and substitute that of chairman with regular review mandatory. I accepted this change without resistance or reservation. Many others did not, and in insisting upon the legitimacy of the post to which they were originally appointed, suffered.

Before immigrating to Canada and taking residence in Edmonton, most of my life had been lived in Michigan. The exceptional years were 1943–1946, when I was overseas. I attended Michigan State College beginning in 1946, and my final degree was awarded in 1958 at Michigan State University. I also stayed there afterwards, first as an Assistant Professor and then as S. Howard Bartley's Research Associate. Bartley, who had been my thesis supervisor, was one of the foremost sensory scientists of that period.

Eventually Bartley would have me seek appointment in an established department or research institute. He enumerated a sizeable range of opportunities, all exciting in different ways. However, I did not enjoy living in highly-urbanized settings, nor working in highly-structured situations. Moreover, I was friendly with 'Dutch' Lambert as a graduate student and upon a number of occasions he had urged me to move to Alberta. A brother-in-law, E.S. Edgington, had been appointed to the Department of Psychology at Calgary and he too wanted me to immigrate. Finally I wrote a letter of inquiry. Shortly afterwards Royce telephoned offering a position as associate professor and we moved to Edmonton in September, 1964.

Unlike Smith, I was far from enthralled by my first glimpse of Edmonton. As the train rolled slowly through the bleak industrial areas of north-east Edmonton and past copses populated with stunted and bare aspen, I vowed not to be there a year hence. I stayed, of course, eventually even refusing offers to return to my Alma Mater as a laboratory director.

The history of the last 14 years is mostly a history of staff development. Royce had placed a premium upon the development of the theoretical and biological sciences sides of the Department. Second priority was the area of personality, third social psychology, and fourth the applied and clinical areas. He intended to carry the areas of lower priority temporarily by appointing sessional, part-time and visiting staff. Eventually they too would be developed.[14]

There was plenty of money for permanent appointments but finding suitable persons was getting hard. The competition for qualified graduates was very keen everywhere and our disadvantages were great enough that progress was noticeably slackening. In 1967 the University was still virtually unknown in psychological circles, the location was remote professionally and the average staff member was young and unproven.

It appeared to me that the priority structure had to be amended if we were to achieve excellence. The modifications I decided upon were as follows: a) highest priority should be theoretical-experimental appointments broadly defined. This meant that social and developmental areas were to be included. Also, persons having clinical and applied interests were not to be excluded on principle. They would qualify where their work and orientation embodied theoretical concepts to a significant degree, i.e., their approach to problems was *interpretative* and not merely empirical. They would, of course, be required to be qualified practitioners too. b) staffing should increase existing areas of strength. Practically this was to be accomplished by giving some of the more productive staff the opportunity to choose another individual in their own area of expertise for appointment. c) appointments in areas of importance not as yet represented in the Department should be established via search committees. Tentatively, the areas to be developed were animal learning, behavior genetics including ethology, and, later, cognitive and information processing.

Overlaying the specific priorities were three generic requirements and one established preference. The requirements were: 1) appointees must hold a Ph.D. degree from a reputable department at the time of, or shortly after, resuming teaching duties,[15] 2) applicants must show strong evidence of becoming publishing scholars, and 3) the best person should be appointed regardless of nationality. Where feasible, preference would be given to biologically-oriented candidates.

On the administrative side, the policy was to establish each new appointee in research as soon as possible. This was to be done by reducing course load the first year, committing space at once, and providing equipment in sufficient quantity and quality to make a fast start possible. We worked to secure adequate sophisticated space in the new Biological Sciences building and strove to provide technical and support services second to none.[16]

In 1970 we were able to move into the new Biological Sciences building where we now occupy five floors. At the same time we established large and sophisticated technical services. In 1966 our shop occupied a space of 450 square feet, serviced by a single technician. It was largely used for construction of wood and metal items. In contrast, in 1979 our technical services were located in a suite of six rooms with a shop supervisor, three technicians, and a full-time Faculty Service Officer, whose job it was to provide design services, in attendance.

In 1967 the staff consisted of 22 members, four part-time. In the

1968–1969 session, R.M. Arvidson (social), A.R. Dobbs (verbal learning) and D. Landy (social) were added but Dean Smith withdrew from teaching for several years. At the end of the year staff listed seven books and 98 articles in their annual report. Students were being prepared for seven degrees, B.A., Honours B.A., B.Sc., Honours B.Sc., M.A., M.Sc., and Ph.D. At the start of 1969 graduate students numbered more than 70. Then as now they typically required two years to complete a masters and an additional three to four years to complete the Ph.D.

In 1969–1970 C.M. Bourassa (perception and sensory psychology) joined the staff and Art Hough moved full-time to the Student Counselling Centre. The graduate program was still structured around the concept of core courses. The actual courses were HISTORY AND SYSTEMS, ADVANCED EXPERIMENTAL PSYCHOLOGY, EXPERIMENTAL DESIGN, and PERSONALITY AND SOCIAL. I was on sabbatical leave and Bill Blanchard was Acting Chairman.

In 1970–1971 the core requirement was increased to six courses. However, since two of these, ADVANCED PSYCHOLOGY OF PERCEPTION and ADVANCED PSYCHOLOGY OF LEARNING, were half courses created by divisioning, there was no real increase in the time required to complete the core. Four new staff were added, namely C.H. Beck (animal psychology), R.C. Hostetter (behavior genetics), L.M. Potash (animal physiology and ethology) and W. Thorngate (decision processing). O.H. Bradbury joined the Centre as Administrative Officer. Ginsberg left the University and Von Bertalanffy accepted appointment as a University Professor. Graduate student enrollment at the end of this academic year was 87, a number which we have not exceeded to date.

By 1971–1972 A. Manes (social psychology) had been appointed. Landy resigned. The next year, 1972–1973, saw three new additions: C. Brainerd (developmental), E. Lechelt (cutaneous perception) and P.F. Zelhart (behavior modification), but B. Schaeffer resigned her position. W.M. Olson became the Department Administrative and Professional Officer, an advancement from the post of Administrative Assistant he had so ably filled since 1967. By this year (1972–1973) Department staff had grown to number 29, of which seven were professors, nine associate professors, twelve assistant professors, and one a Visiting Professor.

The Calendar of 1973–1974 adds the names of D. Curtis (perception psychophysics and scaling) and P. Runquist (learning), but deletes the names of Hostetter and Manes who had resigned. The same year the Department listed 26 undergraduate and honours courses in Arts, 24 in Science and 62 in the Calendar of Graduate Studies. Naturally many of the graduate courses were devoted to seminars, theses, research apprenticeships and special topics.

1974–1975 was quiet. There were no major changes in teaching programs and it was the first time in 25 years that a new appointment is not noted. We were now clearly in the austerity years. Universally funds were being slowly reduced by the provincial government and the major means of economizing was to delay expenditures. Whatever the University did not spend one year could be carried over to the next, serving to buffer the real reductions. But, it served as more than a delay because the monies saved by making a sessional appointment for even one year, instead of a permanent appointment, were enormous. Budgets, therefore, tended to be authorized late in the academic year making it difficult for departments to effectively search out high quality candidates and making it attractive financially to delay appointments until the next academic year.

The Center, now almost totally independent, was also finding it more difficult to flush out funds. It was fortunate to appoint L.P. Mos as its Professional Officer to replace Bradbury, who had become Chairman at the University of Winnipeg. Mos arrived with a broad background (psychology, linguistics, genetics and counselling) that has been of exceptional value to the Center. Center staff included persons from the departments of philosophy, linguistics, computing science, psychiatry, as well as psychology. Rozeboom became half-time with the Center and Royce, once half-time, was made full time Director, The Center offered a well-organized series of international symposia (usually every other year funded by NATO grants), lectures by distinguished visitors and papers by staff related to yearly themes. All of this helped keep the Center highly visible and immune from serious reductions.

The Department became similarly engaged. An annual lecture affair was ably organized by E. Lechelt and officially began in March, 1975, when the first in a series of MacEachran Lectures was delivered by Frank Geldard of Princeton. Geldard delivered a magnificent set of lectures wherein he disclosed the existence of an entirely new sensory phenomenon. These lectures were shortly after published by L. Earlbaum Associates, as have the five given subsequently.

In 1975–1976 A. Buss (behavior genetics and personality) was appointed to the Center and Department, half time each. M. Enzle (social) accepted our offer and Doug Smith returned at one-third time but then retired early after only one year. The effects of budget reductions were becoming more apparent. For the first time, full professors outnumbered those in any other single rank in psychology.

In 1976–1977 E.H. Cornell (infant perception and developmental) and D.C. Heth (conditioned learning) joined the staff to raise the total again to 29 persons. The next year D.S. Grant (animal learning) accepted a position, but much to our regret, Brainerd, now a full professor, resigned, as did Remple.

The year 1978–1979 found G.L. Wells (social) and J.A. Browne (Administrative Officer) appointed. Browne replaced Olson who had resigned to become a hospital administrator. Browne was active in professional matters connected to the Psychological Association of Alberta and came with considerable experience in data analysis, both in research and in business. He promised to be a useful addition. In the spring of 1980 an electrical engineer, L. Osler, was selected to fill the newly created position of Faculty Service Officer. Buss and D. Schaeffer left during this year.

The most recent three years have been very active so far as staffing has been concerned. In 1979–1980 V. Di Lollo (information processing), D.G. Perry (social developmental), W.F. Epling (behaviour modification and animal learning) came to the Department, but Zelhart left. J.H. Bisanz (developmental) and A.R. Friedman (cognition) accepted positions in 1980–1981, while W. Schneiderman and W. Thorngate went elsewhere. Blanchard accepted the position of Registrar full time. Charles Beck was Acting Chairman during this year while I was on study leave.

The 1981–1982 Calendar shows no additions and one subtraction – Osler had resigned. However, we appointed P. Dixon (text processing), C. Hoffman (social memory) and G. Finley as Faculty Service Officer starting July, 1981. The 1981–1982 year will begin with 30 academic staff.

The last years have resulted in general strengthening of all experimental programs and led to staffing in at least three fresh areas. Major changes have not been made in course structure at undergraduate, honours, or graduate levels for a number of years and are unlikely in the near future unless new programs of study are introduced. However, undergraduate enrolment remains at a high level relative to most other departments in the Faculties of Arts and Science. It totalled 6,083 for the 1980–1981 year. Graduate registrations continue to decline. These totalled 39 in 1981–1982 of which 35 were full-time registrants. About 30 people are in all other programs, including Honours and special enrolments.

The Department has international academic recognition and is respected within the University.[17] Course offerings are diversified but not redundant. Research facilities are good and the scholarly output of quality. Establishment of the Center for the Advanced Study in Theoretical Psychology assures that theoretical and humanistic values are being represented in Alberta as at few other places. The last 14 years have put at least 186 theses in the library, 71 of which were at the doctoral level.

Unfortunatly the times demand more. They ask that our working goals make room for broad and useful professional education of students to fill positions created by social legislation and that academic research and theory have significant interpretative dimensions. The question of the moment within the University is how to accommodate the political insistence that universities directly address manpower needs. In our Department the most pressing immediate question is how to accommodate the desire on the part of the provincial government for expanded and upgraded clinical programs. This is only a specific instance of a more general question. To what extent will the Department be capable of devising teaching and research programs that will usefully combine academic rigour with social concern while at the same time avoiding negative features of applied psychology?

While seeking resolutions that are consistent with our real capabilities, we also recognize that we can not ignore the demands made of us. Our society is in rapid transformation and struggling to maintain a favourable productive and intellectual position in the world. We will not be allowed to stand aloof. We are an important part of society and no longer insulated from the shifting needs and demands of government. These problems are not new – MacEachran, Macdonald and Smith faced them in their day – but the demands are becoming more insistent by the hour. Psychological knowledge is no longer unimportant and others know it.

It seems inevitable that renewed integration of psychological research and teaching with problems of community interest will have high priority in the years to come. But we want the solution to redound to the long term benefit of the discipline and the Department as well as to fit the times. The questions are what form will internal change take, and more importantly, *how* will change come about and *who* will mediate it. Shall we whistle our own tune or do we dance to that played by others?

Notes

[1] John Watson, a philosopher specializing in Kant, was his supervisor.

[2] MacEachran mentioned that despite his protests of Canadian nationality, Wundt always regarded the designation of "American" as perfectly proper for anyone residing in North America.

[3] We only have his student book from Leipzig. We do not know what lectures he attented while in Berlin, if any.

[4] The examination was made up of eight questions with instructions to 'Answer any six questions.' Three of the questions had philosophical dimensions but the last five did not.
The questions were the following:
1) Discuss the Greek conception of the soul. What is the conception present in modern psychology?
2) Show how Plato's ethical and political theories were related to his psychology.
3) Explain Plato's theory of "ideas". Point out the difficulties involved in this theory and show how Aristotle seeks to overcome them.

4) Describe the construction of either the eye or the ear.
5) By process of vivisection show how the nerve centres of animals are capable of being specified.
6) How is habit to be explained physiologically? Write a note on the ethical and pedagogical importance of the principle of habit.
7) Discuss the appropriateness of the term "stream of consciousness". What is meant by "topic" and "fringe" of thought? Explain and illustrate the selective character of consciousness.
8) Show how James analyzes the "self as known".

[5] MacEachran stayed in contact with Wundt and on friendly terms. He was one of a number of former students who made contributions toward a piano given Wundt upon the occasion of his 80th birthday. A large and imposing gilt announcement of the event is stored in the University Archives.

[6] Titling of courses in *Psychology* was an innovation. Most Canadian universities long afterwards followed the habit of giving all Psychology courses a philosophical title.

[7] Smith (1975) mentions that he may have gotten some relief in Philosophy from a part-time special lecturer. Smith's manuscript *Development of the Department of Psychology, University of Alberta, 1909–1963* gives personal memories and various detailed information about the development of Psychology. Some biographical information on staff members, a chronological list of courses in psychology, degree programs related to psychology and representative budget items are published in appendices.

[8] MacEachran was also listed as staff with the Faculty of Medicine.

[9] A Catholic college affiliated with the University of Alberta.

[10] Personal communication, Ted Kibblewhite, 2 August 1981.

[11] Personal communication, D.E. Smith, 2 August 1981.

[12] Personal communication, Ted Kibblewhite, 2 August 1981.

[13] The Center for Advanced Study in Theoretical Psychology offers a program of education and research into the theoretical foundations of psychological science. Attempts are made to trace the historical continuities and logical structure of psychology's central concepts, to contribute to the development of substantive theory, and to identify the unities underlying the diversity of current psychological work.

[14] Approximately 22 persons out of a total of about 56 'permanent' part- and full-time appointments made since 1960 have been in the personality-social area.

[15] Ours was possibly the first Department in the Faculty of Arts to have only Ph.D.'s in tenurable positions although it was already the case for a number of departments of the Faculty of Science.

[16] In 1968 we had expanded to 19 separate locations, mostly off-campus. On one memorable day the Chairman of the Board of Governors wanted to assure himself that our need for space was as great as I claimed. He spent six hours with me walking from one unit to another without covering the entire 'empire'. He supported our request for new space in the projected Biological Sciences Building.

[17] Annual awards to students include The MacEachran Humanities Prizes in Philosophy and Psychology, The MacEachran Gold Medal in Psychology and the Dr. John Macdonald Gold Medal in Arts.

References

Alberta and Saskatchewan, the Two New Provinces: 1905–1980, H. Palmer and D. Smith (Eds.), Tantalus, Vancouver, 1981.

Alberta Eugenics Board. *Edmonton Journal*, 13 September 1974.

Alberta Eugenics Board. *Edmonton Journal*, 4 December 1979.

Arvidson, R.M. and Nelson, T.M. Sixty Years of Psychology at the University of Alberta, *Canadian Psychologist*, 1968, *4*, 500–504.

Frost, E.M., *Sterilization in Alberta: 1929–1941*, Edmonton: M.A. Thesis, University of Alberta, 1942.

Johns, W.H. *A History of the University of Alberta: 1908–1969*, Edmonton, 1981.

Macdonald, J. *A History of the University of Alberta, 1908–1958*. University of Alberta Press, Edmonton, 1958.

Macdonald, J. *Some Suggestions Towards a Revised Philosophy of Education*. Studies and Reports, No. 13. University of London Institute of Education, London, 1938.

MacEachran, J.M. A Philosophical Look at Mental Hygiene. *National Committee for Mental Hygiene*, New York, 1932.

MacEachran, J.M. Universities of Imperial Germany, *The Gateway*, February 22, 1945.

MacEachran, J.M. Criminals are not reformed by Brutality or Inhumanity, *Mental Health*, Canadian National Committee for Mental Hygiene, Toronto, 1932.

Nelson, T.M., John M. MacEachran. *The Western Psychologist*, 1972, *3*, 51–62.

Nelson, T.M. The Long Past. *New Trail*, 1971, *27*, 2–5.

Smith, D.E. *Development of the Department of Psychology, University of Alberta, 1909–1963*, Department of Psychology, University of Alberta, Edmonton, 1975.

Further Readings

Anonymous – D.E. Smith. *The Canadian Psychologist*, 1959, *8*, 69–70.

Hough, A.J.B. Historical Links. *The Canadian Psychologist*, 1972, *13*, 71–73.

See also notes in *The Canadian Psychologist*, 1960, *1*, 141; 1961, *2*, 57 and 102; 1962, *3*, 153; 1963, *4*, 68; 1967, *8a*, 245 and 368–369; 1968, *9*, 92 and 386 and 513–515.

Chapter 12

Psychology at British Columbia

by

Donald C.G. Mackay*

A university for British Columbia was envisioned as early as 1872, one year after the Province entered Confederation. Then, on April 26, 1890, "An Act Respecting the University of British Columbia" was passed by the Legislature in Victoria "to establish one university for the whole of British Columbia, for the purpose of raising the standard of higher education in the Province, and of enabling all denominations and classes to obtain academical degrees." This act was, however, repealed in 1908 and a new act established and incorporated the university.

The University opened for classes in the autumn of 1915 in temporary buildings in Vancouver in the vicinity of the Vancouver General Hospital in Fairview. The move to the present large campus on Point Grey outside the city limits did not occur until the session of 1925–26. The University was planned at that time for a maximum enrolment of approximately 2500 daytime students. Since then the campus has increased to almost 1000 acres in area and the enrolment to 23,161 (1979–80) with 6132 students enrolled in psychology courses.

Initially it was planned to establish in the University a Department of Philosophy and Psychology as in so many other Canadian universities. The first President of U.B.C., Dr. Wesbrook, in procuring the original faculty of the University, was authorized to negotiate with Doctor William McDougall of Oxford University. Dr. McDougall had earlier carried out psychophysiological research at University College, London, and was well known in Britain and abroad for such books as *Physiological Psychology* (1905), *Social Psychology* (1908), and *Body and Mind* (1911). He

* Professor Mackay joined the Faculty of the University of British Columbia in 1947 and was an active member of the Department of Philosophy and Psychology, and later the Department of Psychology, there until his retirement in the late 1970s.

was predisposed to move to the new world partly because he felt that the British climate had contributed to the death of one of his children. He was offered the headship of the proposed Department of Philosophy and Psychology at U.B.C. (Professors at that time received $3500 to $5000 and Deans $5000 to $7500.) Mail travelled slowly and negotiations with U.B.C. were very protracted. In the end Dr. McDougall declined the offer largely because of the absence of a pension plan for U.B.C. faculty! He later (1920) accepted the headship of the Psychology Department at Harvard University, a post that had become vacant with the death of Professor Münsterberg in 1916. Had Dr. McDougall accepted the U.B.C. position, it is most probable that psychology would have had not only an early but also a vigorous start in those areas in which he had already become prominent. However, in the absence of a distinguished psychologist to head the new department, arrangements worked out rather differently and less to the advantage of the development of psychology on the campus.

A Department of Philosophy was established at U.B.C. in 1915 and it offered the first course in psychology in that same year. It was called Psychology 1A and was offered during the autumn semester. Philosophy 1B (Logic) was given during the spring semester. Professor James Henderson, M.A. a graduate of the University of Glasgow and whose field of specialization was logic, was the sole staff member of the infant department. The entire teaching staff of the University consisted of only 34 men and women of whom 2 were away on active service, and the administrative staff consisted of 12 and the university library contained only 22,000 volumes and 700 pamplets in contrast to the present 1,600,000 volumes.

In November, 1915, Dean L.S. Klinck, Dean of Agriculture, presented the report of the Committee on Graduate Studies. This report advised against having the university offer the Ph.D. degree in any field and recommended concentration on the M.A. and M.Sc. degrees.

By 1916 the University enrolment had increased to 369, of whom 179 were women. Three hundred and twenty-one of these were in the Faculty of Arts.

In 1920 Dr. H.T.J. Coleman became Head of the Department of Philosophy as well as Dean of Arts. He came from Queen's University where he had been Dean of Education. Because of one of his other accomplishments he has been described as the "ungarlanded Poet-laureate of the faculty."

The department continued to be called the Department of Philosophy and the only course in psychology continued to be Psychology 1A until 1926 when Mrs. Jennie Benson Wyman (later Dr. Jennie Wyman Pilcher), a New Zealander, became assistant professor. Philosophy 8 (Social Psychology) was added at that time. She also taught introductory psychology, child psychology, and educational psychology at various times. In her lectures she is said to have frequently used her own child as the example of what she was discussing and to have shown a strong desire to help students and friends with their psychological problems. Dr. Pilcher was an enthusiastic follower of Professor Lewis M. Terman of Stanford University under whom she had studied, and her main interest appears to have been in psychological testing in connection with education. She resigned when her husband, who represented a New Zealand company, was transferred to San Francisco.

Dr. Joseph Morsh joined the department in 1935 while Dr. Coleman was still the Head although no longer Dean. Professor Morsh had obtained his Ph.D. in Experimental Psychology at the Johns Hopkins University working under Professor Knight Dunlap three years before joining U.B.C. He rose in rank from Lecturer to full Professor and at various times he taught experimental, elementary, abnormal, applied, social, physiological, child, and educational psychology as well as elementary statistics. His research interests included motor performance of the deaf, eidetic imagery, Morse code, and conditioned responses. He served as Director of Research for the Canadian Army Signal Corps during the period of 1944–46. Classes were often extremely large at the end of the war and the class room facilities very inadequate. Dr. Morsh taught one of the largest of these classes which happened to be in elementary psychology with 700 students. Another course that he taught, the psychology of adjustment, had between 200 and 300 students crowded into an agricultural laboratory. Much amusement resulted from one occasion when two of his students were noticed busily taking notes while sitting under a cow. On another occasion a prize pig wandered into one of his lectures and was told that she was late for class but that she had come to the right place!

It was not until 1936 that the Department's name was officially changed to the Department of Philosophy and Psychology. In that year the number of psychology courses was increased to include: elementary, experimental, social, personality, abnormal, and clinical psychology. The departmental staff at that time consisted of only three – Professors Coleman, Pilcher, and Morsh.

In 1939 courses in the psychology of adjustment, tests and measurements, and applied psychology were added. Professor J.A. Irving, who had joined the faculty in 1937, became Department Head in 1940 replacing Dr. Coleman. With a staff of only four the Department then added courses in child psychology, the psychology of culture, and the first psychology seminar. The introduction of a course in the psychology of culture is interesting in that it was an unusual type of course in psychology. It was described in the U.B.C. Calendar for 1940–41 as a "psychological analysis of social life from the point of view of culture. Topics included are the meaning of culture, its psychological relevance to personality, its value relativity, and the problem of reconciling personality variations and cultural variations." The instructor in this course was Professor Irving, a philosopher. The course in experimental psychology, taught by Professor Morsh, appears to have been fairly ambitious when one considers the inadequate facilities that were then available. The Calendar description of this course for 1940–41 includes the following: "The work will include performance of individual and group experiments involving the various sense modes, images, illusions, motor performance, reaction time, hand-eye coordination, attention, learning, memory, and reasoning."

By 1943 the staff of the Department had increased to five with the addition of Dr. Alexander Maslow, a philosopher and Russian emigré. There was no change in the course offerings in psychology.

From this point on there was to be a rapid expansion in the Department with increases in staff, students and courses in psychology. Professor S.N.F. Chant, who had risen to the rank of Group-Captain in the R.C.A.F., succeeded Professor Irving, one of his former students, as head of the Department in 1945. Profesor Chant had become a widely known psychologist with many important papers to his credit before the second World War and during the war he had rendered important services in the selection of pilots for the Royal Canadian Air Force. Towards the end of the war he served with the Department of Veterans Affairs and became Director General of Rehabilitation for Canada (1943–44). In 1944 he was awarded the O.B.E. in recognition of his services in the R.C.A.F. in which service he had been Director of Personnel Selection and Research during the period of 1941–45. When he came to U.B.C. to be Head of the Department of Philosophy and Psychology, teaching loads were particularly heavy and Professor Chant recalls teaching two huge sections of the introductory psychology course as well as a course in advanced statistics. Dr. Fred Tyler, who had joined the staff in 1939 as assistant professor of psychology and education, taught the fourth year seminar and for a number of years he was to teach mental measurements and statistics.

When Professor Chant first arrived at U.B.C. there were 2200 students in the entire university. With the influx of veterans the total enrolment rapidly rose to 9000, then declined somewhat, only to increase again when the children of the wartime "baby boom" reached college age.

A new course numbering system using hundreds instead of consecutive numberings beginning with "1" was adopted in 1946 and the first 500 course (graduate course) was offered during the session of 1946–47. It was a seminar in the History of Psychology with Dr. D.C.G. MacKay the instructor. By 1951–52 the number of 500's courses listed in the calendar had increased to eleven.

Until shortly after the arrival of Professor Chant as Head, the staff were scattered around the campus both for offices and class-rooms. Rushing from one building to another, often in the rain, was a constant occurrence and sometimes the distances to be covered were considerable. Professor Chant managed to improve this situation by persuading the University to make available to the department a number of temporary huts that had been built and equipped for the use of engineering students. These huts were to remain in use by psychologists as offices, class-rooms and laboratories for a decade and a half. They were noisy, dirty, and small. However, they represented a real step forward in bringing the department together in one place.

Edwin S.W. Belyea joined the Department in the spring of 1946 after service in the Royal Canadian Navy. He shared in the teaching of large classes and conducted a laboratory course similar to one that he had taught at the University of Toronto. The course was conducted in a small former army hut that bore the sign, "Psychology Laboratory." The hut was a well known landmark to students and faculty until it burned to the ground in December, 1948. Books, research material, and equipment were all lost. A short time later a box arrived from Dr. Bott of the University of Toronto Psychology Department. It contained a kymograph and other pieces of equipment to help the psychology laboratory to function once more.

Professor Belyea was particularly interested in the field of industrial psychology. His untimely death in his 54th year occurred while he was on study leave at the University of Edinburgh in April, 1972.

Professor Chant became Dean of Arts and Sciences at U.B.C. in 1948 and, because of his new duties, was no longer able to devote his full time to psychology. He remained, however, Head of the Department with Dr. Barnet Savery, a philosopher, functioning as chairman. For several years the psychologists and philosophers held separate meetings with Dr. Savery in the chair.

The faculty increased relatively rapidly as the student body increased. Dr. D.C.G. MacKay joined the Department in 1947, Dr. Edro Signori in 1949, Dr. and Mrs. Douglas T. Kenny in 1950, and Dr. Donald Sampson in 1951. Dr. MacKay had had a longtime interest in comparative psychology (the behaviour of white mice, crabs, and Pacific salmon) in which field he was to teach a course for many years as well as teaching the first graduate seminar and the first undergraduate course on the History of Psychology. During the period 1943–1946 he had been Assistant Director of the International Pacific Salmon Fisheries Commission where his chief research interest had been in the analysis of the results of tagging more than 21,000 sockeye salmon in British Columbia waters. It may be of interest to note that more than 50% of the tags were recovered either by fishermen or on the spawning grounds where the salmon had died after spawning. Professor Signori joined the U.B.C. Department after having served from 1942 to 1946 as an administrative officer in the Directorate of Personnel Selection and Research, R.C.A.F. headquarters in Ottawa, and having taught briefly at Queen's University in Kingston. His many interests include the psychology of personality and its applications, industrial and personnel selection, counselling, and psychological factors in marriage.

While Professor Chant was Head of the Department no special psychological orientation was adopted or followed. Each intructor was free to teach as he saw fit. During this period, however, there came to be a majority of faculty who had shared the University of Toronto Psychology Department experience as graduate students or staff. For a time the only psychologists in the Department who had taken their doctoral work elsewhere were Dr. Douglas Kenny (U. of Washington), Dr. W.G. Black (U. of Chicago), and Dr. D.C.G. MacKay (Stanford and the U. of Chicago). The others, Chant, Signori, Belyea, Sampson, and Potashin, as well as at least one part-time instructor, had taken their graduate work at the University of Toronto.

A book by Chant and Signori entitled *Interpretive Psychology: The Nature of Human Activity*, published by McGraw Hill in 1957, was used as the text in introductory psychology for several years. It was usually accompanied by another book of the instructor's choice to provide the student with supplementary material on experiments, techniques, and points of view. Dr. Donald Sampson took over the teaching of the course in Social Psychology after Dr. William Black resigned to become Regional Liaison officer for B.C. for the Citizenship Branch of the Canadian Department of Citizenship and Immigration.

Application to the Faculty of Graduate Studies was made on October 5, 1950 to authorize the Department of Philosophy and Psychology to offer the Ph.D. in clinical psychology. Approval was given in the following year but it was not until 1968 that the first candidate successfully fulfilled the requirements for the degree. This was Mr. John Huberman of Vancouver who is now an Honorary lecturer in psychology and the author of two recent articles in the Harvard Business Review.

The U.B.C. Counselling Service was organized in 1954 by Dr.

Gordon Shrum, a physicist. Professor Chant was an advisor to the Service and for many years a majority of the Counsellors have been psychologists, several of them teaching sections of the introductory psychology course. The present Director of the Counselling Service, Mr. A.F. Shirren, is a psychologist and teaches a course in the Department.

The long-awaited division of the Department into two departments was authorized by the U.B.C. Senate on February 12, 1958 and the 1958–59 U.B.C. Calendar shows Professor Chant as Head of Psychology and Professor Savery as head of Philosophy. Professor Signori then became Acting Chairman of the Department of Psychology, a position that he was to hold until 1961 when he became Acting Head of the Department and a committee began to search for a permanent head.

Dean Chant had become Chairman of the Royal Commission on Education in B.C. and Dr. Signori, Director of Research for the Commission with two full-time and four part-time assistants. Their report, often referred to as the "Chant Report" was published early in 1961. A tribute read to Dean Chant at the U.B.C. Senate meeting of February, 1964, the last meeting of the Senate that he attended as Dean, in referring to the Chant report stated that "No document has had such an impact upon education in this province. Exhaustive, critical, and constructive, it became and remains the blueprint for the spectacular improvements and reforms now being introduced into the school. These, of course, have and will have an impact upon the University."

Professor Belyea was collaborating at this time with Dr. Michael Beddoes of the Department of Electrical Engineering on the development of a reading device for the blind. Dr. Kenny had completed a series of studies on the influence of stimulus deprivation on fantasy behavior as well as two research studies of the influences of the stimulus variable on perceptual responses. A number of other research projects were in progress or had been completed and Mr. Kenneth Craig had been awarded a fellowship at Purdue University. Professor Belyea was President of the B.C.P.A. having followed Professors Black, Morsh and MacKay in this position.

Student enrolment in psychology courses had been increasing rapidly. By September, 1963, the enrolment in undergraduate courses in the Department had reached 3846. In addition there were 50 students in graduate courses. Twelve full-time faculty members of whom one was on leave as well as six instructors who served on a part-time basis mainly teaching sections of the introductory course, made up the staff of the Department.

It may be of interest to note what had become of many of those who had taken graduate degrees in psychology up to this time. Professor

Belyea made a tabulation of what he referred to as the "fates of the 109 persons awarded the M.A. in psychology for the period 1945–1964." This showed that 23, or 32%, had followed the M.A. at U.B.C. with a Ph.D. obtained elsewhere. These individuals were then (1965) working in an academic field with such specialties as experimental (5), clinical (4), clinical-experimental (3), industrial (2), developmental (2), educational (2), and comparative-physiological (2). Another 8 had become clinical psychologists, one an industrial psychologist, and one a non-university researcher. Twenty-four, or 22%, had followed the M.A. at U.B.C. with work towards a Ph.D. at U.B.C. or elsewhere. Ten of these were in the clinical field and two each in experimental, social, and personality psychology. Thirty, or 27%, without a Ph.D. were employed in work involving psychology. Eighteen of these were in clinical, 4 in industrial, 3 in counselling and 2 each in public service and the armed forces. Another 13, or 12%, without Ph.D.'s were employed in professions other than psychology.

The search for a new head ended in 1965 with the appointment of Dr. Douglas T. Kenny who had been on leave for two years at Harvard University where he had been a visiting professor. Previous to his leave at Harvard he had been a member of the U.B.C. Psychology Department since 1950. It is worth observing that he had done his undergraduate work at U.B.C., received his M.A. under the supervision of Dr. Tyler, and also served as the first graduate assistant of Professor Chant when he came to U.B.C. Dr. Kenny is an individual with wide-ranging interests in psychology, specializing in personality research and socialization practices of parents.

During the four years of Dr. Kenny's headship, the Department changed markedly and grew both in terms of students and faculty. In 1965 when he assumed his new position, there were 4285 course registrations in psychology, an increase of 258 over the previous year, 16 full-time and 4 part-time staff, and 35 students working towards advanced degrees. The teaching program of the Department was broadened especially at the graduate level. No particular school or approach to the problems of behaviour was espoused. The program was truly eclectic in the best sense of the term. However, Dr. Kenny focussed his attention upon the recruitment of experimental psychologists, building up the laboratory equipment of the Department, establishing the first animal laboratory, attracting research funds, and revamping the graduate program at the doctoral level. One important change that was made in the program for majors was that Experimental Psychology became a required course in the second year in order to make possible a more orderly sequence of courses in the third and fourth years as well as to emphasize the increasing importance of this aspect of psychology. Funds for research were still insufficient. However, there was an encouraging increase in such funds from approximately $42,000 in 1965 to $72,000 in 1966. These funds came mainly from the Dominion-provincial Mental Health Grant ($20,600), the U.B.C. Committee on Research ($17,200), U.S. Federal sources ($14,800), and the National Research Council ($12,700). One of the largest research grants was awarded to Dr. Robert Hare in the form of a Dominion-provincial Mental Health Grant to conduct a three-year study of the physiological and psychological factors underlying psychopathic behaviour. Another source of funds resulted from a bequest of $118,030 from the will of the late Dr. Gladys C. Schwesinger, a former U.B.C. graduate, "to establish and maintain a modern Department of psychology including as many fields of psychology as possible."

An event that made life more pleasant and efficient for students, faculty, and secretaries of the Department was a move after 15 years occupancy and with only 8,380 square feet of space, from the old converted huts to new quarters in the Henry Angus Building in 1965. Here we had 12,884 square feet of space and the new quarters were clean and elegant in contrast to the old converted huts. In my own office in the huts there was at one time a small roof leak immediately above my desk and the room was too small to re-arrange the furniture! The old building had been for a time infested with wild mice. However, it was not possible to arrange heating and ventilation suitable for maintaining experimental animals. This had made it virtually out of the question to carry out investigations in Comparative Psychology. The new quarters made a tremendous improvement in morale and in efficiency but space was still insufficient for the needs of a rapidly growing department. As a result, only one year later part of the Department was once again housed in a converted army hut. This was a depressing necessity in view of having had only one year altogether in the new quarters.

During these years a significant number of new staff appointments had been made in order to strengthen the Department in such fields as sensory processes, physiological psychology, learning, abnormal, and social psychology. There was a marked increase in publications by the Faculty (18 in 1965–66; 32 in 1966–67). One major decision during 1966–67 related to the future of clinical psychology which had been a matter of debate and indecision for some time. It was decided to continue the graduate program in clinical psychology but to restrict it to doctoral students only.

In 1969 Dr. Kenny resigned as Head of the Department to become Associate Dean of Arts; Dr. Signori became, once again, Acting Head. Then, in 1970, Dr. Kenny became Dean of Arts and in 1975, the seventh President of U.B.C. succeeding President Walter Gage, a mathematician.

Following Dr. Kenny's resignation, a new search committee was organized to look once more for a permanent head. Many names were submitted to this committee and a number of promising candidates visited the University and were interviewed. Finally, the search seemed to have ended when the University Gazette, the official organ of the University, announced that Dr. J.A. Keats had been appointed Professor and Head from January 1, 1971. However, it was not over after all and Professor Keats withdrew. The search began again. Meantime, Dr. Edro Signori was appointed Acting Head.

During the ensuing school year (1971–72), the Psychology Annex was opened and provided excellent facilities for research in comparative and physiological psychology as well as space for animal colonies and faculty offices for those engaged in such fields of research. Research grants amounted to over $118,000 and 80 papers were published. Ten M.A.'s and 3 Ph.D.'s were awarded.

The new "search for a head" ended with the appointment of Dr. Peter Suedfeld as Professor and Head of the Department of Psychology from July 1, 1972. Dr. Suedfeld had headed the Department of Psychology, University College, Rutgers University since 1967. Previous to that he had taught at the University of Illinois and his graduate work had been taken at Princeton University. Dr. Suedfeld is primarily an experimental social psychologist and has carried out research in human cognitive and information processes, sensory deprivation, human attitudes and health psychology. He is the author of one book, the editor of three, and has contributed more than seventy journal articles. In addition he is the co-editor of the Journal of Applied Social Psychology.

Since the appointment of Dr. Suedfeld as Head, the Department has made strides and has grown rapidly. At the May, 1974 graduation ceremony, and again in 1975, more Bachelor of Arts degrees were earned by honours and majors students in psychology than in any other department. This trend still continues. It has also become possible to earn a B.Sc. degree in psychology and the first such degree was awarded to Perry Fainstein in May, 1975.

Other changes included the reorganization of the clinical program in a direction more closely related to current trends. There is now greater involvement with institutions for the care of the mentally retarded, community mental health centres, etc. and a program in environmental psychology is offered. The University of British Columbia is in an excellent position to make such an offering inasmuch as the University has six psychologists interested in environmental psychology, four of whom are members of the Department. There are in addition outstanding groups of researchers in the fields of Biopsychology, Cognition, Perception, and Personality.

The undergraduate curriculum has been completely reorganized with the result that there is now a more rational sequence of courses. Fourth year laboratory courses have been introduced to follow the third year courses which concentrate on theory and concepts.

The Psychology Club, a student organization with a 1978–79 membership of more than 400 has been in existence for more than 30 years. The Club is administered by a steering committee of students and holds weekly meetings with talks by invited speakers.

Over the years there have come to be a number of awards that are open to students in psychology at U.B.C. For example, the British Columbia Psychological Association every year awards a gold medal for outstanding achievement in the field of psychology to a student in the graduating class. This was won in 1975 by Philip Tetlock who also won the Governor-General's Gold Medal and went on to Yale University where he received his Ph.D. in 1979. He has since been appointed an assistant professor in the Department of Psychology at the University of California in Berkeley. Another award is the Morris Belkin Prize, a cash prize of $1,000 awarded annually and split among the student authors of the three best essays written in psychology during the year. There is also the David Bolocan and Jean Bolocan Memorial Prize which is awarded each year to the student judged to be the most outstanding in his graduating year.

Both undergraduate and graduate enrolment in psychology courses, which had been increasing markedly, have now levelled off somewhat. In the fall of 1974 alone, the increase in undergraduate enrolment was about 10% and the number of lecture sections had increased from 78 to 86. By 1978–79 117 separate lecture sections were being offered including 16 sections of the introductory psychology course. One of the factors that contributed to this increase was the new B.Sc. program in psychology which brought in many students who were primarily interested in the biological and experimental aspects of the discipline.

At the time of writing (1979) there are in the Department 11 full professors, 17 associate professors, 13 assistant professors, and 20 lecturers from other departments, a total of 41 full-time and 20 part-time faculty. The writer is at the present time the only emeritus professor and he is acting as the departmental archivist. Professor S.N.F. Chant has been Dean Emeritus of Arts and Sciences since 1964. By 1978–79 the number of publications by faculty had risen to approximately 150 per year and funds in support of research had risen to $1,000,000. Fifty-nine students are in the graduate programme of whom 28 are doctoral candidates. A number of visiting, part-time, and honorary staff appointments have been made. They include scholars from Great Britain, Japan, the United States, and Canada. This shows both the growing recognition and diversity of the Department.

The areas of specialization for graduate study within the Department at the time of writing are: Biopsychology, Clinical/Community Psychology, Cognitive Processes, Developmental Psychology, Environmental Psychology, Learning, Perception and Sensation, Personality, and Social Psychology.

Many forms of recognition and honours have been received by graduates, faculty, and the department as a whole. Some examples are the following: Dr. Albert Bandura, a former president of the American Psychological Association, who received his B.A. in psychology from U.B.C., was awarded an honorary doctorate by his Alma mater in 1979. Another U.B.C. alumnus John R. Anderson, shared the 1978 Early Career Award of the American Psychological Association with Dr. Gary E. Schwartz who had been Visiting Associate professor at U.B.C. during the year 1975–76. Dr. Suedfeld was Visiting professor at the University of New South Wales in 1977 and Visiting Fellow at Yale University in 1978. He is now listed in Who's Who in America. Dr. Park O. Davidson, who joined the staff in 1973, was President of the Canadian Psychological Association during 1975–76. The Department was the host body for the 1976 Conference of the Environmental Design and Research Association. This was the first time that the Conference had been held outside the United States as well as the first time that the host organization had been a psychology department. President Douglas T. Kenny was appointed to the Canada Council and then to the new Social Sciences and Humanities Research Council of Canada.

In recent years four major psychological journals have had their editorial offices in the Department. These are: The Canadian Journal of Behavioural Science, editor, Dr. Park O. Davidson; the Journal of Research in Personality, co-editor, Dr. Jerry S. Wiggins; the Journal of Applied Social Psychology, editor, Dr. Peter Suedfeld; and Human Development, editor, Dr. Klaus Riegel. This is certainly a remarkable achievement for one department in any university.

The present excellence of the Psychology Department at U.B.C. is further indicated by the results of a recent study (1978) by Endler, Rushton and Roediger. In this investigation the productivity and scholarly impact of 180 psychology departments in Canada, the United States, and Great Britain were compared. The results show that the U.B.C. Department ranked as the first in Canada in median and total scientific publications and median citations by other authors.

For the future the Department plans to intensify the recent trend toward covering a wide range of specializations and approaches. The faculty will continue to be encouraged to pursue diversified psychological interests. Theory and laboratory research will continue to be coupled with field research and the application wherever possible, of psychological methods and insights. These pursuits will, in turn provide data for analysis and investigation. Some further growth of the faculty is anticipated. New faculty members will be chosen to fill some missing specialities, to strengthen existing areas, and to reduce the faculty-student ratio which is still among the highest of any department on the Campus. Undergraduate and graduate students will be trained for flexible roles in academic and non-academic pursuits.

Except for a short period following the move into new quarters in the Henry Angus Building in 1965, the Department has been scattered around the campus in a number of locations including the new annex for Social and Developmental Psychology, opened in 1974. This has become a serious problem and the Psychology Department has once again become the most widely dispersed one in the entire university. A new building to provide more space, to increase cohesiveness, communication, efficiency, and cross-fertilization of ideas is urgently needed and has already been approved at a size of approximately 90,000 square feet. An architect has been selected and the building is expected to be completed by late 1981 or early 1982.

References

Endler, N.S., Rushton, J.P., and Roediger, H.L. Productivity and scholarly impact of British, Canadian, and U.S. departments of psychology. York University Department of Psychology Reports, Report No. 69. July 1978.

Logan, Harry T. Tuum Est. A history of the University of British Columbia. Vancouver, The University of British Columbia, 1958.

Soward, F.H. The Early History of the University of British Columbia. Unpublished manuscript in the U.B.C. library. Written in 1930.

PART IV

The Great Expansion of the 1960's

Epilogue: The End of an Era and A New Beginning

The great expansion of Canadian Universities in the 1960's could have been predicted, and it was – but not on the grand scale that actually materialized. However, few, if any, foresaw in advance, that psychology would enjoy the "growth spurt" that it did during that decade. Although after World War II, when the universities were flooded by veterans, whose advanced training was supported by grants from the federal government, a disproportionate number of them chose to study psychology, this was not recognized as a portend of what was to come. When, two decades later, their children, the products of the so-called post-war "baby-boom", enrolled in university, they too chose psychology in disproportionate numbers.

The great expansion of the universities was not, however, entirely due to the "baby-boom". During the late 1940's and the 1950's, Canada enjoyed a period of prosperity during which the economy expanded rapidly. Jobs were plentiful, there was little or no inflation, and the country was an attractive place for displaced and disillusioned Europeans seeking a new home. Immigrants poured in from seemingly everywhere, and Canadian professors found themselves confronted by class lists in which the Smiths and the MacDonalds were few and far between, and tongue-twisters like Kusyszyn, Vansteenkiste, Tsiapalis, Reintjes, and Zapotochny had to be mastered. These new immigrants, like their counterparts of a century before, were determined to see that their children obtained the education which they themselves had been, in so many cases, denied.

During the late 1950's and 1960's old universities were expanded and/or new universities were created in every province across the land. In the Maritimes, a new university replaced colleges on Prince Edward Island and a new French language university was established at Moncton in New Brunswick. The University of Quebec was established with campuses located in several different parts of the province. Ontario increased the number of its universities from 5 to 15, adding Windsor,

Carleton, Sir Wilfrid Laurier, Waterloo, York, Laurentian, Trent, Brock Guelph, and the Lakehead. Manitoba created the Universities of Brandon and Winnipeg; Saskatchewan the University of Regina; and Alberta the Universities of Calgary and Lethbridge. In British Columbia, Victoria College became a University and Simon Fraser was established.

What happened to psychology in Canadian universities in the 1960's was startling. It was caught up in a wave of popularity which produced extraordinarily large increases in enrolments in psychology everywhere. In many places "Psychology" became the largest department in the university. Why psychology was the choice of so many students is difficult to understand. It may have been due to the affluence of the country which freed the young to seek an education rather than job-oriented training. Most students did not need to work during their summers and instead travelled widely. It may also have been due to the fact that the 60's were a time of ideological turmoil, during which all "sacred-cows" were suspect, and students were preoccupied with social issues and the human condition. Whatever the reason the weight of numbers gave psychology the opportunity it needed to "come of age".

The increases in enrolments in psychology were not limited to undergraduates. They were matched at the graduate level. By 1967 psychology was, of the traditional academic disciplines, the third largest producer of Canadian Ph.D.'s (Wright, 1969, p. 231). This astonishing feat was not accomplished without tremendous effort and support from a variety of sources. Early in the 1960's the supply of Canadian psychologists, qualified for university appointments, had been virtually exhausted and foreign talent had to be imported. High salaries were not, however, sufficient to attract the kind of talent required. More important were funds to support research and suitable facilities in which to conduct it.

Until well into the 1960's most of the psychological research done in Canada was financed from sources in the United States. Although both the National Research Council of Canada and the Canadian Defence Research Board had, since World War II, provided some support for research in psychology, and some funds were available for mental-health-related research from the Canadian Department of National Health and Welfare, these were insufficient. By the mid-1960's psychologists in Canada found it increasingly difficult to obtain research support from the United States. The needs of the rapidly expanding universities in that country forced its granting agencies to limit their support of research done abroad. This was not a tragedy without benefit. Canadian granting agencies were forced to assume their responsibilities. By 1968 the funds allocated by the National Research Council of Canada for the support of psychological research were 24 times the amount allocated for this purpose in 1960 (Wright, 1969, p. 232). Perhaps more important was that, in the mid-1960's, the Canada Council assumed responsibility for funding research in social, child, and educational psychology, areas which had been almost bereft of such support until that time and were, therefore, very poorly developed in Canada. Also some provinces established effective and generous research foundations.

Traditionally, psychology, which was little understood in the academic community, was assigned one of the lowest ranks in the academic pecking order and occupied space, unwanted by others, in cellars, attics, and old houses. In the 1960's this began to change. Most departments of psychology were enabled to move into new buildings, with properly equipped laboratories which were designed for modern psychological research.

In the decade of the 1960's the number of graduate departments of psychology in Canada more than doubled (Wright, 1969, p. 230). Concern about the inability of Canada to staff its faculties with its own citizens moved the federal government, as well as the provincial governments, which were responsible for higher education in their jurisdictions, to provide training funds for graduate students. The National Research Council expanded its scholarship and bursary program, the Canada Council established doctoral fellowships and some provinces also offered graduate student fellowships.

Thus, the extensive support system for graduate training, which was mounted in the 1960's, marked the end of an era for psychology, and a new beginning. This support system made it possible for some of the newest universities to develop "instant" departments of psychology which, in strength, shortly rivalled some of the older departments on which this volume has focused. Noteable among these were Laval, Carleton, York, Waterloo, Calgary, Simon Fraser, and Victoria.

The scope of this volume has not permitted due credit to be given to the new departments of note, referred to above, or some of the oldest Canadian Universities of significance in psychology. Among the latter are Acadia, in Wolfville, Nova Scotia, and the University of New Brunswick, in Fredericton, which have offered graduate training at the Master's level for many years, the former since the 1940's and the latter since the 1950's. In order to compensate in small measure for these omissions, an attempt has been made to compile a chronology, which follows, of all of the departments of psychology in Canadian universities (other than those dealt with in depth in this volume), which are known to the writers, except those which are specialized departments of applied psychology.

It is recognized that there are, in most of the larger Canadian universities some very important Departments of Applied Psychology, in addition to the formal academic departments of psychology. These offer training in educational, clinical or industrial psychology. By far the largest number of these are Departments of Educational Psychology. In Alberta, for example, there are large and strong Departments of Educational Psychology at both the University of Alberta in Edmonton and the University of Calgary in Calgary. In Ontario a unique development took place in Toronto when that province established the Ontario Institute for Studies in Education (OISE). This was an independent Institute, but affiliation arrangements were made with the University of Toronto, through its School of Graduate Studies, so that it could offer graduate training. This Institute has a large Department of Applied Psychology. Unfortunately, the scope of this book has not permitted a detailed description of the history of these specialized departments.

Chronology

The following is an attempt to provide, province by province, a brief sketch of the Canadian universities which have Departments of Psychology, other than the 12 described in detail in this volume. One of the resources found most useful for this purpose was Harris (1976). The authors were also assisted by the Ontario Council on Education. The information about the departments, such as the dates of their founding, and when their first degrees in psychology were conferred was provided by the respondents to the questionnaire sent to all departments of psychology in Canada in 1975.

Newfoundland

Memorial University of Newfoundland is the only university on the island, although it now has two campuses: the main campus in St. John's, and a secondary campus at Corner Brook on the west coast of the island. The first higher education available in Newfoundland was offered in 1952 by Memorial University College in St. John's. This was a "junior" college established there by St. Dunstan's (PEI). Memorial University of Newfoundland was chartered in 1949, the year that Newfoundland became a province of Canada. The first separate Department of Psychology was established in 1960. The first degrees in psychology were awarded in 1966 (B.A.) and 1970 (M.A.). In the 1970's, training to the doctoral level was also begun. Further information about Memorial may be obtained from notes published in the *Canadian Psychologist* (1968, *9*, p. 82 and *9*, p. 384). One of these tells of National Research Council support for the establishment of the Institute for Studies in Human Abilities, and the other of the start of graduate training in psychology to the M.A. level.

Prince Edward Island

The University of Prince Edward Island is now the only university serving this small province. It was chartered in 1967, and resulted from the union of two older institutions; St. Dunstan's University, Roman Catholic, which had been established in 1892 as an affiliate of Laval, and Prince of Wales College, which had been until that time primarily a "normal school" for the preparation of teachers. In 1967 when this university started, it had a separate Department of Psychology. The first B.A. degree in psychology was awarded in 1969, and a start was made at offering graduate training to the Master's level in the 1970's.

Nova Scotia

Besides Dalhousie, Nova Scotia has four other degree-granting universities with separate departments of psychology. These are Acadia in Wolfville, established in 1839 by Baptists; St. Francis Xavier in Antigonish, founded in 1853 by Roman Catholics; Mount St. Vincent in Halifax, founded in 1914 as a "junior college for women" by Roman Catholics; and St. Mary's in Halifax, founded in the 19th century by Roman Catholics, but closed for a time, and given degree-granting powers in 1925. Also the College of Cape Breton in Sydney, which was founded in 1951 as a junior college by St. Francis Xavier, but which now grants undergraduate degrees in affiliation with that University, has had a separate department of psychology since 1971. Of these, Acadia has made the longest, and probably the greatest contribution to Canadian psychology. Its first separate Department of Psychology was one of the earliest in Canada, being established in 1926, and as early as the 1940's was offering graduate training to the Master's level. The first Acadia M.A. in psychology was awarded in 1950. For further information about Acadia, see A.M. MacMillan (1949).

New Brunswick

There are four universities with separate departments of psychology in New Brunswick. The oldest of these is the University of New Brunswick, in Fredericton. It was first chartered in 1800, but offered no university level work for two decades. It was granted a second charter as the "King's College of New Brunswick" in 1928, and its third charter when it was re-organized as the University of New Brunswick in 1859. The other universities are Mount Allison, in Sackville, founded by the Methodists and chartered in 1886; St. Thomas, in Fredericton, founded by Roman Catholics and chartered in 1934; and Moncton University, in Moncton, a French-language university, founded as "St. Joseph's College" in 1864, and chartered as the University of Moncton in the early 1960's. Of these, only the University of New Brunswick (UNB) was offering graduate training in psychology before the 1960's, and this was only to the Master's level. The first UNB M.A. degree in psychology was awarded in 1956. After 1960, the University of Moncton also offered training to the Master's level, and awarded its first M.A. degree in psychology in 1966. As far as we know, the other two universities have never offered any graduate training in psychology.

In both Nova Scotia and New Brunswick, the multiplicity of small universities, far more than their population warrants, is a consequence of the early denominational feuding that occurred there in the 19th century, and was the main reason why those Maritimers, who went to take important academic positions in Western Canada (e.g., W.C. Murray who became the President of the University of Saskatchewan and H.M. Tory, who became the President of the University of Alberta in Edmonton) were so opposed to a proliferation of church-based colleges there. They "successfully imparted, at least in their lifetimes, the notion of one province, one university" (MacNutt, 1973, p. 447).

Quebec

Besides McGill University and the University of Montreal, Quebec has five other degree-granting universities. These are: Laval University in Quebec City (French), Bishop's University in nearby Lennoxville (English), Sherbrooke University in Sherbrooke (French), Concordia University in Montreal (English), and the University of Quebec (French) with several campuses throughout the province.

Laval was chartered in 1852. Although a "Chair" in psychology seems to have been endowed there as early as 1945 (*Bulletin* of the Canadian Psychological Association, 1945, 3, p. 9), a separate Department of Psychology was not established until 1965. The first graduate degrees in psychology were awarded in 1966 (M.A.) and 1972 (Ph.D.).

Bishop's was founded by the Church of England in 1845, and chartered as a degree-granting university in 1853. It offers undergraduate, but no graduate training in psychology.

Sherbrooke was chartered as a University in 1954, but it began as a Classical College much earlier, in the latter part of the 19th century. It established a separate Department of Psychology in 1968 which immediately began to offer graduate training at the Master's level. The first M.A. degrees in psychology were awarded in 1970. As yet Sherbrooke does not offer graduate training in psychology at the doctoral level.

Concordia was chartered in 1973, but was the result of the amalgamation of two older institutions of higher education in Montreal. These were: Loyola (Roman Catholic) established in 1896, and Sir George Williams (Protestant) which was incorporated as a YMCA College in 1934. Sir George Williams established a separate Department of Psychology in 1961, awarded its first M.A. in psychology in 1969, and began doctoral training in the 1970's.

The University of Quebec was the first "instant" university created by the Province of Quebec. Departments of Psychology were established on its campus at Montreal and its campus at Three Rivers. The Department at Montreal awarded its first M.A. in psychology in 1972, and began doctoral training in psychology in the 1970's.

Ontario

Besides the five older universities (Ottawa, Queen's, Toronto, McMaster, and Western), Ontario now has ten other degree-granting universities. These are: Windsor in Windsor, Carleton in Ottawa, Sir Wilfrid Laurier in Waterloo, Waterloo in Waterloo, York in Toronto, Laurentian in Sudbury, Trent in Peterborough, Brock in St. Catharine's, Guelph in Guelph, and Lakehead in Thunder Bay.

Windsor University was chartered in 1953, but was founded by the Jesuits in 1857 as Assumption College. It was temporarily closed two years later, but re-opened by the Basilians in 1870. From 1919 to 1953, it was affiliated with The University of Western Ontario. A separate Department of Psychology was created at Windsor in 1944, and the first M.A. and Ph.D. in psychology were awarded in 1961 and 1967 respectively. Those readers who may be especially interested in psychology at Windsor should see a note in the *Canadian Psychologist* (1960, *1*, 141) and two published accounts (Cervin & Crews, 1967, and Bringman, Fehr & Mueller, 1969).

Carleton University was chartered in 1957, but had a separate Department of Psychology as early as 1952. In psychology, the first graduate degrees were awarded there in 1961 (M.A.), and 1968 (Ph.D.). Those especially interested in psychology at Carleton, should see three notes in the *Canadian Psychologist* (1963, *4*, 67; 1967, *8a*, 136–137; and 1968, *9*, 520). Being located in Ottawa where the Public Archives of Canada are housed, and being part of a University that launched a program of Canadian Studies in 1957, are factors which have led the Department at Carleton to specialize in the history of Canadian Psychology.

Sir Wilfrid Laurier University was chartered as Waterloo-Lutheran

University in 1959, and re-named in 1973. It began as Waterloo College, a Lutheran Seminary. From 1925 to 1960 it was affiliated with the University of Western Ontario. It has had a separate Department of Psychology since 1956. It began offering training to the Master's level in the 1960's and conferred its first M.A. degree in psychology in 1967.

Waterloo University was chartered in 1959, but had a separate Department of Psychology in 1958. It awarded its first Ph.D. in psychology in 1965. Readers especially interested in psychology at Waterloo should see notes in the *Canadian Psychologist* (1963, *4*, 123; 1964, *5*, 69–70; 1966, *7*, 49–50, and *7a*, 492–495; 1967, *8a*, 43–47) two articles (Walters 1963 and 1964) and a note in the *Quarterly* of the Ontario Psychological Association (1967, *20*, 143).

York University was chartered in 1959, and opened in September, 1960, first as an affiliate of the University of Toronto, but shortly thereafter as an independent university. It established a separate Department of Psychology in 1962, and awarded its first graduate degrees in psychology in 1966 (M.A.) and 1969 (Ph.D.). Those especially interested in psychology at York should see a note in the *Canadian Psychologist* (1965, *6*, 71)

Laurentian University was chartered in 1960 as a bilingual university. It began as the College of Sudbury which was founded in 1913. It established a separate Department of Psychology in 1969, but still offers only undergraduate instruction. Those especially interested in psychology at Laurentian should see a note in the *OPA Quarterly* (1963, *16*, 21) and an article (in French) by Farrant & Thibaudeau (1968).

Trent University was chartered in 1960, and was one of the "instant" universities created by Ontario. It established a separate Department of Psychology in 1964, but still does only undergraduate teaching. Those especially interested in psychology at Trent, should see the citation for Julian Blackburn in the *Canadian Psychologist* (1960, *1*, 87) who, after his retirement from Queen's, helped create this Department.

Brock University was chartered in 1962, and was another of the "instant" universities created by Ontario. It established a Department of Psychology in 1968, but still offers only undergraduate instruction in psychology.

Guelph University was chartered in 1964, but the older institutions which came together to form this University have a longer history. These were: The Ontario Veterinary College (OVC) originally established at Toronto in 1862, The Ontario Agricultural College (OAC) established in 1874, and Macdonald Institute at Guelph which joined OAC in 1929. OVC moved from Toronto to Guelph in 1922. All three of these institutions were affiliated with the University of Toronto until they became part of the new University of Guelph in 1964. Guelph established a separate Department of Psychology in 1966, awarded its first graduate degree in psychology in 1967 (M.A.), but offers no doctoral training in psychology (see also Bowen and Yarmey 1970).

Lakehead University was chartered in 1965. It began as the Lakehead Institute of Technology which was established in 1948. It has a separate Department of Psychology, but offers no graduate training in psychology.

Manitoba

The provinces of western Canada clung as long as they could to the idea that one university was enough for one province, but partly as a result of the threatening post-war "baby boom", and partly because of the ambitions of secondary campuses to become independent, all have now more than one university.

Besides the University of Manitoba, the province now has two other degree-granting universities. They are: Brandon University in Brandon and the University of Winnipeg, both chartered as independent universities in 1967.

Brandon was originally established in 1890 as Brandon College. In 1899, the Baptists assumed full responsibility for Brandon College, and it was affiliated with McMaster University in Ontario from 1911 to 1939, when it became an affiliate of the University of Manitoba. Psychology was first taught in 1939 as part of the program in the Department of Philosophy and Psychology. The first appointment of a psychologist (E.J. Tyler) occurred in 1949, but a separate Department of Psychology was established there in 1946.

The University of Winnipeg was formed out of Wesley College and United College – two affiliates of the University of Manitoba. A separate Department of Psychology was established in 1937, but it offers only undergraduate instruction.

Saskatchewan

Besides the University of Saskatchewan in Saskatoon, the province has one other degree-granting university: Regina University in Regina. Until Regina was chartered in 1961 as a completely separate university, it was a secondary campus of the University of Saskatchewan. It established a separate Department of Psychology in the late 1960's and the first graduate degrees in psychology were awarded there in 1966 (M.A.) and 1969 (Ph.D.).

Alberta

Besides the University of Alberta in Edmonton, Alberta now has two other degree-granting universities with departments of psychology: the University of Calgary in Calgary and the University of Lethbridge in Lethbridge.

Calgary was chartered in 1966. It was incorporated originally in 1911 as Calgary College, and at that time was denied degree-granting powers. For a long period prior to becoming a separate university, it was an affiliate of the University of Alberta in Edmonton. A separate Department of Psychology was established in the year in which it was chartered (1966) and the first graduate degrees in psychology were awarded in 1966 (M.A.) and 1971 (Ph.D.). Those especially interested in psychology at Calgary should see a note in the *Canadian Psychologist* (1967, *8a*, 246–250).

The University of Lethbridge was chartered in 1967. Before that, like Calgary, it was a college affiliated with the University of Alberta in Edmonton. A separate Department of Psychology was established there as soon as the university was chartered, but only undergraduate work is offered. Those interested in psychology at Lethbridge should see a note in the *Canadian Psychologist* (1968, *9*, 84).

British Columbia

Besides the University of British Columbia (UBC) in Vancouver, this province also has two other degree-granting universities with departments of psychology. These are: the University of Victoria in Victoria on Vancouver Island, and Simon Fraser University in Burnaby (near Vancouver).

The University of Victoria was chartered in 1963, but long before that it was Victoria College, affiliated first with McGill University (1902–1915), and then with UBC (1915–1963). It had a separate Department of Psychology as early as 1948, and awarded its first graduate degrees in psychology in 1968 (M.A.), and 1969 (Ph.D.). Those interested in psychology at Victoria should see a note in the *Canadian Psychologist* (1963, *4*, 120).

Simon Fraser was also chartered in 1963. A separate Department of Psychology was established there in 1965, and the first graduate degrees in psychology were awarded in 1969 (both M.A. and Ph.D.). This was the only "instant" university created by British Columbia. Those interested in psychology at Simon Fraser should see notes in the *Canadian Psychologist* (1965, *6*, 298 and 1968, *9*, 86).

References

Arvidson, R.M., & Nelson, T.M. "Sixty Years of Psychology at the University of Alberta". *Canadian Psychologist*, 1968, *9*, 500–504.

Beach, H.D., & Page, F.H. "Psychology at Dalhousie". *Canadian Psychologist*, 1960, *1*, 9–14.

Bowen, N.V., & Yarmey, A.D. "Psychology at Guelph". *Canadian Psychologist*, 1970, *11*, 367–372.

Bringman, W.C., Fehr, R.C., & Mueller, R.H. "Psychology at Windsor". *Canadian Psychologist*, 1969, *10*, 371–382.

Cervin, V.B., & Crews, W. "Psychology at the University of Windsor". *Canadian Psychologist*, 1967, *8a*, 193–201.

Farrant, R.H., & Thibaudeau, G. "L'Enseignement de la Psychologie". (at Laurentian). *Canadian Psychologist*, 1968, *9*, 1–5.

Harris, R.S. *History of Higher Education in Canada: 1663–1960*. University of Toronto Press, Toronto, 1976.

Macmillan, A.M. "Psychology at Acadia". *Acadia Bulletin*, 1949, *35*, 5–9.

MacNutt, W.S. "A Glance Backward at the Universities of the Maritimes". *Dalhousie Review*, 1973, *53*, 431–448.

Walters, R.H. "Psychology at the University of Waterloo". *OPA Quarterly*, 1963, *16*, 5–9.

Walters, R.H. "Psychology at the University of Waterloo". *OPA Quarterly*, 1964, *17*, 75–77.

Wright, M.J. "Canadian Psychology Comes of Age". *Canadian Psychologist*, 1969, *10*, 229–253.

Index

Professional Psychology in Canada

K Dobson & J G Dobson, Department of Psychology,
University of Alberta, Edmonton, Alberta, Canada (Editors)

- *Invaluable for*
- *Practitioners*
- *Students*
- *Professors*

What is the future, and indeed what are the current realities facing the practice of psychology in Canada? In quite a readable format, the diverse specialists who have contributed to this book:

- explain the nature of the various practical fields in which psychologists are engaged on a day-to-day basis
- provide understandable explanations of the current regulatory and legal issues faced by practitioners
- present reviews of the various training programs presently available throughout the country
- explain the details of how the practice of psychology in Canada is organized.

Audience: This title will be productive for all for all practicing psychologists in Canada, including therapists and academics who train future clinicians, as well as specialists in government, industry, and school psychology. In addition, students who are in, or are seriously considering, long term training programs in this field will find the material here to be an invaluable guide to the many important aspects of a career in professional psychology.

Dr Keith Dobson is currently the President of the Canadian Psychological Association, and is based at the University of Calgary, where he is a professor of psychology. Dr Deborah Dobson is a staff psychologist and director of clinical training at the Foothills Medical Centre, Calgary, as well as an adjunct assistant professor in the departments of psychology and psychiatry at the University of Calgary.

From the Contents

Overview of the Field • Training Issues in Psychology • Important Regulatory Issues in the Practice of Psychology • Specific Applications of Professional Psychology • Community-Based Mental Health Services: Current Status and Future Directions • The Future of Professional Psychology • Appendix

1993 / 480 pages / hardcover
ISBN 0-88937-043-5 / **US $49.00 / CAN $58.00**

Hogrefe & Huber Publishers

North America: PO Box 2487 • Kirkland, WA 98083-2487
Phone (206) 820-1500 • Fax (206) 823-8324
Worldwide: Rohnsweg 25 • D-37085 Göttingen • Germany
Phone (0551) 49609-0 • Fax (0551) 49609-88